Programs in Aid of the Poor

Programs in Aid of the Poor

Sar A. Levitan

Garth L. Mangum

Stephen L. Mangum

Seventh Edition

The Johns Hopkins University Press
Baltimore and London

© 1998 The Johns Hopkins University Press
All rights reserved. First edition 1973
Seventh edition 1998
Printed in the United States of America
on acid-free paper
07 06 05 04 03 02 01 00 99 98 5 4 3 2 1

The Johns Hopkins University Press
2715 North Charles Street
Baltimore, Maryland 21218-4319
The Johns Hopkins Press Ltd., London

Figures 1.1, 1.2, 1.4, 1.8, 1.10, and 1.11 are used by
permission of M. E. Sharpe, Publishers, Inc.

ISBN 0-8018-5688-4
ISBN 0-8018-5713-9 (pbk.)

Library of Congress Cataloging-in-Publication Data will
be found at the end of this book.

A catalog record for this book is available from the
British Library.

Contents

Preface and Acknowledgments

In the preface to the sixth edition of this work, published in 1990, Sar Levitan cited the continual expansion of programs designed to aid America's poor during all of the federal administrations from Johnson through Carter, programs that subsided into mere maintenance during the Reagan and Bush years. Seven years later, what was once declared as a war on poverty can now be described with only mild exaggeration as a war on the poor. Some explain the transformation as a withdrawal after a failure to win that war after thirty years of trying. But failure to achieve program objectives is rarely sufficient reason for ending a government program. No one really expected to eliminate poverty. We had it on the highest authority that "you have the poor with you always" (Mark 14:7). And few doubt that the poor are fewer today than they would have been in the absence of the programs, if only because of the transfer payments accompanying them. More telling is the fact that a nation whose Statue of Liberty still trumpets "Give me your tired, your poor, your huddled masses yearning to breathe free" has also declared war on its legal as well as its illegal aliens. Our collective hearts are simply harder today than they were in 1964. It is worth asking why. To paraphrase comedian Jackie Gleason's comment after President Lyndon Baines Johnson spoke at Howard University: "They wouldn't have dared declare war on poverty when I was a boy. There were so many of us poor people we would have won it hands down." The more pertinent question is, What political forces explain the popularity of an antipoverty effort during the 1960s, its promotion during the 1970s, its maintenance of effort during the 1980s, and its rising unpopularity during the following decade?

Despite the less than impressive accomplishments of many of the programs involved as weapons in the War on Poverty, to be documented in this seventh edition, we believe the answer will be found in the straightforward self-interestedness of the American voter.

During the 1960s the War on Poverty required no apparent sacrifice. The productivity of the American worker was increasing at nearly 3 percent per year, potentially doubling the standard of living in less than a quarter-century and almost quadrupling it in a working life-time. High tax rates as hangovers from World War II and the Korean conflict were pinching off economic growth before full employment, then assumed to be around 4 percent unemployment, could be achieved. The concept of a nonaccelerating inflation rate of unemployment (NAIRU) had not yet been invented. In 1964 income tax rates could be reduced at the same time that government expenditures were being increased and even reduce the federal budget deficit in the process. It was potential income not yet realized that was being diverted for antipoverty and other programs. The voter could have his cake and eat it too.

Soon the Vietnam conflict was siphoning off some of that "fiscal dividend," but the high productivity increase supported both wars—foreign and domestic—and kept real incomes rising until the energy cost revolution of the 1970s. In retrospect, the blue collar support of George Wallace in 1968 indicated some disgruntlement with the potential of affirmative action, but none of that was yet felt in the pocketbook. Also in retrospect, both productivity increases and real income began deteriorating after 1973. However, accustomed to the war and postwar upward income trajectory and with the real impact hidden by inflation, most households did not begin to feel the pain and react politically before 1980, and it was into the early 1990s before the signals became clear. A Democratic candidate promising, in order to win, to "end welfare as we know it" in 1992, and a Republican Congress winning in 1994 by declaring war on the War on Poverty brought the issues full circle.

Only their forgetting that the median household income was $36,000 instead of $100,000 stifled the Republican revolution. Now the enemy was those with lower incomes or anyone threatening to compete for the jobs, two of which were often required to achieve that median income. Corporate welfare was an unfamiliar concept to these new members of Congress, but public welfare was a perceived reality. Welfare was "their" entitlement at "our" expense; it was either "them" or "us," and the devil take the hindmost. Social security and Medicare, promised to those in their sixties when the average age at death was in the fifties and continued unabated as life expectancy advanced into the seventies, was "our" entitlement and therefore sacrosanct. By the mid-1990s it was clearly evident that the real incomes of those in the middle of the income distribution had been on a downhill slide for more than twenty years. Yet the political animosity was directed toward those immediately below, among whom there was danger of falling, rather than toward those far above, who were out of reach. Hence a war on the poor and the immigrant.

The following chapters follow closely the format of the earlier editions, critiquing poverty measurements and describing the populations identified by them, characterizing and evaluating the programs, and recommending both improvements and substitutes. But the forward thrust of the first five editions and the holding action of the sixth will give way to strategic retreat in the seventh: What can be preserved to chop away at poverty's problems now in the hope of returning to the battle in full array on a future day?

We undertake this seventh edition of *Programs in Aid of the Poor* as a labor of love, in a spirit of nostalgia for and devotion to our respected colleague and mentor Sar A. Levitan. We have changed all that requires updating after the passage of some six or seven years, but most of the words are still his. He left in midstride shortly before his eightieth birthday in 1994. If we can in some modest way further the cause of poverty alleviation, which he pursued throughout his long career, our efforts will be justified.

The authors acknowledge and express appreciation for the research assistance of Cissy Horton, Brad Alge, Nancy Waldeck, and Scott Lazerus, the manuscript assistance of Judy O'Flaherty, and funding to compensate them from the National Council for Employment Policy persuant to a bequest from the estate of Sar A. and Brita Levitan.

Programs in Aid of the Poor

1. The Poor: Dimensions and Programs

If all of the afflictions of the world were assembled on one side of the scale and poverty on the other, poverty would outweigh them all.

Rabba, Mishpatim 31:14

According to the Bible, "The poor shall never cease out of the land" (Deuteronomy 15:11). Rather than a pessimistic forecast, this prophecy is an acknowledgment that each society defines poverty in its own terms. Primarily because poverty is a relative concept, more than one American in eight is considered poor according to government statistics. In less affluent countries poverty is equated with living at the brink of subsistence. In this country even the lowest-income families are rarely confronted with the specter of starvation, though many have inadequate diets.

As a relative concept, poverty will always be with us because inequality has persisted throughout recorded history. No system distributes income evenly, nor necessarily should it. The reasons for inequality of income are many, some worthy and others unconscionable. The operative question for public policy is what degree of inequality is politically acceptable at any point in time in a viable democracy. Sar Levitan reported in the sixth edition of this work that "income distribution in the United States today is little different from the pattern just after World War II. The average income of the poorest 20 percent of families is less than one-fifth that of the top 5 percent, and there is some evidence that these figures may actually understate the full extent of inequality." He could not know at the time of that writing that that ratio had already fallen to one-sixth and would be one-seventh by 1994 (figure 1.1). Nor could he know that every income group except the top 5 percent would lose real income over the following five years (table 1.1).

Measuring Poverty

Poverty can be defined as insufficient resources for an "adequate" standard of living. However, because standards of adequacy vary with societal wealth and public attitudes toward deprivation, there

1

Figure 1.1. Ratio of family income, top 5 percent to lowest 20 percent, 1973–1994

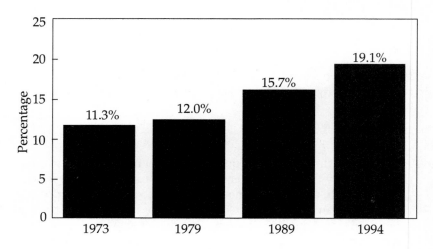

Source: Lawrence Mishel, Jared Bernstein, and John Schmitt, *The State of Working America, 1996–97* (Washington, D.C.: Economic Policy Institute, 1996), 52.

Note: Part of the increase in 1994 is attributable to changes in the way data are collected.

is no universally accepted definition of basic needs. The amount of money necessary to provide for any agreed-upon set of basic needs is equally difficult to determine. For example, government programs such as free education and medical care or subsidized food reduce the amount of cash required to support a family. Differentials in the cost of living between urban and rural areas or among regions raise the income requirements for some people and lower them for others. It is no wonder, then, that experts differ over the purchasing power necessary for an individual or family to achieve a minimally acceptable living standard. From the standpoint of public policy, however, there must be some barometer to measure whether matters are getting better or worse and some means of determining who needs help and who should be considered self-reliant.

Despite conceptual and technical measurement problems, the federal government has devised a poverty index that has gained wide acceptance. The Social Security Administration in 1964 developed an index based on a 1955 Agriculture Department survey that estimated the cost of an economy food plan for a four-member

Table 1.1. Real Family Income and Annual Growth Rate by Income Group, 1947–1994 (Upper Limit of Group in 1995 Dollars)

Year(s)	Bottom Fifth	Second Fifth	Third Fifth	Fourth Fifth	Top 5 Percent	Average
Real family income						
1947	$ 9,975	$16,096	$21,827	$30,971	$ 50,834	$22,331
1967	17,251	28,318	37,964	52,060	83,648	37,865
1973	19,634	32,398	45,203	62,164	96,913	43,983
1979	20,183	33,287	47,141	64,889	103,484	45,959
1989	19,668	34,413	50,145	73,189	121,629	51,012
1994	18,448	32,187	48,332	71,982	123,445	50,738
Annual growth rate						
1947–67	2.8%	2.9%	2.8%	2.6%	2.5%	2.7%
1967–73	2.2	2.3	2.9	3.0	2.5	2.5
1973–79	0.5	0.5	0.7	0.7	1.1	0.7
1979–89	−0.3	0.3	0.6	1.2	1.6	1.0
1989–94	−1.3	−1.3	−0.7	−0.3	0.3	−0.1

Source: Mishel, Bernstein, and Schmitt, *The State of Working America, 1996–97*, 53.

Table 1.2. Federal Poverty Thresholds, 1979–1996

Family Size	1979	1989	1991	1993	1995	1996
1	$3,629	$ 6,310	$ 6,392	$ 7,363	$ 7,761	$ 8,163
2	3,723	8,076	8,865	9,414	9,935	9,484
3	5,727	9,225	10,860	11,522	12,156	12,273
4	7,412	12,674	13,924	14,763	15,570	16,183
5	8,775	14,990	16,456	17,449	18,407	19,516
6	9,915	16,921	18,586	19,718	20,808	22,447

Source: U.S. Bureau of the Census, 1997.

family with two school-age children. Because families of three or more persons spent one-third of their income on food at the time, the analysts set the poverty level for these families at three times the cost of the economy food plan. The multiplier was set at higher than three for smaller families and persons living alone in order to compensate for their relatively larger fixed expenses. The poverty thresholds are weighted by family size, with a larger family having a higher poverty threshold, and by the age of the householder, with an elderly head presumed to need 10 percent less than those under 65 years of age. When first established in 1964 the poverty threshold for a family of four was an annual income of $3,100. Starting from that base and adjusting for changes in the cost of living, table 1.2 indicates the poverty threshold for families of up to six persons from 1979 to 1997.

Even though the thresholds have been adjusted to reflect changes in the level of consumer prices, it is too much to expect that consumption patterns and relative prices would stay constant over such a long period of time. Unfortunately, the poverty classification system is quite out of date. When it was introduced more than thirty years ago the poverty index established by the food cost criterion was about one-half of the national median family income; now it is about one-third. Housing costs, which were then assumed to be about one-quarter of a low-income budget, are now at least one-third and rising. Other living costs have risen more rapidly than food costs, so that the latter are now closer to one-fourth than to one-third of the expenditures of the average low-income family. And even in the 1960s the food budget was based on a "temporary or emergency" diet, not one expected to maintain health over time. Therefore, on the basis of the changing weight of food costs alone one might argue for a one-third increase in the poverty index in order to provide the equivalent of the 1964 poverty standard of living.

However, given that the index has been increased during the intervening years based on the consumer price index rather than on the changing balance of food costs, the issue is more complex than that.

In addition, the poverty index, although offering a constant yardstick to measure progress, is imprecise at best. By varying the index only for family size, the threshold ignores both higher prices in inner cities (where many of the poor are concentrated) and the added resources available to farmers. The complexity of adjusting the poverty index to reflect regional price differences has impeded further refinements. It remains important to recognize that official statistics provide only a rough guide to income inadequacy across the nation. Overstating inflation, as the consumer price index is accused of doing, could understate progress against poverty. The survey used to ascertain the poverty rate tends to undercount income slightly because of underreporting and therefore also exaggerates the extent of impoverishment. The reliance on cash income without regard to its source also tends to distort the official poverty count. By focusing solely on a family's gross income, the poverty index fails to account for differences in tax burdens and other expenses that affect the amount of disposable income available to meet basic needs. An earning family might be classified as nonpoor yet have its take-home pay reduced by taxes to a point below the tax-exempt disposable transfer income received through such programs as Aid to Families with Dependent Children (AFDC), Supplemental Security Income (SSI), and state general assistance by a family classified as poor. The exclusion of family assets in official poverty calculations further weakens the link between a family's poverty status and its ability to secure an adequate standard of living because a small proportion of households with limited incomes can rely upon savings or property to fulfill basic needs. For these reasons the distinction between the poor and the near poor is a loose and imperfect one. Concerned with all of this, the National Research Council (NRC) sponsored a study examining the poverty threshold in light of changes in consumption, work patterns, taxes, and government benefits (table 1.3).[1]

The study recommended an increase of 3.6 percent in the 1992 poverty index, but without an assurance of parity with 1964 living standards. However, the NRC alternative deals only with a few near-cash benefits. A more serious conceptual shortcoming of the current poverty index lies in its failure to take into account in-kind benefits in determining the extent of poverty. Although food stamps, health care, subsidized housing, and other needs-tested assistance account for more than three-fourths of all federal aid to the poor, the

Table 1.3. Alternative Poverty Rates Applied to 1992 Data

	Official Index	*Alternative Index*[a]	*Percentage Change*
Age			
Children under 18	21.9%	26.4%	4.5%
Adults 65 and over	12.9	14.6	1.7
Race/ethnicity			
White	11.6	15.3	3.7
Black	33.2	35.6	2.4
Hispanic (any race)	29.4	41.0	11.6
Illustrative contrasts			
Receiving cash benefits[b]	59.4	53.4	−6.0
One or more workers	9.1	13.7	4.6
No health insurance	32.0	44.9	12.9
Total	14.5	18.1	3.6

Source: Constance F. Citro and Robert T. Michael, eds., *Measuring Poverty: A New Approach* (Washington, D.C.: National Academy Press, 1995), 265.

[a]The alternative index updates consumption requirements, includes the cash value of near-cash benefits, and subtracts medical and work-related expenses.

[b]The poverty rate of recipients of AFDC or SSI (i.e., means-tested benefits) is reduced, in contrast to child care and health insurance costs of working single parents.

value of in-kind aid is disregarded in the official poverty count. Table 1.4 illustrates this fact with data from 1979–92, taking into account the cash value of food and housing benefits received by the poor. When that analysis is extended to 1995 but without the full detail available for the earlier years, all social insurance programs combined would cut the poverty rate by 6.9 percent, all means-tested benefits combined would reduce the poverty rate by another 2.9 percent, and the impact of the enlarged earned income tax credit (EITC) would cut another 0.5 percent, for a total reduction in the poverty rate of 10.4 percent. Yet the poverty count based only on cash income is the one generally used because it carries the advantage of continuity, making it easier to compare the ups and downs of poverty over the years.

In addition to problems with the index itself, the poverty count is understated because it is based on a survey of households. For instance, the homeless—the most destitute of the poor, whose numbers have increased substantially in recent years—are left uncounted. The 1990 decennial census was the first to make an effort to enumerate the homeless, although the Census Bureau does not deny the incompleteness of that first effort.

Table 1.4. Effects of Federal Transfers and Taxes on the Poverty Rate, 1979–1992

	1979	1983	1989	1990	1991	1992
Cash income before transfers	19.2%	22.8%	19.9%	20.5%	21.8%	22.5%
Plus social insurance (other than social security)	18.3	21.4	19.3	19.7	20.8	21.4
Plus social security	12.8	15.9	13.8	14.4	15.2	15.6
Plus means-tested cash transfers (official measure)	11.6	15.1	12.8	13.5	14.2	14.5
Plus food and housing benefits	9.7	13.7	11.2	11.8	12.4	12.9
Less federal taxes	10.0	14.6	11.8	12.3	12.6	13.0
Combined effect	−9.2	−8.2	−8.1	−8.2	−9.2	−9.5

Source: House Committee on Ways and Means. *1994 Green Book: Background Material and Data on Programs within the Jurisdiction of the Committee on Ways and Means* (Washington, D.C.: U.S. Government Printing Office, 15 July 1994), 1172–73.

Others question the adequacy of the official standard because it provides an absolute, or static, rather than a relative measure of poverty in America. The official measure is adjusted only to reflect changing price levels and not to reflect productivity gains or rising standards of living. It therefore fails to reflect changes in aspirations and relative concepts of poverty. For example, a home without indoor plumbing—the norm in earlier generations—is now considered substandard or unfit for habitation. Yet such shifts in societal norms and expectations, driven by real income gains achieved through greater productivity, are not captured by a static poverty measure that is adjusted only for changes in the cost of living over time. Note, for instance, the misperceptions of federal politicians during 1995 and 1996 as they advocated a "middle-class" tax cut but could not decide whether to set an annual income of $85,000 or of $100,000 as its ceiling, when any statistician could have told them that the median household income in the United States was closer to $36,000.

A flexible or relative poverty index pegged to median family income would reflect productivity gains as well as changes in the cost of living. For example, if the poverty threshold were set at 50 percent of the median family income for a family of four, the poverty threshold for 1994 would have been $23,378, or 54 percent higher than the official level, and the poverty rate would have been 22.6 percent rather than the official 14.5 percent. Thus, because the poor have not kept pace in income growth with the rest of the population over the past two decades, their share of the national income has declined substantially.

Figure 1.2 illustrates the extent to which the poor have failed to profit from economic growth in recent years. The dotted line traces the correlation over the years between the poverty rate and economic indicators such as unemployment, inflation, income, and government transfers. The dotted line for 1983–94 predicts what would have happened to the poverty rate had the same relationship to these indicators prevailed. Yet as unemployment fell, inflation lessened, and government transfers shrank during the post-1983 period, the poverty rate stayed high, reflecting a marked departure from past relationships.

Static and relative poverty indexes address two distinctly different concerns, and it is actually possible for one index to show an increase in poverty while the other indicates a diminution. A static measure like the official index reveals how the fortunes of low-income households have changed and demonstrates that substantial progress was made during the 1960s and 1970s in lifting families

Figure 1.2. Predicted and actual poverty rates, 1960–1993

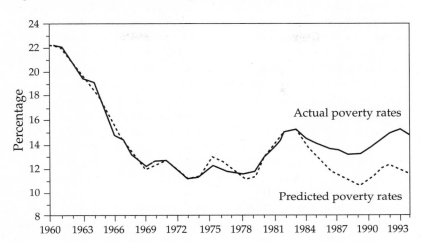

Source: Mishel, Bernstein, and Schmitt, *State of Working America, 1996–97,* 294.

above a fixed (albeit somewhat arbitrary) minimum income standard but has reversed since then. A relative poverty measure gauges shifts in income distribution, offering a reminder that there has been little progress in sharing the benefits of a prosperous economy more equitably. The widely accepted official poverty standard will no doubt remain the basis for the government's data collection because its static measure provides a sense of continuity in assessing how low-income Americans are faring. A relative measure offers an alternative perspective, but its practical use is limited. For example, setting a program eligibility guideline at half of the median income would make it difficult to target limited resources to the most needy. Nevertheless, after the passage of one-third of a century, it seems worthwhile to establish a new and corrected static measure for comparisons through the years ahead.

Our understanding of the level and causes of poverty also can be enhanced through the use of measures that link poverty and employment data and provide a more comprehensive picture of labor market conditions and problems. The official poverty index alone fails to reveal whether the poor suffer deprivation as a result of low wages, lack of job opportunities, or nonparticipation in the labor force. A labor market–related economic hardship measure could shed light on these important questions, yielding valuable information on levels of employment and earnings among the poor as well as on the extent of deprivation among the unemployed and underemployed. Reporting on Labor Day, 1979, the National Commission on Employment and Unemployment Statistics, chaired by Sar Levitan, recommended the launching of such a "hardship index." In response to what became known thereafter as the Levitan Report, the Bureau of Labor Statistics (BLS) published annual reports on "employment problems and economic status" for the years 1979–82, dropping the series thereafter because public and professional interest were lacking. In 1983 the Census Bureau inaugurated a survey of income and program participation, which provides some data linking economic hardship with labor force status. Then in 1989 the BLS resumed publishing an annual *Profile of the Working Poor,* the first covering data from 1987 and the 1996 report covering data from 1994.[2] The focus of the reports is on workers who spent more than half the year in the labor force, either working or looking for work, but remained in poverty. In 1994 such workers numbered 7.7 million, or 20 percent of the 38.1 million persons in the Census Bureau poverty count.

Such data make clear that the incidence of poverty in the United States extends well beyond the indigent into working families. Robert Haveman and Lawrence Buron have calculated that even if the adult members of every American family were making the fullest use of their physical and human capital in the labor market, 6.9 percent of the population would still be poor. In other words, the state of the labor market, together with the earning capacity of the population, has created a situation in which more than one out of fifteen Americans must be poor, no matter how hard they work.[3]

Identifying the Poor

Annual Census Bureau estimates of the poverty population are currently available for years from 1959 onward. More sketchy information indicates that, by the current poverty benchmark, more than half of the population was poor at the turn of the century. Economic growth lowered the poverty rate to about two-fifths of the population by 1929, but the Great Depression during the 1930s again impoverished half the nation. A booming economy during World War II reduced the poverty rate to a third of the population, and continued economic growth brought the rate to a low of slightly above 10 percent in the 1970s before it leveled off and then reversed (figure 1.3).

In 1960 nearly 40 million persons, or 22 percent of the popula-

Figure 1.3. Poverty, 1959–1995

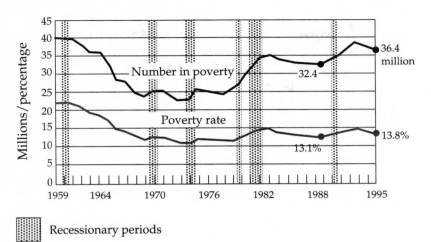

Source: U.S. Bureau of the Census, March Current Population Survey, 1959–95.

tion, were classified as poor. By 1969 this number had been reduced to 24.1 million, or 12 percent of the population. Most of this progress occurred during the second half of the decade, when American troops were in Vietnam, jobs were plentiful, and the federal government mounted special efforts to reduce the ranks of the poor.

If in-kind assistance had been counted, some additional headway against poverty was made during the 1970s. Regardless of how the poverty count is measured, the number of poor has climbed since 1978. Between 1978 and 1983, 10.8 million Americans were added to the poverty rolls—an increase of 44 percent—as the poverty rate rose from 11.4 percent to 15.2 percent of the population. This sharp rise was due to back-to-back recessions in 1979–80 and 1981–82 and to the failure of public assistance benefits to keep pace with inflation. During the subsequent prolonged economic recovery the poverty rate dropped to 13.1 percent by 1989, which was still higher than the rate in any recovery year since the 1960s. With another recession, the poverty rate climbed again in the early 1990s. At the time of the 1992 presidential elections the poverty rate stood at 14.5 percent, growing to 15.1 percent, or 39.3 million people, in 1993 and returning to 14.5 percent in 1994. The poverty rate appeared to be less responsive to each economic recovery. By 1995 the poverty rate had fallen to 13.8 percent. In that year 36.4 million people were classified as poor, 1.6 million fewer than in 1994 but a full 4 million more than in 1989. The experience since 1970 would lead us to expect a poverty rate fluctuating over the business cycle between 13 percent and 15 percent but with persistently rising numbers as the overall population increases. However, the slower response to the post-1992 economic recovery may portend even higher rates in the years ahead.

Political rhetoric to the contrary, without government assistance the poverty situation would be far bleaker; 27.3 million Americans would have been poor in 1995 had no government benefits been included in their incomes.[4] Poverty among the elderly was reduced from 15.8 million to 2.8 million by that means; among children the reduction was from 17.1 million to 11.4 million. The proportionate differences between poverty reduction among the old and among the young provide a significant insight. Of the 27.3 million individuals removed from poverty by government programs in 1995, 18.2 million were freed by social insurance—social security and unemployment compensation—and only 7.7 million by means-tested programs such as AFDC and Supplemental Security Income. Another 1.4 million were released from poverty by tax policy, primarily the EITC. Of course, 12.1 million of the 13.0 million elderly saved from poverty were saved by social insurance. In contrast, of the 5.7 million children removed from poverty by government programs in 1995, only 1.4 million were saved by social insurance, compared with 3.2 million by means-tested programs and 1.0 million by tax policy.

Differentiating on another axis between the impact of cash and in-kind benefits from government programs, almost 18 percent of all families and 35 percent of all unrelated individuals in the United States would live in poverty in the absence of cash benefits. These rates are in sharp contrast to the respective post-cash-transfer poverty rates of 10 percent and 21 percent. If the value of food, housing, and medical in-kind assistance were also included, the poverty rate for all persons would decline further to an estimated 10.3 percent of the population. The 1995 antipoverty gains were made despite substantial cuts in antipoverty expenditures, cuts that have deepened since, as documented below.

The difference between the family income of the poor and the poverty line—the poverty gap—generally shows that poor families and unrelated individuals have become relatively poorer since the 1970s (table 1.5). Once again, that poverty gap would be much

Table 1.5. Aggregate and Mean Poverty Gap and Annual Growth Rate, 1967–1994 (1995 $ millions)

	Families		Persons Not in Families	
Year(s)	Aggregate Poverty Gap	Mean Poverty Gap	Aggregate Poverty Gap	Mean Poverty Gap
1967	$30,597	$5,398	$16,612	$3,322
1973	26,104	5,406	14,950	3,200
1979	30,914	5,660	18,009	3,136
1983	48,633	6,158	22,500	2,674
1989	43,103	6,107	23,582	3,486
1994	50,491	6,270	30,457	3,675
Annual Growth Rates				
1967–73	−2.6%	0.0%	−1.7%	−0.6%
1973–79	2.9	0.8	3.2	−0.3
1979–89	3.4	0.8	2.7	1.1
1989–94	3.2	0.5	5.2	1.1

Source: Mishel, Bernstein, and Schmitt, *The State of Working America, 1996–97*, 304.

wider without the saving impact of government programs. The poverty gap was $59.4 billion in 1995, but it would have been $194.5 billion without government programs. The $5.4 billion poverty gap faced by the elderly would have been $68.8 billion, and the $15.7 billion poverty gap burdening children would have been $42.2 billion.[5]

The same point can be illustrated by the rising percentage of the poor whose income is below 50 percent of the poverty threshold (figure 1.4). The incidence of poverty is related to race, age, sex, household type, and educational attainment (figure 1.5). Despite a much lower poverty rate, the largest racial group among the poor are whites. Non-Hispanic whites constituted 44.7 percent of the poverty population in 1995. Blacks and Hispanics are two and one-half times as likely as whites to be poor (figure 1.6). They constituted 27.1 percent and 23.5 percent, respectively, of the poverty population. The greatest concentration of poverty is among individuals in female-headed households. Although members of this group constitute one-fifth of the U.S. population, they account for one-half of the poverty population. They are nearly six times as likely to be poor as two-parent families. Children have the highest poverty rate of any age group. Although they make up 27 percent of the U.S. pop-

Figure 1.4. Percentage of poor persons below 50 percent of poverty level, 1975–1994

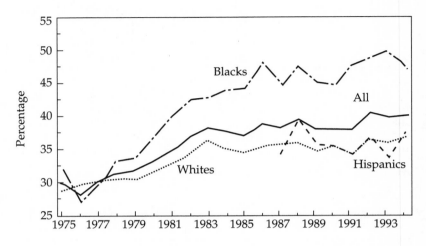

Source: Mishel, Bernstein, and Schmitt, *State of Working America, 1996–97,* 305.

ulation, children are 40 percent of the poor. Finally, adults with fewer than twelve years of schooling experience an incidence of poverty four times that of those with some college education.

The relative stability of the poverty rate and the characteristics of the poor mask considerable variability in poverty experiences and the movement of persons into and out of poverty. For example, 37.6 million Americans were poor in an average month in 1993, a poverty rate of 14.6 percent. However, Census Bureau statistics show that 52.7 million people, or 20.8 percent of the population, were poor for two months or more during that year. One in five persons who were poor in 1992 (21.6%) were not poor in 1993. The 6.3 million people leaving poverty were offset by 6.5 million who moved into poverty during the same period. Whites experienced significantly higher exit rates than did Hispanics, whose exit rates were higher than those of blacks. Individuals 18 to 64 years of age had a higher exit rate than that of individuals under age 18, and the rate for married-couple households exceeded that for all other household types (figure 1.7). Finally, one in four (24%) poverty spells in the years 1992 to 1994 lasted more than twelve months, and 13 percent lasted more than two years. These findings suggest that a large segment of the American population is susceptible to at

Figure 1.5. Selected poverty rates, 1995

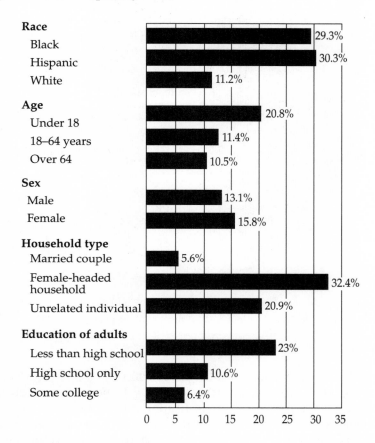

Source: U.S. Bureau of the Census.
Note: The total percentage poor in 1995 was 13.8 percent.

least temporary deprivation and that poverty is more pervasive than annual poverty rates indicate.

Yet for most households poverty is not a long-term affliction. Periods spent in school, accidents or poor health, job loss, family breakup, and many other temporary factors may be involved. Nearly one-half (46%) of poverty spells in 1992–94 lasted four months or less, and 67 percent lasted less than eight months. However, persistent poverty plagues a significant proportion of the poor; 11.9 million, more than one-third of the 38 million poor in 1992, were

Figure 1.6. Composition of the poor, by race, 1995

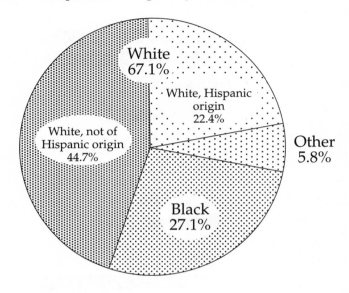

Source: U.S. Bureau of the Census, March Current Population Survey, 1995.
Note: Persons of Hispanic origin are 23.5 percent of the poor.

poor for all twenty-four months of 1992 and 1993. One-fourth of all poverty spells last five or more years, and 12 percent last a decade or more. Lengthy periods of destitution for a minority of the poor translates into an average duration of approximately four years. Whites and two-parent families experience primarily transitory poverty, but blacks and children born into poor families often experience long-term destitution. For example, if we use poverty in every month of 1992 and 1993 as a proxy for persistent poverty, 15.1 percent of blacks were persistently poor, compared with 10.3 percent of Hispanics and 3.1 percent of whites. Similarly, 17.2 percent of individuals in female-headed families were persistently poor, compared with 1.6 percent in married-couple families and 8.1 percent among unrelated individuals. Although poverty may often be persistent, evidence from longitudinal surveys and the experience of immigrants and their descendants suggest that destitution is infrequently lifelong or intergenerational. Nevertheless, though a few, such as those experiencing poverty while completing their educa-

Figure 1.7. Number of persons in poverty in 1992 and 1993 (poverty rates in parentheses)

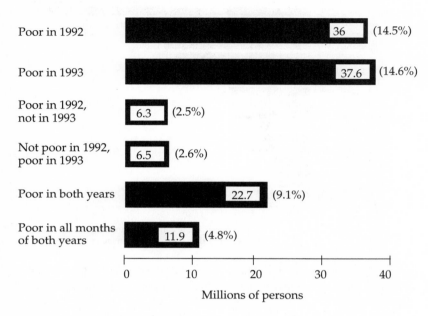

Millions of persons

Source: U.S. Bureau of the Census.

Note: The incidence of poverty reported here is lower than in the official estimates because these data are derived from the Survey of Income and Program Participation. "Poor in . . . " refers to those who were poor in an average month in the year.

tion, leave poverty far behind thereafter, most of the entry and exit is by those whose marginal earnings result in their fluctuating just above and just below the poverty threshold.

The International Context

The most recent comparative international poverty data available are for children during the late 1980s and the early 1990s (figure 1.8). Whether poverty is measured in relative terms (half of each nation's median income) or by an absolute standard (the U.S. thresholds modified for other countries by purchasing power parity), the incidence of poverty was higher in the United States than in any other developed industrial country.

The relatively high American poverty rates result from less equal

Figure 1.8. Relative poverty rates for children, mid-1980s to early 1990s

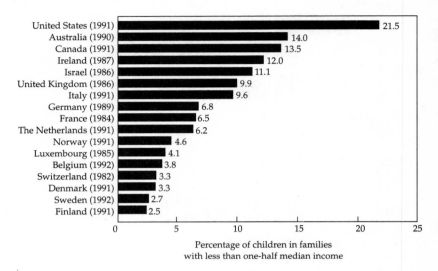

Percentage of children in families
with less than one-half median income

Source: Mishel, Bernstein, and Schmitt, *State of Working America, 1996–97,* 303.

Note: Income is post-tax and includes near-cash transfers such as food stamps and housing assistance.

income distribution, low earnings, a less generous income support system, and a high proportion of single-parent families. Despite America's overall high standard of living, poor American families with children earn less than the poor in other major countries for which data are available except in the much less affluent Australia. Cash or quasi-cash transfers (e.g., food stamps) and tax breaks were more effective in all countries in reducing the poverty rate among the elderly than in assisting families with children.

Even though they are now nearly a decade old, the figures in table 1.6 illustrating this point are still valid. More than one-fourth of poor American families with children received no income support, whereas virtually all poor families in the other countries studied obtained some help. The comparatively high proportion of single-parent families in the United States exacerbates this country's poverty rates. However, this factor has not similarly affected poverty rates in Scandinavian countries, where single-parent families are as prevalent as in the United States.

Table 1.6. Comparative Impact of Government Programs in Reducing Poverty, Early 1980s

	Pre-Tax/Transfer Poverty Rate		Reduction of Poverty Rate Due to Government Efforts	
	Families with Children	*Elderly*	*Families with Children*	*Elderly*
United States	17%	59%	17%	68%
Australia	18	72	15	67
Canada	14	57	37	90
Germany	8	81	13	79
Sweden	10	88	58	97
United Kingdom	14	78	40	47

Source: Timothy Smeeding, Barbara Boyle Torrey, and Martin Rein, "Patterns of Income and Poverty: The Economic Status of Children and the Elderly in Eight Countries," in *The Vulnerable*, ed. John Palmer, Timothy Smeeding, and Barbara Boyle Torrey (Washington, D.C.: Urban Institute Press, 1988), 96, 113.

Wealth and Poverty

Government poverty indicators have been based on income rather than on wealth because the latter concept is more difficult to quantify. However, the distribution of wealth is even more inequitable than that of income. In contrast to the general long-term decline in poverty, the concentration of wealth has fluctuated during the twentieth century. The proportion of wealth held by the richest 1 percent climbed during the 1920s, dropped to a low point after World War II, stabilized there, and then rose rapidly during the 1980s and early 1990s. For instance, the top 1 percent had 33.4 percent of the country's total wealth in 1983 and 37.2 percent in 1992. During the same years, the next 4 percent saw their proportion of the country's wealth rise moderately, from 21.2 percent to 22.8 percent, but the proportion of wealth held by all income groups below the top 5 percent declined. In 1992 the top 10 percent owned 71.8 percent of all wealth, leaving only 28.2 percent for the remaining 90 percent.[6] More than half of the poor have no assets at all, and another quarter have assets worth less than $1,000. Thus, if necessary, most of the poor could stave off only brief poverty spells by converting assets into cash. The elderly poor, some of whom have paid off their home mortgages, may be in a better position, but only in recent years have innovative financing schemes permitted a few of the elderly to remain in their homes and simultaneously use this resource to ameliorate poverty.

Causes of Poverty

The erosion of the traditional family structure in the past three decades, sluggish economic growth and scant productivity increases since 1973, growing income inequality since the late 1960s, and less generous social welfare assistance since 1980 have all contributed to the nation's inability to reduce impoverishment since the late 1970s. Changing family composition and fluctuating earnings account for most transitions into and out of poverty. Since none of these events appear to be declining, the poverty level is not likely to decrease significantly in the near future.

The Eroding Family

The close connection between poverty and family breakdown is a fairly recent development; before 1960 the vast majority of poor families were intact. However, since then the divorce rate has more than doubled and the proportion of births out of wedlock has increased fivefold. During the 1980s and into the 1990s the divorce rate dropped slightly, but out-of-wedlock births continued to increase rapidly (figure 1.9). Consequently, from 1960 to 1994 the proportion of families with children headed by a single parent has risen from 9 to 23 percent. However, a countertrend may be setting in, though it is too early to be certain. In 1995 the rate of births to teenagers fell for the fourth year in a row and out-of-wedlock births fell for the first time from 46.9 live births per 1,000 unmarried women in 1994 to 44.9 per 1,000 in 1995.

The high rate of divorce and out-of-wedlock births means that 60 percent of all children will spend some time in a single-parent family before reaching adulthood; nine of ten black children are expected to do so. Single-parent families are economically vulnerable because usually only one adult is available to provide income, the parent is often too young or lacking in salable skills to command sufficient wages, and the absent parent often contributes little, if any, support. Individuals who live independently of their families tend to increase the poverty rate because they cannot readily pool resources with other family members to take advantage of economies of scale. Many elderly individuals who once would have lived with their families have taken advantage of rising social security and private pension income and other benefits to establish separate households. However, the trend toward solo living apparently

Figure 1.9. Divorce and out-of-wedlock birth rates, 1975–1992

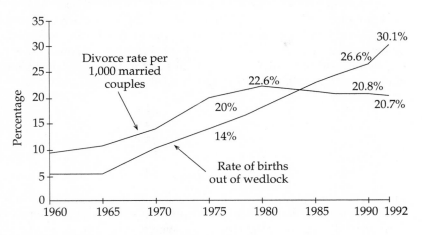

Source: U.S. National Center for Health Statistics.

peaked and leveled off during the 1980s and therefore probably did not significantly contribute to the rising poverty during the early 1990s:

	One-person households (%)	Persons 65 and older living alone (%)
1960	13	19
1970	17	27
1980	23	30
1990	25	31
1994	24	30

On the other hand, smaller families, the mass entrance of married women into the work force, and the increasing reluctance of young people to leave the nest have helped to restrain poverty in recent decades. The connection between family size and poverty is well documented: the larger the family, the more likely it is to be counted among the poor. Average family size has decreased from 3.7 in 1960 to 3.2 in 1994, but because most of this decline occurred during the 1970s it had little impact upon poverty in the succeeding decades. Young people have been particularly hurt by sluggish income growth. Between 1973 and 1995 the median real weekly earnings of all 16- to 24-year-old young men employed full-time declined by 31 percent, and those for young women in the same age group declined by 13.3 percent, even though they had become better educated—there was a sharp decline in the share who were school dropouts and a substantial rise in the share who had received postsecondary education.[7] Perhaps in part for that reason, a growing proportion of youths aged 18 to 24 elect to live with their parents rather than establish their own households:

1960	43%
1970	47
1980	48
1990	53
1994	53

The poverty rate would undoubtedly be higher if these young adults had left the nest. But it is still an open question whether family structure is the cause or the victim of poverty. How many males disappear because they cannot support the children they have fathered? Are single-parent families poor because they are headed by a woman or because the wage structure allows few mothers to earn their way out of poverty? For instance, Mary Jo Bane and David Ellwood argue that only one-fifth of the poverty spells of female-headed families result directly from the family breakup, the remainder being a direct result of job loss, wage cuts, or other labor market phenomena impacting upon such families.[8]

Joblessness or Low Earnings

Trends in earnings, which constitute the lion's share of personal income, significantly influence the extent of poverty. During the postwar period average earnings steadily rose, but since 1973 they have stagnated and declined in real terms. Figure 1.10 shows the trends in men's hourly wages by percentile between 1973 and 1995. Only the top 10 percent of earners (the 9th percentile) were able to maintain their real-wage level. All other employed men were paid less for their work on the average year by year. In the case of women, on the other hand, though starting from a far lower base, all but those in the lowest two percentiles experienced improving real wages, but those in the lowest two percentiles—those most likely to have been in poverty—saw their real wages decline (figure 1.11). As a result the gender wage gap declined persistently until women who on the average earned 63.1 percent of male wages in 1973 were earning 76.7 percent in 1995.

Applying the wage analysis more directly to the poverty level,

Figure 1.10. Hourly wages of men by wage percentile, 1973–1995

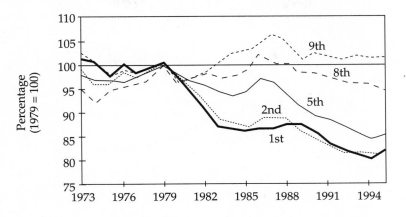

Source: Mishel, Bernstein, and Schmitt, *State of Working America, 1996–97,* 143.

the proportion of jobs paying wages less than, at, and just above the poverty level has risen markedly since the early 1970s. In 1995, 30 percent of the work force received wages at or below the poverty line, compared with 23.5 percent in 1973. In addition, 13.3 percent of the work force received wages at between 100 percent and 125 percent of the poverty level in 1973, compared with 14.6 percent in 1995. More than 36 percent of all males employed received wages at less than 125 percent of the poverty level in 1995, compared with 21.5 percent in 1973. In contrast, females receiving wages below 125 percent of the poverty level declined from 57.7 percent in 1973 to 53 percent in 1995.[9]

Of course, these wage shares represent only those of the poor who are working. While the number of poor persons in the prime working-age group, those aged 25 to 54, increased from 7,659,000 in 1979 to 12,312,000 in 1994, the percentage of those who were not employable rose from 17.6 percent to 24.4 percent, primarily because of illness or disability. Thus, those who were employable fell from 82.4 percent to 75.6 percent. But of the employable, the proportion unable to find jobs rose from 3.7 percent to 5.1 percent. The proportion who worked stayed nearly constant, falling from 53.4 percent in 1979 to 51.1 in 1994. At the same time, work commitment rose moderately, with the proportion working full-time year-round increasing from 13.9 percent to 16.2 percent, offset by a drop from 39.5 percent to 34.9 percent among those working part-time or part-

Figure 1.11. Hourly wages of women by wage percentile, 1973–1995

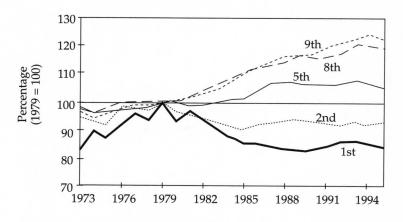

Source: Mishel, Bernstein, and Schmitt, *State of Working America, 1996–97,* 145.

year. However, the part-time employed continued to outnumber the full-time employed, as is to be expected among a population including so many single-parent families.

Multiple Problems among Poor Families

The poor tend to suffer more than their share of most social ills—family breakup, teen pregnancy, inadequate housing, ill health, drug and alcohol abuse, child and spouse abuse, juvenile delinquency, and involvement as either victims or perpetrators of crime. Single-parent poor families are much more likely than two-parent poor families to face multiple difficulties, given the interactions between being a single parent and being jobless, poor, ill-educated, and on welfare. Poor married parents generally face less severe difficulties than poor single parents, but they are not free of multiple barriers to self-sufficiency.

Surveys of inmates in state juvenile institutions (which house the more serious youthful criminal offenders) indicate a close connection between crime, family breakdown, drug abuse, and limited education. Seven of ten inmates grew up primarily in a one-parent household. More than 60 percent had used drugs regularly, and of those who had ever used drugs (80%), two out of five began before age 12. Of inmates over age 18 who remained in juvenile institutions, only 10 percent had a high school diploma. More than half

Table 1.7. Demographic Characteristics of the Poverty Population, 1959–1995 (millions)

	1959	*1970*	*1980*	*1988*	*1995*
Total					
Number poor	39.5	25.4	29.3	31.9	36.4
Percentage poor	22.4	12.6	13.0	13.1	13.8
Aged					
Number poor	5.5	4.8	3.9	3.5	3.3
Percentage poor	35.2	24.6	15.7	12.0	10.5
Children					
Number poor	17.6	10.4	11.5	12.6	14.7
Percentage poor	27.3	15.1	18.3	19.7	20.8
Nonaged adults					
Number poor	16.5	10.2	13.9	15.8	18.4
Percentage poor	17.0	9.0	10.1	10.5	11.4
Individuals in female-headed households					
Number poor	10.4	11.2	14.6	16.2	14.2
Percentage poor	50.2	38.2	33.8	32.2	36.5
Blacks					
Number poor	9.9	7.5	8.6	9.4	9.5
Percentage poor	55.1	33.5	32.5	31.6	29.3
Whites					
Number poor	28.5	17.5	19.7	20.8	24.4
Percentage poor	18.1	9.9	10.2	10.1	11.2

Source: U.S. Bureau of the Census.

of the inmates reported that another family member also had been incarcerated. The characteristics of adult prisoners also indicate a clear connection between crime, inadequate education, low income, and alcohol or drug abuse. Although a majority of inmates are working at the time of arrest, their limited incomes place most of them in the ranks of the working poor.

A Profile of America's Poor

The demographic characteristics of the poor have changed significantly during the past generation. Two phenomena are particularly striking: the increased poverty rate of persons living in female-headed households and the declining poverty rate of the elderly poor (table 1.7).

For the purposes of this survey, the poor can be divided into four major groups; the elderly; the working poor; adults not in the work force; and children, particularly those in families headed by women. Although all these individuals have limited incomes, the causes contributing to their penury vary, and different programs are often required to lift them out of poverty.

The Aged Poor

Poverty among the elderly is an enlightening success story, though that very success may eventually backfire politically as the younger realize they are paying for it. Traditionally the elderly have been among poverty's most frequent victims. Throughout recent decades, however, the economic status of older Americans has improved, largely because they have transformed themselves into the most formidable voting bloc in the nation. While the size of the aged population continued to rise, the number of aged poor dropped from 4.8 million in 1970 to 3.3 million in 1995. The decline in the number of poor has left the incidence of poverty among persons aged 65 and over slightly lower than the incidence in the rest of the population despite their exit from the work force (figure 1.12). This downward trend in poverty levels for the aged is due largely to more generous social security benefits, which are indexed for inflation, and the growth of private pensions. The impact of social security is demonstrated by a decline of 9 percent in the elderly poverty rate during the 1970s alone due to successive increases in benefits that more than compensated for inflation. The percentage of those 65 and over below the poverty line fell from 24.6 percent in 1970 to 15.7 percent in 1980, 12.0 percent in 1988, and 10.5 percent in 1995. However, that development has not totally solved the poverty problems of the aged. Even though the roughly 2.5 million elderly unrelated individuals whose poverty rate was 47.2 percent in 1970 have seen their poverty rate cut, it was still 24.1 percent in 1993. The older among the poor, especially the rising number over 85, include many who are not eligible for social security pensions and dependent upon the less generous SSI program discussed in chapter 2. Also, poverty is more persistent among the elderly than among the younger population. A quarter of the elderly who become poor remain so for a decade or more; this is more than double the proportion for the nonelderly.

It is uncertain whether progress against poverty among the aged will continue as the economic strains of sustaining a growing elderly population increase in future years. Politicians of neither party were prepared to discuss the issue in an election year, but, as

Figure 1.12. Poverty rates by age, 1959–1995

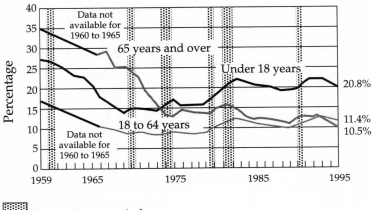

Recessionary periods

Source: U.S. Bureau of the Census, March Current Population Survey, 1959–95.

noted in chapter 2, the issue must be faced in the near future. When it is, the nonpoor elderly will be much better prepared than their low-income peers to protect themselves politically.

The Working Poor

Lack of employment opportunities is often the cause of poverty, but even a full-time job may not guarantee an adequate income. Year after year more than 40 percent of poor persons 16 years of age or older worked, one out of ten of them year-round (table 1.8). More than one-half of the family heads who were poor in 1994 worked during that year. Sixteen percent of all poor families had two or more persons working at some time during the year but remained poor. Some combination of low wages, spells of unemployment, limited hours, and large families kept these persons and their families in poverty despite their work effort. Nevertheless, the rising share of workers earning poverty-level wages demonstrates the commitment of the poor to work despite declining compensation for it. In 1995, 18.7 percent, 33.8 percent, and 44.5 percent of white, black, and Hispanic male workers, respectively, earned less than poverty-level wages. Each figure was dramatically larger than at any time since 1973. For female workers the corresponding statistics were 33.9 percent, 43.7 percent, and 53.5 percent, respectively.[10]

Table 1.8. Workers as a Proportion of All Poor Persons, 1978–1995, 16 Years and Over (thousands)

| | | Worked Year-Round | | | |
| | | Worked | | Worked Full-Time | |
Year	Total Number	Number	Percentage	Number	Percentage
1978	16,914	6,599	39.0	1,309	7.7
1980	18,892	7,674	40.6	1,644	8.7
1982	22,100	9,013	40.8	1,999	9.0
1984	21,541	8,999	41.8	2,076	9.6
1986	20,688	8,743	42.3	2,007	9.7
1988	20,323	8,363	41.2	1,929	9.5
1990	21,242	8,716	41.0	2,076	9.8
1992	23,951	9,739	40.6	2,211	9.2
1994	24,108	9,829	40.8	2,520	10.5
1995	23,077	9,484	41.1	2,418	10.5

Source: U.S. Bureau of the Census, March Current Population Survey.

Declining real wages since 1973 are the primary cause. Among prime-age male workers (25–54 years old) working or looking for work at least fifty weeks per year the annual earnings of 8.1 percent for a family of four in 1974, 9.0 percent in 1979, 12.3 percent in 1989, and 15.2 percent in 1994 did not reach the poverty line. For women in the same age group the percentages of those earning less than poverty wages despite full-time work were 26.4 percent, 24.6 percent, 23.8 percent, and 25.5 percent, respectively. For women, the presence of children made a difference, not only in their commitment to the work force but also in the wages they were able to earn in a full-time, year-round labor force attachment. Of female household heads, 37.5 percent in 1974, 34.4 percent in 1979, 34.4 percent in 1989, and 40.0 percent in 1994 worked or looked for work year-round without exceeding poverty-level earnings.

The working poor are heavily concentrated in a few low-paid occupations. In addition, although the link between joblessness and poverty is often overstated, it remains a major cause of poverty. Poor family heads are almost two and one-half times more likely than nonpoor family heads to experience joblessness. The majority of the working poor who drop out of the work force encounter other labor market difficulties. Some leave the work force because of illness or disability, and others become discouraged by low-paying jobs and drop out of the labor force voluntarily.

Employment and training programs designed to smooth the operation of the labor market, enhance the productivity of low-income workers, and open opportunities for employment and advancement can alleviate the plight of the working poor. The acquisition of job skills and work experience are often essential for workers seeking access to higher-paying jobs. The primary shortcoming of such training efforts has been that they spread too little money among too many trainees, with the result that few are in training long enough for it to make a sufficient impact on their posttraining wages. Effective enforcement of antidiscrimination legislation is also required to ensure that opportunities for advancement and self-sufficiency are not closed on the basis of race, sex, age, disability, or national origin.

The Nonworking Poor

Disability, long-term illness, and family responsibilities are common barriers to employment among the nonworking poor. The disabled are especially prone to work limitations and poverty. Some 24 percent of individuals 15 years old and over with severe disabilities were poor in 1992, compared with 14 percent of those with disabilities classified as nonsevere and 12 percent among their nondisabled counterparts. Among individuals receiving some form of cash assistance in 1992, 62.4 percent had a disability. For example, the disability rate among food stamp recipients was 48 percent, and the rate among public housing recipients was 30.7 percent.

In March 1996, 27.5 percent of individuals 25 to 64 years of age and with work disabilities were employed, 18 percent of them full-time. The unemployment rate among the disabled was 11.4 percent. Among the severely disabled only 9 percent were employed, 4 percent full-time, with an unemployment rate in this group of 41 percent. In contrast, the employment rate among the nondisabled was over 80 percent and the unemployment rate was below 6 percent.

Data on the interaction of poverty, disability, and employment are not published routinely. The most recent available publication on this interaction dates back to the late 1980s.[11] At that time more than two-fifths of poor males and one in six poor females aged 22 to 59 who did not work at all during 1987 were disabled. Only 13 percent of poor working-age disabled worked, only 5 percent of those full-time; a third of those in the labor force were unemployed, and those with jobs earned an average of only $2,400. In addition, more than three out of five females in this age group cited home responsibilities as the obstacle to outside work. The problems facing female household heads are particularly acute because the presence of children not only increases income needs but also hinders employment, as has already been discussed.

Some of the nonworking poor could and should be lured or goaded into employment. With appropriate assistance, work effort and earnings by this group could be enhanced and prospects for self-sufficiency increased. The 1988 Family Support Act tried to address some of the obstacles to self-sufficiency for those on welfare, and the 1996 welfare reform legislation, described in chapter 2, attempted to make that mandatory. For the vast majority of welfare mothers, however, jobs alone are not the answer because in the absence of income support and other assistance their chances of escaping deprivation are limited. For the disabled the self-reliance opportunities are even more limited. The Americans With Disabilities Act of 1990 will help. More can always be done with sheltered workshop alternatives, but the fact must be faced that the workplace cannot provide places for everyone. There will always be need for the equivalent of Supplemental Security Income and public assistance for those for whom the Temporary Assistance to Needy Families (TANF) 20 percent exemption discussed in chapter 2 is designed. Only experience can determine whether that window is of adequate width.

Children in Poverty

In 1995 two-fifths of the poor were under 18 years of age and more than one in every five children in the United States lived in poverty. The number of children under age 6 living in poverty rose from 3.5 million in 1979 to 6.1 million in 1994, an increase from 18 percent to 25 percent of all children that age. The proportion of young children living in extreme poverty—less than 50 percent of the poverty threshold—doubled from 6 percent to 12 percent. Forty-five percent of all children under age 6 live in households with incomes between 101 percent and 185 percent of poverty.[12] Child poverty rates dropped until the early 1970s and then plateaued. The resurgence of child poverty in the 1980s and 1990s has long-term consequences because children raised in poor families are almost inevitably denied opportunities from the very start and are thus impeded in preparing themselves for productive adult lives.

Contrary to stereotypes, poverty among young children has grown much faster in the suburbs than in either urban or rural areas—60 percent compared with 34 percent and 45 percent, respectively, between 1979 and 1994. Young white children experience the most poverty—2.2 million in 1994 compared with 1.9 million black children and 1.7 million Hispanic children, but with the number of Hispanic children increasing by 43 percent compared with 38 percent for whites and 19 percent for blacks during 1979–94. But whereas only 6 percent of young white children were extremely poor in 1994 (less than 50% of the poverty threshold), 30 percent of young black children were. In 1994, 62 percent of young children lived in households in which at least one adult worked. Less than one-third of young poor children lived in households relying exclusively on public assistance. Although poverty rates were of course higher in fractured families, young children living in traditional nuclear families with two parents at least one of whom was employed full-time were two and one-half times as likely to be poor in 1994 as in 1975, their poverty rate having increased from 6 percent to 15 percent.

The poverty rate for young children is at least one-third higher and usually two to three times as high in the United States as in any other Western industrialized nation. The rate of poverty for young children also ranges from 11 percent in New Hampshire to 41 percent in Louisiana and from 14 percent in San Jose to 60 percent in Detroit.

Many children live in poverty because they are its cause; that is, low-income families are frequently driven into poverty by the addition of family members. There is a close relationship between family size and poverty (figure 1.13); half of families with five or more children live in poverty (table 1.9). A higher incidence of poverty among larger families is not surprising in a society where need is not a factor in wage determination and where the absence of child care facilities often hinders mothers from earning needed income.

Not only are children the most poverty-impacted age group but they are the most likely to remain in poverty for long periods (table 1.10). This is especially true of black children. Children living with a single or disabled parent are particularly likely to experience long-term poverty. However, black children in two-parent families live in poverty on average for about as long (3 years) as do white children in single-parent families.

Poor children have special needs over and above those that can be fulfilled through income maintenance. Preventive health care, adequate nutrition, compensatory education, and vocational training are particularly important in providing permanent exits from poverty. Not only do children in poor families suffer material deprivation but they are more likely to suffer abuse and neglect than children from more affluent families—and that abuse and neglect appear to be increasing. It is not possible to know for certain

Figure 1.13. Poverty and family size, 1993

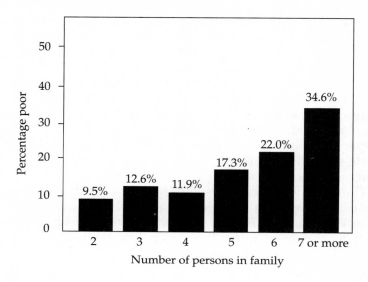

Source: U.S. Bureau of the Census.

whether abuse is increasing or whether reporting is improving or even whether abuse is more likely to be reported when the family is poor, nor is it possible to know the relationship between the number of reported instances and the total.

But considering those limitations, the trends are disquieting, to say the least. Since the late 1970s the U.S. Congress has required the National Center on Child Abuse and Neglect to conduct periodic surveys of child protection specialists to obtain estimates of the number harmed and endangered in a sample of U.S. counties. Such surveys were conducted in 1979–80, 1986–87, and 1993–94. The 1,553,800 children shown to be harmed by abuse or neglect in the latest survey represented a 67 percent increase over the previous survey and a 149 percent increase over the first survey. The 1993–94 total included 743,200 abused and 879,000 neglected children. Adding the number of children considered by the professionals to be endangered to the number reported as actually harmed raised the abuse and neglect number for 1993–94 to 2,815,600, a 98 percent increase over 1986–87. By type, 614,000 were physically abused, 300,200 sexually abused, 532,000 emotionally abused, 1,335,000 physically neglected, and 585,100 emotionally neglected. That

Table 1.9. Poverty and Family Size by Race, 1993

Family Size	Whites	Blacks	Hispanics
2	7.5%	26.2%	21.9%
3	9.7	29.7	25.9
4	9.1	30.6	27.4
5	13.2	41.3	30.2
6	18.0	40.2	34.8
7+	28.6	52.9	41.1

Source: U.S. Bureau of the Census.

Table 1.10. Duration of Child Poverty for Black and Nonblack Children Aged 18 in 1988–1990

Duration of Poverty	All Children	Blacks	Nonblacks
Never poor	65%	28%	73%
Ever poor	35	72	27
1–5 years	21	26	20
6–10 years	6	19	4
11–16 years	7	22	4
17 years	1	6	Less than 1

Source: Mishel, Bernstein, and Schmitt, *The State of Working America, 1996–97*, 307.

breakdown becomes relevant to the current study because children from families with an annual income below $15,000 were twenty-two times more likely to experience harm and twenty-five times more likely to be endangered than children from families with an annual income above $30,000. Children from the lowest-income families were eighteen times more likely to be sexually abused, nearly fifty-six times more likely to be educationally neglected, and twenty-two times more likely to be seriously injured from maltreatment than their higher-income counterparts. The perpetrators were more likely to be women than men except in sex abuse cases. Children of single parents were 77 percent more likely to be harmed by physical abuse, 87 percent more likely to be harmed by physical neglect, and at an 80 percent greater risk of serious injury than children in two-parent families.[13] There were no significant differences by race.

Family Structure and Poverty

As noted earlier, a major cause of the rise in child poverty has been the substantial increase in the numbers and proportions of households headed by single female parents. Sixty percent of all poor families are now headed by women, and female-headed families with children are six times more likely to be poor than two-parent families. Impoverished families headed by women are as a group heavily dependent upon welfare for support, and many female heads of households have scant prospects of earning enough to lift their families out of poverty even if they are able to obtain full-time work.

Nevertheless, it should also be noted that while the number of female-headed families has continued to rise, the pace of that increase has markedly slowed and the poverty rates of those families have remained relatively static since the late 1960s (table 1.11). In fact, the phenomenon spoken of as the feminization of poverty has emerged primarily because the poverty rate for female-headed households has decreased less over time than that of other households.

That the numbers of single-headed families who are poor has not increased more rapidly is largely attributable to the fact that the average number of children in such families has been falling (from 2.36 in 1970 to 1.80 in 1992, below the 1.85 average for all two-parent families and 2.26 for those in poverty) at the same time that the number of female-headed families has been rising. Those two phenomena just offset each other for whites, while the declining births offset the impact of a little more than half of the rise in female headship among black families.[14]

Their higher rate of single-parent families—46 percent in 1995—of course impedes economic progress among blacks. Nevertheless, it is notable that the poverty rate of black female-headed families has been headed downward in recent years, decreasing from 52.8 percent in 1973 to 46.1 percent in 1994. At the same time, the trend for white female-headed families has been persistently upward, though at lower rates, increasing from 24.6 percent in 1973 to 29 percent in 1994.

It is also worth noting that despite the regrettable rise in the number of never-married female household heads, the consequence of a rising incidence of out-of-wedlock births, divorce accounts for well over one-third of single-parent families. The never-married category continues to rise, while the divorce proportion has stabilized and even the rate of increase in the never-married incidence

Table 1.11. Changing Family Structure and Poverty, 1959–1994

	Percentage of Persons			Poverty Rates of Persons			
Year	In Female-Headed Families	In Married-Couple and Male-Headed Families	Not Living in Families	In Female-Headed Families	In Married-Couple and Male-Headed Families	Not Living in Families	All Persons
1959	8.0%	85.9%	6.1%	49.4%	18.2%	46.1%	22.4%
1967	9.1	84.2	6.7	38.8	9.6	38.1	14.2
1973	10.5	80.7	8.8	37.5	6.0	25.6	11.1
1979	12.1	76.2	11.7	34.9	6.4	21.9	11.7
1989	13.5	72.3	14.3	36.4	7.5	19.3	13.1
1994	14.2	71.0	14.7	38.6	8.3	21.5	14.5

Source: Mishel, Bernstein, and Schmitt, *The State of Working America, 1996–97,* 315.

Table 1.12. Marital Status of Female Heads of Households, 1973–1994

Year	Married, Husband Absent	Widowed	Divorced	Never Married	Number (000)
1973	23.9%	37.7%	25.9%	12.6%	6,535
1979	21.0	29.8	33.0	16.2	8,220
1989	17.1	23.9	36.4	22.6	10,890
1994	17.8	19.5	36.1	26.6	12,406

Source: Mishel, Bernstein, and Schmitt, *The State of Working America, 1996–97*, 323.

is slowing (table 1.12). As noted, the family structure may be the consequence as much as the cause of the poverty.

The feminization of poverty—the analytical warning of the 1980s—still deserves a prominent place on the nation's social welfare agenda. It threatens children as well as their mothers and could contribute to a dependent underclass with little hope of economic advancement and self-sufficiency. Nevertheless, the narrowing income gap between males and females resulting from the general decline in male wages over the past two decades is tending to make poverty equally threatening to both genders.

The Underclass Specter?

The threat of a growing underclass has captured increasing attention in recent years. The term is often used loosely, but it is usually applied to young people with criminal records, unmarried welfare mothers, ghetto residents, or some combination of these groups, who undergo lengthy impoverishment. Another trait frequently attributed to the underclass is "a willingness to flout the traditional norms of what society generally considers to be acceptable behavior."[15] Analysts have divided the underclass into several types, including the violent underclass, the reproductive underclass, the educational underclass, the jobless underclass, and the impoverished underclass.[16] Focusing upon what he perceives as an inner-city underclass, William Julius Wilson explains the phenomenon by labor market changes, including the decline in well-paid jobs and their movement out of congested urban areas, the resultant decline in the availability of marriageable males able to support a family, declining marriage rates and an increase in out-of-wedlock births, a rise in welfare dependency, migration of the middle class to the suburbs, and the impact of deteriorating neighborhoods on children and youths.[17] In the absence of a rigorous "official" definition of the underclass, its magnitude cannot be determined and estimates range widely. Ronald Mincy, after reviewing the literature on the subject, posited a range from 1 million to 4 million, at most about 4 percent of the total population and one-fourth of the poor.[18] William Kelso, who tends to stress the magnitude of social breakdown and pathology, estimates that 30–40 percent of the poor are in that underclass.[19] But that conclusion requires a very expansive definition of the term.

Despite the widespread media and academic attention, the underclass appears to constitute a small part of the poverty population. About a quarter of the impoverished at a given time are nonelderly, able-bodied individuals who experience lengthy deprivation. In 1995, 41 percent of the poor 16 years of age and older worked, 11 percent of them full-time, year-round. In the most highly concentrated poverty areas one-third of working-age adults worked regularly and two-thirds of the households did not receive public assistance. As noted earlier, in 1995, 45 percent of the poor lived in inner cities, compared with 30 percent of the total U.S. population. The poverty rate was 13.4 percent in metropolitan areas, compared with 15.6 percent in nonmetropolitan areas, and the inner-city poverty rate was 20 percent. Concern for these concentrations of poverty is appropriate and should receive policy attention. Nevertheless, that concern should not be allowed to detract attention from the primary problems of the majority of the poor.

Strategies for Helping the Poor

Poor people need money. Whatever their characteristics, their immediate problem is a lack of income to purchase basic goods and services. Beyond this, however, the various groups of the poor have different needs, many of which cannot be fulfilled by cash payments at a level the public is willing to support. Family heads and young people with their life's work ahead of them need not only daily subsistence but also encouragement and support to acquire salable skills. Children also need health care and basic education to fulfill their potential. Medical and nursing home care are primary concerns of the aged. All poor people may need income supplements, including housing, medical care, food, and other assistance.

Beginning with the New Deal of the 1930s, the United States developed an extensive though far from comprehensive array of programs to assist the economically disadvantaged. Throughout their history there has been tension between programs designed to rehabilitate the poor and bring them to self-reliance and programs prepared to support the poor in their poverty. The New Deal not only provided work relief programs for its own time but also put together the Social Security Act, with its combination of social insurance and means-tested public assistance, for the future. The 1960s War on Poverty emphasized employment and training but never came near to the 1930s programs in scale. Although all of these programs have come under increasing criticism in recent years, only one—AFDC—has actually been abolished, and even it has been replaced by a federal block grant to the states from which to provide sustenance to at least some of those who cannot become self-sufficient. This antipoverty system was based on the assumption that special-purpose programs were required to take care of the diverse needs of the poor. While some programs single out one or more segments of the poverty population for special attention, other programs provide broader coverage. Therefore, aid to the poor is more readily classified by the assistance received than by who is served.

Federal programs in aid of the poor fall into four broad categories: (1) cash support; (2) direct provision of necessities such as food, shelter, and health care; (3) preventive and compensatory programs targeted at children and youths; and (4) employment-related efforts designed to expand opportunities for work, advancement, and self-sufficiency.

Income maintenance programs provide the foundation of federal assistance to the poor because poverty can be ameliorated most directly by cash support. The family unit itself is often the best judge of how its limited resources should be allocated, and income maintenance is a more flexible form of assistance than the provision of goods and services. Cash support is flawed, however, by the probability that employable recipients will become less motivated to work. In addition, income subsidies may not be used for the intended goal of providing basic sustenance. Finally, political support for income maintenance can fluctuate greatly, sometimes depending upon its purpose and the characteristics of the recipients but more often according to the attitudes of the voting public.

The major cash income maintenance programs include old age, survivors, and disability insurance (OASDI), unemployment insurance, general assistance, veterans' pensions, workers' compensation, and, until 1996, AFDC. Because public sentiment against income payment to employable persons remains strong, these programs are designed primarily for persons considered too old or too disabled to work, those who have been forced out of jobs, and those burdened by child care responsibilities, though sympathy for the last is declining. More comprehensive programs, such as a guaranteed income, negative income tax, or family allowance, have occasionally been proposed to provide income subsidies without regard to labor force status but have never been given serious political consideration.

Another group of programs provides the needy with goods and services as a supplement to their cash income. Whatever the relative merits of helping the poor with cash versus in-kind benefits, political realities frequently dictate the latter. In order to mobilize societal resources, public attention usually needs to be focused on a specific and visible problem. For example, only after a highly publicized investigation in the late 1960s stressed the persistence of hunger in the United States did Congress increase food appropriations and tailor the resulting program to address this specific problem. In response to high unemployment in the mid-1970s the federal government expanded the food stamp program. It would have been infinitely more difficult to gain additional support for direct cash payments to the poor. However, in addition to the symbolic connection between food stamps and hunger, there was the political support of farmers expecting some impact on agricultural demand.

Not only is in-kind aid more palatable politically but in some instances goods need to be provided directly because they are not available in the market. For example, in the absence of policies to stimulate construction of low-cost units, housing subsidies to the poor would tend to raise rent levels on existing units while doing little to increase the supply of affordable housing, particularly for victims of discrimination and the homeless. Finally, because certain economies are possible in large-scale enterprises, the government can in some cases provide goods and services more efficiently than the private sector.

Other services are provided directly by the government not only to make life easier for today's poor but to give their children a better chance of escaping poverty. Helping families prevent unwanted children is one of the most effective ways of reducing poverty, but it conflicts with strongly held moral values. Proper health care and nutrition for mother and child ensure that the young will have a better chance for a productive life, and they actually reduce health care and other costs in the long run. The federal government also supports compensatory education programs from preschool through college, providing poor children with the basic competencies necessary to obtain good jobs. However, despite the relatively small portion of the federal budget involved, all of these programs now find themselves caught between the simultaneous demands to reduce federal deficits and cut taxes.

Efforts to expand work opportunities and improve the functioning of labor market institutions are critical components of antipoverty programs. These initiatives are designed to eliminate the causes of poverty rather than to merely mitigate its symptoms. For the most part, programs are directed at the employable poor and concentrate on economic institutions, although giving the poor the opportunity to design and participate in the implementation of noneconomic programs on their behalf can facilitate economic opportunity. Employment-related initiatives can be divided into three groups: (1) education, occupational training, job search assistance, and subsidized private-sector jobs; (2) attempts to restructure the labor market through a minimum wage, public employment, and antidiscrimination laws; and (3) economic development programs to rejuvenate depressed urban and rural areas. The effectiveness of all of these has been challenged in recent years.

At best, these various programs complement and reinforce each other. It is necessary not only to assuage poverty through cash and in-kind aid but also to prevent deprivation by promoting self-sufficiency in the first place. Many programs serve both ends. Birth control may reduce child care burdens, and child care itself may be designed primarily to give the young a better start in life, but both also enable the mother to better contribute to her family's support. Similarly, the difference between cash support and "rehabilitative" programs is often blurred in reality, as in the case of wage subsidies or tax incentives to employers to support on-the-job training. These interrelationships both caution against narrow evaluations of program benefits and offer a reminder that no single strategy can hope to address adequately the complex and multiple impediments to self-sufficiency that the poor face. However, survival depends more upon public perceptions than upon actual evidence of effectiveness.

The Scale of Antipoverty Efforts

The cost of programs in aid of the poor is substantial but elusive because social security, Medicare, and many lesser efforts serve the nonpoor as well as the poor. From President Johnson's declaration of war on poverty in 1964 until the end of the 1970s the antipoverty budget grew dramatically, with most of the increase occurring under Republican administrations (table 1.13). The total budget for an-

Table 1.13. Total Antipoverty Expenditures and Outlays Per Poor Person (1992 dollars)

Year	Expenditures (billions)			Expenditures per Poor Person		
	Total	Federal	State/Local	Total	Federal	State/Local
1968	$70.0	$49.5	$20.5	$2,758	$1,949	$ 809
1973	125.6	91.4	34.2	5,471	3,977	1,494
1978	196.0	149.0	47.0	8,000	6,082	1,494
1983	192.2	143.6	48.6	5,444	4,065	1,379
1987	211.8	153.3	58.5	6,508	4,712	1,796
1992	288.9	207.6	82.3	7,964	5,702	2,262

Source: U.S. General Accounting Office.

tipoverty programs has continued to grow since 1978, but its growth has not been commensurate with the increasing number of the poor, and most of the increase has been due to rising health care costs, which are primarily due to inflation. Although not all low-income programs restrict eligibility to those below the poverty line, adjusting expenditures for the size of the poverty population provides a fair approximation of trends over time. In the decade following 1968 antipoverty spending per poor person (adjusted for inflation) nearly tripled, but it dropped by almost a third by 1983 before rising slightly by 1987 and substantially by 1992, returning to the 1978 level. By 1992, government programs aimed specifically at the low-income population carried a $289 billion price tag with the federal government contributing 72 percent of the total (table 1.13). Nevertheless, though federal antipoverty spending fluctuated, that of state and local governments marched steadily upward.

Viewed in the context of the increase in the gross national product, the proportion of antipoverty spending declined in the 1980s but recovered in the early 1990s. Antipoverty expenditures rose from 1.8 percent of GNP in 1968 to 3.9 percent in 1980 and then dropped slightly to 3.5 percent in 1987 before rising to 4 percent in 1992. As a proportion of the federal budget antipoverty spending increased from 6.4 percent in 1968 to 14.0 percent in 1978, declined to 11 percent by 1985, and then returned to 14.0 percent by 1992. In 1992, federal spending for the elderly under the old age and survivors insurance (OASI) and Medicare programs alone amounted to $396.6 billion—over $100 billion more than total antipoverty spending, although some of the poor also benefited from these programs. By 1995, social security and Medicare spending had reached

$495.7 billion. Unlike antipoverty expenditures, social security and Medicare costs per elderly person have risen steadily.

	OASI and Medicare outlays (billions)	Per elderly person
1960	$ 73.5	$ 3,920
1970	113.8	5,658
1975	168.6	7,429
1980	207.4	8,070
1985	267.7	9,381
1990	346.7	11,093
1995	495.7	14,681

Federal and state governments finance more than seventy-five programs specifically for individuals with limited incomes (table 1.14). Programs providing cash shrunk from 47 percent to 24 percent of the total between 1968 and 1992, and medical and food programs grew correspondingly (figure 1.14). Job and training expenditures doubled, from 4.7 percent to 10.2 percent, by 1979 but then diminished to only 1.7 percent of total antipoverty spending by 1992. Concerned about undermining the work ethic of able-bodied working-age individuals and arousing resentment among nonpoor workers, American policymakers traditionally have been wary of providing cash. Therefore, the expansion of antipoverty programs emphasized noncash assistance. In addition, escalating medical care costs during the three decades—far outstripping the overall inflation index—have obliged governments to invest more resources to maintain the same level of health care for the poor.

Who Is Helped?

Government aid to the poor is targeted toward the elderly, the disabled, and families headed by single mothers. The system generally neglects the needs of the working poor and nonaged adults without children. Poor single parents are much more likely than married parents to receive government assistance, although that longstanding commitment appears to be waning. However, poor married parents are more likely to obtain social insurance benefits through unemployment insurance or workers' compensation, largely because they work more. Altogether a quarter of poor families with children do not receive help from any program. Although they are eligible for a variety of benefits, no more than a third of poor single parents obtaining AFDC also receive Medicaid, food stamps, and housing assistance.

Impact of Antipoverty Efforts

The impact on the poor of income support and in-kind aid is difficult to assess because the availability of assistance influences individuals' behavior. For example, old age insurance was partly intended to make retirement a general practice: without social security more elderly individuals would have remained in the work force, and many would return to it today if the program were curtailed. That some of the elderly aged 62 to 70 who continue to work lose part or all of their benefits provides another incentive to retire, yet saving the social security system will require a general delay in retirement. Demonstration projects conducted in the 1970s found that nonelderly individuals who were provided a guaranteed income also reduced their work effort.

With this caveat in mind, the evidence indicates that social programs substantially reduce the number of poor individuals and significantly raise the income of those remaining in poverty. As noted above, in the absence of government assistance 57.6 million people rather than 30.3 million would have been poor in 1995, and their average income would have been nearly $3,400 below the poverty line (the poverty gap). Health care assistance to the poor added substantially to the amelioration of poverty, but its exact impact is difficult to measure. The 1995 antipoverty contribution was the largest on record and represented a restoration of an impact substantially moderated during the 1980s (table 1.15).[20] The impact of the EITC after it was strengthened in 1993 is especially significant. The critical question for the late 1990s is the likely impact of subsequent cuts in government assistance, an issue addressed in the following section.

National averages obscure significant differences in the incidence of poverty among the states and the effectiveness of government antipoverty programs. Apart from social security, Supplemental Security Income, and veterans' benefits, state governments effectively control the level of all other major cash assistance programs. According to the latest available data for 1993–94, averaged over two years because of the small samples available in noncensus years, state poverty rates ranged from 8.4 percent in Hawaii and 8.8 percent in New Hampshire and Vermont to 22.3 percent in Mississippi and 23.8 percent in Washington, D.C. No measure of antipoverty effectiveness of government programs is available by state.

The adequacy of antipoverty resources remains a matter of controversy. The level of support depends ultimately upon perceptions

Table 1.14. Expenditures and Recipients for Means-Tested Assistance Programs, FY 1992 ($ millions)

Benefit Category/Program	Federal	State	Total	Recipients (000)[a]
Income support				
AFDC	$ 13,569	$ 11,354	$ 23,923	13,754
SSI	18,744	4,030	22,774	5,559[b]
EITC	9,553	0	9,553	39,909
Pensions for needy veterans/dependents	3,667	0	3,667	969
Foster care	2,233	1,937	4,170	202
General assistance (nonmedical)	0	3,340	3,340	1,205
Adoption assistance	221	181	402	66
Cash assistance to refugees	139	0	139	31
Emergency assistance	134	134	268	158[c]
Dependent parents of deceased veterans	68	0	68	34
General assistance to Indians	46	0	46	41
Total income support	48,374	20,976	69,350	
Medical care				
Medicaid	67,827	50,240	118,067	30,776[b]
Medical for veterans (non-service related)	7,838	0	7,838	580
General assistance (medical component)	0	4,850	4,850	
Indian health services	1,431	0	1,431	1,160
Maternal and child services block grant	646	413	1,059	
Community health centers	537	0	537	
Title X family planning services	150	0	150	5,675[b]
Migrant health centers	58	0	58	4,000[b]
Medical assistance to refugees	42	0	42	545[b]
Total medical care	78,529	55,503	133,032	44

Food and nutrition

Food stamps	23,540	1,378	34,198	26,900
School lunch program	3,895		3,895	13,000
Supplemental women, infants, children	2,600		2,600	5,400
School breakfast program	782		782	4,500
Child and adult care food program	624		624	1,019
Nutrition program for the elderly	591	68	659	3,349[b]
Emergency food assistance program	250		250	7,500[c]
Summer food service for children	203		203	1,919
Commodity supplemental food program	90		90	343
Food distribution on Indian reservations	84		84	119
Special milk program	2		2	60
Total food and nutrition	32,661	1,446	34,107	34,107

Housing units

Section 8 low-income assistance	12,307	0	12,307	2,797
Low-rent public housing	5,008		5,008	1,409
Low-income energy assistance	1,500	94	1,594	6,200
Rural housing loans	1,468	0	1,468	26
Section 236 interest reduction	652	0	652	511
Rural rental housing loans	573	0	573	5
Rural rental assistance	320	0	320	29
Weatherization assistance	174		174	87
Section 101 rent supplements	54	0	54	20
Section 235 home ownership assistance	45	0	45	98
Farm labor housing loans/grants	29	0	29	1

Table 1.14., cont'd

Benefit Category/Program	Federal	State	Total	Recipients (000)[a]
Housing Units, cont'd.				
Farm labor housing loans/grants	29	0	29	1
Rural housing repair loans/grants	24	0	24	5
Rural housing preservation grants	23	0	23	4
Indian housing improvement grants	20	0	20	1
Rural self-help technical assistance	9	0	9	50
Home investment partnerships	3	0	3	182
Total housing	22,209	94	22,303	
Education and training				
Stafford loans	5,683	0	5,683	5,135
Pell grants	5,374	0	5,374	4,259
Head Start	2,202	551	2,753	621
College work-study program	595	0	595	827
Supplemental opportunity grants	520	0	520	835
Federal TRIO programs	385	0	385	649
Chapter 1 migrant education	308		308	417
Perkins loans	156	0	156	688
State student-incentive grants	64	64	128	213
Fellowships for graduate/professional study	63	0	63	6
Health professions student loans/scholarships	48	0	48	34
Follow Through	9		9	
Migrant high school equivalency	8		8	4
Ellender fellowships	4	0	4	6
College assistance migrant program	2	0	2	.4
Child development associate scholarships	1	0	1	5
Subtotal, education	15,423	614	16,037	

Training for disadvantaged adults/youths	1,774	0	1,774	602
Summer youth employment and training	1,183	0	1,183	783
Job Corps	995	0	995	65
JOBS	623	387	1,010	510
Senior community service employment	395	44	439	65
Foster grandparents	66	29	95	23
Senior companions	29	16	45	12
Subtotal, training	5,024	476	5,500	
Total, education and training	20,447	1,090	21,537	
Services				
Social services block grant	2,800	2,619	5,419	
Child care/development block grant	825	0	825	570
AFDC and transitional child care	438	317	755	265
At-risk child care	335	269	604	
Community services block grant	438	0	438	
Legal services	350	0	350	
Emergency food and shelter	134		134	
Social services for refugees	26	0	26	340
Total, services	5,346	3,205	8,551	
Grand total	207,566	82,314	288,880	

Source: U.S. General Accounting Office.

Note: 1992 is the most recent fiscal year for which all of these data are available. More recent data for specific programs are included in subsequent chapters.

[a]Unless otherwise noted, the average monthly number of individual recipients are indicated.

[b]Annual number of recipients.

[c]Number of households.

Figure 1.14. Percentage distribution of means-tested federal programs, FY 1992

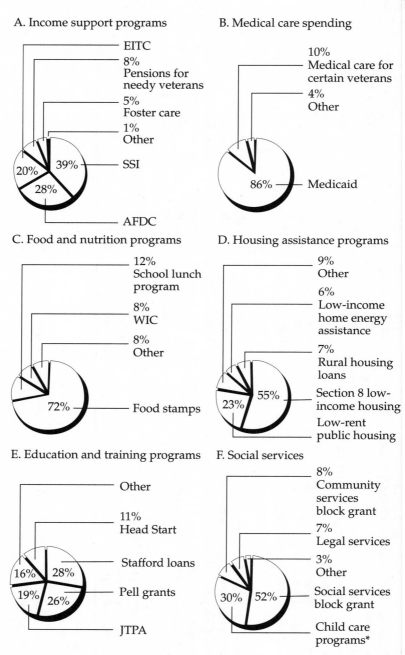

A. Income support programs

EITC
8%
Pensions for needy veterans
5%
Foster care
1%
Other
39% — SSI
20%
28%
AFDC

B. Medical care spending

10%
Medical care for certain veterans
4%
Other
86% — Medicaid

C. Food and nutrition programs

12%
School lunch program
8%
WIC
8%
Other
72% — Food stamps

D. Housing assistance programs

9%
Other
6%
Low-income home energy assistance
7%
Rural housing loans
Section 8 low-income housing
Low-rent public housing
55%
23%

E. Education and training programs

Other
11%
Head Start
Stafford loans
Pell grants
JTPA
16% 28%
19% 26%

F. Social services

8%
Community services block grant
7%
Legal services
3%
Other
Social services block grant
Child care programs*
30% 52%

Source: U.S. General Accounting Office.

*Includes the child care and development block grant, AFDC and Transitional Child Care, and At-Risk Child Care.

Table 1.15. Impact of Governmental Benefit Programs on Poverty, 1979–1995

	1979	1983	1989	1993	1995
Number in millions removed from poverty by					
All government benefit programs	20.7	19.2	20.1	25.2	27.3
Social insurance programs	14.6	16.0	14.9	18.6	18.2
Means-tested programs	6.7	5.3	6.5	7.6	7.7
Federal taxes	−0.7	−2.0	−1.3	−0.6	1.4
Percentage removed from poverty by					
All government benefit programs	47.6	36.1	40.3	41.7	47.4
Social insurance programs	33.7	30.0	29.9	30.1	31.6
Means-tested programs	15.3	9.9	13.0	12.5	13.3
Federal taxes	−1.4	−3.8	−2.7	−0.9	2.4
Reduction in poverty rate by					
All government benefit programs	9.3	8.3	8.1	9.7	10.4
Social insurance programs	6.6	6.9	6.0	7.0	6.9
Means-tested programs	3.0	2.3	2.6	2.9	2.9
Federal taxes	−0.3	−0.9	−0.5	−0.2	0.5

Source: Wendell E. Primus et al., *The Safety Net Delivers: The Effects of Government Benefit Programs in Reducing Poverty* (Washington, D.C.: Center on Budget Policy Priorities, 15 November 1996).

of the severity of deprivation, the confidence that government aid can make a difference, and the willingness of public officials and taxpayers to accept responsibility for being their "brothers' keeper." Current attitudes toward alleviating the state of the poor offer ample cause for concern. President Reagan repeatedly undermined public confidence in the ability of government to help the poor. His administration thus hindered both recognition of the nation's prior progress and further improvements in the welfare system. President Bush, despite abandoning his pledge not to raise taxes, undertook no significant antipoverty initiatives. At the end of the 1980s there were some indications that the American public was ready to support new antipoverty efforts. Shortly after President Bush's election, two-thirds of adults indicated that the government devoted too few resources to helping the poor. In August 1989 a majority disapproved of the president's handling of the poverty problem, and only a third approved of his record in this area.[21] Nevertheless, his 1992 campaign opponent, Arkansas Governor William Jefferson Clinton, was able to attract substantial support through his promise to "end welfare as we know it." Two years later President Clinton was under attack and the Republicans won control of the Congress in part based on his failure to keep that promise. Two years thereafter the president joined that same Congress in abolishing the oldest of antipoverty entitlements.

During the crucial years 1995–96 reducing the federal budget deficit had become a high political priority for both Congress and the administration, but the choice remained whose ox to gore. Government programs existed favoring almost every component of the population. To no one's surprise, the cuts were distributed in reverse order of political power. The bulk of entitlement programs— those to which individuals and households are automatically entitled by various personal characteristics, regardless of appropriation levels—are guided by other characteristics than income, notably social security and Medicare. Only 23 percent of all entitlements in 1996 were targeted toward those with low incomes. Nevertheless, focusing on the period 1996–2002, $65.6 billion was cut from entitlement programs; 93 percent of those cuts came from entitlements targeted at low-income households, $54.4 billion being cut by the August 1996 welfare reforms and the remainder through other changes in EITC, SSI, Medicaid, and appropriations provisions.[22] For the final year, 2002, $16.3 billion was deleted from entitlements, 87 percent of it from low-income entitlements.

Though less dramatic, the same intent was evident in discretionary spending. Low-income programs accounted for 21 percent of all funding for nondefense discretionary programs at the beginning of the 104th Congress; 34 percent of the cuts in discretionary spending came from those low-income programs, which therefore bore one and one-half times their proportionate share of the cuts. Low-income housing and employment and training programs were the primary targets of discretionary cuts. Entitlements and discretionary programs combined, which before the 1995–96 legislation would have constituted 23 percent of the total nondefense budget for the 1996–2002 period, absorbed 53 percent of the cuts imposed if the discretionary cuts are adjusted for expected inflation and 89 percent if they are not.

It is impossible to determine all of the reasons for that sharp right turn in public opinion. But one major factor was undoubtedly the fact that those in the middle of the income distribution and those just below were becoming painfully aware that their real income had been declining for two decades. In the 1960s a war on poverty could be painlessly declared by allocating a small portion of the substantial rate of economic growth, essentially buying the weapons to aid the poor with dollars the nonpoor could potentially have received but had not and therefore did not feel deprived of. But by the 1990s everyone knew that a dollar given to anyone else was a dollar right out of their pocket. Fighting poverty had become a zero-sum game, that is, unless the poor could be lifted to self-reliance.

Poverty as a Public Concern

In 1990 Sar Levitan could say that "the role of the federal government in helping the poor is accepted today by all segments of society." That cannot be said with equal assurance seven years later. The notion of federal government responsibility for aiding the poor emerged only under the strains of the Great Depression. Prior to the 1930s, assistance to the poor was largely left to religious organizations and other private charities, supplemented at the local level by public poorhouses, orphanages, harsh institutions that cared for the gravely handicapped, and some public assistance, usually administered by county personnel as the beginning of a social work vocation. Poverty was perceived primarily as the consequence of the individual's shortcomings, and alleviating it was seen as a local responsibility as a last resort.

Reliance on private alms and limited community assistance was a natural outgrowth of Calvinist doctrine. Seventeenth-century English poor laws assumed that poverty was the consequence of personal inadequacies—physical frailty, mental deficiencies, or moral and behavioral defects. Although alms were considered appropriate to relieve the suffering of the sick or disabled, the destitution of the corrupt or weak in spirit was perceived as retribution for their misdeeds. In accordance with the notion of individual responsibility, aid to the poor has traditionally emphasized different treatment for the deserving poor and the deviant, calling for subjective moral judgments by neighbors and community leaders to determine appropriate responses to the needs of the poor. In the United States assistance was provided on a neighbor-to-neighbor basis in small communities, but urbanization soon precluded such assistance, and growing numbers and interpersonal distance soon fostered those same stereotypes. Settlement houses such as Chicago's famous Hull House did carry over some of the village compassion into the urban setting, and the social work profession grew out of such experiences and spread into county-level assistance to the poor. Still, the stereotypical concepts of worthy and unworthy poor predominated.[23]

The widespread unemployment and economic deprivation during the Great Depression destroyed public faith in a rigid link between individual responsibility and penury, but traditional beliefs continued to shape government efforts in aid of the poor. Income maintenance programs still categorize the poor according to labor force status in an attempt to distinguish between the deserving and the slackers. Most federal antipoverty initiatives continue to rely upon state or local discretion and administration. Faced with unfavorable income distribution trends, the nonpoor increasingly see aid to the poor as an additional reduction in their own real income. In a cyclical fashion, many of the attitudes characteristic of the 1920s have returned during the 1980s and 1990s to challenge all over again the public acceptance of antipoverty responsibility apparently endorsed over the previous two decades.[24]

Restrictive eligibility and work requirements for those deemed employable, benefit reductions to offset earnings, and low benefit levels for the able-bodied nonworking poor all are designed to prevent or discourage the "undeserving" poor from relying upon government assistance. Ironically, by forcing an all-or-nothing choice between uncertain earnings and the minimal security of welfare, these restrictions have made welfare more attractive than work for many low-skilled, low-wage workers and have increased the risk of dependency as well as the financial burden borne by the taxpayer. Welfare reforms at the state level during the first half of the 1990s were made possible only by the willingness of the Department of Health and Human Services to waive the very regulations it and the Congress had imposed to prevent supposed abuses.

Even on theoretical grounds it is difficult to distinguish individuals who should be expected to work from those who should be provided income support. For example, should a jobless single mother with an infant be required to work in return for assistance, or should the state support her family? Would society and the family itself be better served if government found or provided work for the mother—or if it provided sufficient income to allow the mother to concentrate on raising her children? As the proportion of working women with young children has increased among the nonpoor, though more often than not they work part-time and belong to two-parent families, the latter alternative on behalf of the poor has become harder to defend. Yet, providing employment and child care for needy, low-skilled female family heads can also be costly. In fact, all of the welfare reform proposals of the sixties, seventies, and eighties died hoisted on that petard—it was simply cheaper to maintain the dole than to provide the job.

The notion that society as well as relief recipients would be best served by encouraging those recipients to work without taking away all of their welfare benefits gained acceptance during the 1970s. Proposals for combining work and welfare recognized that low-wage jobs often leave families in poverty and that incentives to work while receiving some welfare offer hope for an eventual escape from dependency. Moreover, many poor people move in and out of the work force in response to changing economic conditions over which they have no control. But in the early 1980s, Congress, on President Reagan's urging, sharply reduced and in some cases eliminated work incentives for welfare recipients. Assistance to the working poor was cut under the rationale of targeting benefits to those most in need. These policies forced low-income Americans to make no-win choices between employment and dependency and contributed to the travails of the working poor. The 1988 Family Support Act took some halting steps to revive the notion that in some cases a combination of work and welfare is an effective strategy for reducing dependency. However, the failure of the 1988 act to make a major difference in the proportion of adult AFDC recipients becoming employed and self-supporting motivated the Congress in 1996 to abrogate the AFDC entitlement, which since 1935 had guaranteed income support to impoverished single mothers and their children.

Thus, during the past three decades the nation's approach to administering antipoverty efforts has come full circle. Prior to President Johnson's Great Society most government assistance to the poor was provided at state and local levels. Federal social programs were few in number, and their budgets were correspondingly slim. The federal government provided matching funds for some purposes, including public assistance, but administration was largely left to the states. Even when virtually all financial support came from Washington, as in the case of employment services, states and localities ran the programs with minimal federal intervention.

The Great Society's architects believed that federal expertise and resources should play an active role in strengthening government programs and in designing strategies to aid the poor. The many initiatives of the 1960s frequently specified detailed approaches and priorities, providing direct funding to public and private local sponsors and often bypassing state and local officials. Narrowly specified grant-in-aid programs proliferated, and funds flowed from a variety of federal spigots. By targeting federal assistance to underserved groups and conditioning financial support on the fulfillment of numerous program requirements, the enhanced federal role spurred action on problems long ignored by state and local officials. The expansion of federal categorical programs, however, also resulted in an uncoordinated tangle of services, funding arrangements, and operating guidelines, and the needy sometimes fell through the cracks.

By the early 1980s a reaction against the presumed unwieldiness of Washington's dictates had gathered considerable steam. The Reagan administration's New Federalism gave what turned out to be primarily lip service to the notion of shifting program responsibility to state and local authorities and allowing these officials more discretion over how to spend the funds Washington continued to provide, although in reduced amounts. The Reagan and Bush administrations championed both these goals by reasserting the traditional principle of subsidiarity, which holds that the federal government should not undertake actions that can be performed by a lower level of government. In the realm of social welfare policy this philosophy claimed that state and local officials and private groups—by virtue of their proximity to the needy—are better able to design and administer solutions to problems in their own states and communities. Nevertheless, the state and local program operators were required to function within narrow federal mandates and requirements.

In 1981 the Reagan administration partially succeeded in advancing the New Federalism goals by consolidating dozens of social welfare programs into six block grants covering education, job training, health care, and social services, but again within narrow constraints. It also attempted to shift responsibility for certain welfare programs back to state and local governments, but this initiative failed in large part because of state and local reluctance to accept the additional financial burden. President Bush championed vaguely defined voluntary action by private groups and individuals in place of government effort—a "thousand points of light." However, the public's persistent belief in the importance of federal programs to address unmet national needs, as well as questions regarding the ability and willingness of state and local officials to satisfactorily match federal efforts, largely left intact the division of responsibilities that had previously evolved. But increasing public dissatisfaction with the persistence of poverty after decades of antipoverty programs was marked by a Democratic presidential candidate's choosing as one of his campaign slogans in 1992 the promise to "end welfare as we know it." That was followed after 1994 by the commitment of the first Republican-dominated House as well as Senate in over forty years to return most antipoverty responsibilities to state and local governments aided by fixed and limited amounts of federal block grant aid. At this writing, when the devolution legislation has just taken effect and has no experience, the consequences are anyone's guess. But clearly, programs in aid of the poor are in the midst of changes as dramatic as those that occurred during the 1930s or the 1960s, though apparently in the opposite direction.

Views will always differ on the appropriate balance among federal, state, local, and private responsibility for aid to the poor. Concerns over equitable financing and state or local inaction may once again in the future fuel calls for federal initiatives, while demands for manageable administration and responsiveness to community needs will ensure some measure of flexibility and discretion for state and local officials and private groups. The American federal system derives its strength from this balance of competing claims and abilities; the danger lies in ideological attempts to push the nation to either extreme. Careful attention will have to be given to the results of what appears to be a counterrevolution in care for the poor to assure that the apparent war on the war on poverty does not turn into an unconscionable war on the poor themselves.

Even though recent political leaders have failed to take credit for its accomplishments and the media have failed to publicize it, the Great Society and subsequent antipoverty initiatives made major strides toward the reduction of poverty in America. The official poverty rate fell sharply during the late 1960s, and the failure of official data to measure the impact of expanding in-kind assistance to the poor in the 1970s and after masked further progress. A closer examination of programs in aid of the poor holds open the prospects of future gains. If and when the nation rejects the pessimistic notion that government is powerless to help the poor to help themselves, the lessons of the past thirty and more years can provide a solid foundation from which to launch a more effective and comprehensive assault on poverty in America.

Notes

1. Constance F. Citro and Robert T. Michael, eds., *Measuring Poverty: A New Approach* (Washington, D.C.: National Academy Press, 1995).

2. Monica Castillo, *A Profile of the Working Poor, 1994,* U.S. Department of Labor Report 986 (Washington, D.C.: U.S. Department of Labor, Bureau of Labor Statistics, July 1996).

3. Robert Haveman and Lawrence Buron, "Escaping Poverty through Work: The Problem of Low Earning Capacity in the United States, 1973–88," *Review of Income and Wealth* 39 (June 1993): 141–57.

4. Wendell E. Primus et al., *The Safety Net Delivers: The Effects of Government Benefit Programs in Reducing Poverty* (Washington, D.C.: Center on Budget and Policy Priorities, 15 November 1996), 6–12.

5. Ibid., 11.

6. Lawrence Mishel, Jared Bernstein, and John Schmitt, *The State of Working America, 1996–97* (Washington, D.C.: Economic Policy Institute, 1996), 282.

7. Andrew Sum, W. Neal Fogg, and Robert Taggart, *From Dreams to Dust: The Deteriorating Labor Market Fortunes of Young Adults* (Baltimore: Sar Levitan Center for Labor Market Studies, Johns Hopkins University, August 1996), 6.

8. Mary Jo Bane and David Ellwood, "Slipping Into and Out of Poverty: The Dynamics of Spells," *Journal of Human Resources* 21 (winter 1986): 1–23.

9. Mishel, Bernstein, and Schmitt, *The State of Working America,* 148.

10. Ibid., 337.

11. U.S. Bureau of the Census, *Labor Force Status and Other Characteristics of Persons With Work Disabilities, 1981 to 1988* (Washington, D.C.: Government Printing Office, July 1989).

12. Columbia University Center for Children in Poverty, *One in Four: Child Poverty in America* (New York, 1996), 12–14.

13. U.S. Department of Health and Human Services, Administration for Children, Youth and Families, National Center on Child Abuse and Neglect, *Executive Summary of the Third National Incidence Study of Child Abuse and Neglect* (Washington, D.C., 1995), vi, 4–5, 8, 10.

14. Peter Gottschalk and Sheldon Danziger, "Family Structure, Family Size, and Family Income," in *Uneven Tides: Rising Inequality in America* (New York: Russell Sage Foundation, 1993), 167–93.

15. William A. Kelso, *Poverty and the Underclass: Changing Perceptions of the Poor in America* (New York: New York University Press, 1994), 25.

16. Christopher Jencks and Paul E. Petersen, eds., *The Urban Underclass* (Washington, D.C.: Brookings Institution, 1991), 28–102.

17. William Julius Wilson, *The Truly Disadvantaged: The Inner City, the Underclass, and Public Policy* (Chicago: University of Chicago Press, 1987); *When Work Disappears: The World of the New Urban Poor* (New York: Knopf, 1996).

18. Ronald B. Mincy, "The Underclass: Concept, Controversy, and Change," in *Confronting Poverty: Prescriptions for Change,* ed. Sheldon H. Danziger, Gary D. Sandefur, and Daniel H. Weinberg (Cambridge: Harvard University Press, 1994), 109–46.

19. Kelso, *Poverty and the Underclass,* 28.

20. Primus et al., *The Safety Net Delivers,* 20.

21. Thomas Edsall, "Consensus Builds to Expand Aid for Working Poor," *Washington Post,* 21 August 1989, A1; "Poverty Is Perceived as Increasing and State of the Poor Unimproved," *New York Times,* 23 August 1989, A14.

22. Robert Greenstein, Richard Kogan, and Marion Nichols, *Bearing Most of the Burden: How Deficit Reduction during the 104th Congress Concentrated on Programs for the Poor* (Washington, D.C.: Center on Budget and Policy Priorities, 3 December 1996).

23. Merritt Ierley, *With Charity for All: Ancient Times to the Present* (New York: Praeger, 1984), 39–86.

24. Stuart Butler and Anna Kondratas, *Out of the Poverty Trap: A Conservative Strategy for Welfare Reform* (New York: Free Press, 1987).

2. Cash Support Programs

If there is among you a poor man . . . you shall not harden your heart or shut your hand against your poor brother . . . and lend him sufficient for his need, whatever it may be. . . . You shall open wide your hand to your brother, to the needy, and to the poor in the land.

Deuteronomy, 15:7–8, 11

Despite attempts at reduction, nearly three of every ten Americans receive assistance from public programs. The total cost of the programs, excluding education, exceeds $600 billion. Despite the trends in the direction of in-kind benefits, three-fifths of that assistance is in the form of cash payments. The poor are much more likely to receive cash transfer payments than are the nonpoor, although an estimated 17 million of the latter would have been poor without these transfers. Earnings account for roughly one-half of the income received by the nonaged poor, compared with four-fifths of the nonaged, nonpoor's income (figure 2.1).

The Social Security Act

The Social Security Act, the product of more than six decades of evolution since its enactment in 1935, has accounted for almost all of the public cash support received by both poor and nonpoor Americans. The Social Security Act provides two types of income support: (1) social insurance programs—including Old Age, Survivors, and Disability Insurance (OASDI) and unemployment insurance—which distribute payments on the basis of prior earnings and payroll tax contributions; and (2) public assistance programs—for the elderly, the blind, the disabled, and families with dependent children—which provide income support on the basis of need alone (figure 2.2).

OASDI

The social security system is vast. Old age, survivors, and disability insurance expenditures alone totaled $332.6 billion in 1995 (excluding expenditures for hospital and medical insurance, dis-

Figure 2.1. Sources of income for poor and nonpoor, aged and non-aged families, 1993

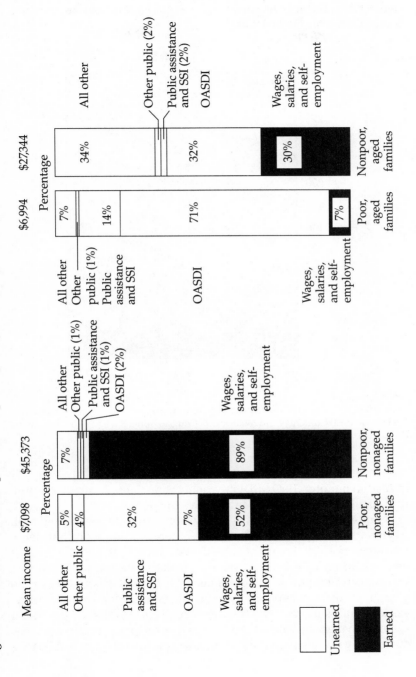

59

Figure 2.2. Value of government outlays for major income-security programs, 1975–1994 (1988 dollars)

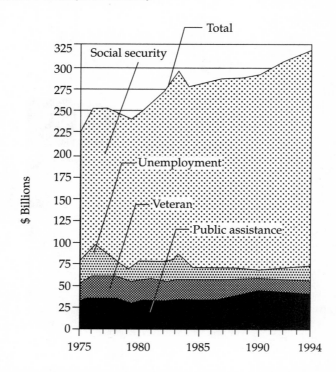

Sources: U.S. Office of Management and Budget, Budget of the U.S. Government; House Committee on Ways and Means; U.S. Congressional Research Service; Social Security Administration.

cussed in chapter 3). OASDI payments represented more than one-fifth of all federal government outlays in 1995.

Some 43.6 million persons—one American in six—received cash payments in August 1996. Some 61 percent of these recipients were retired workers, 9.9 percent were disabled workers, and 8.7 percent were children of retired, disabled, or deceased workers; the rest were surviving spouses. The average 1995 benefit was $7,700 for the year. In addition, a separate system covers retired railroad employees and their survivors. By the time Congress established the social security system in 1935 about four of five railroad employees were covered by private pensions—hence a separate program for the railroad industry. Once established, the railroad retirement program survived despite a decline in covered employment from 1.2 million, when the program was established, to fewer than 300,000 in 1995.

OASDI covers 96 percent of the work force. Almost all children and their mothers would receive benefits if the fathers were to die. Of those who now reach age 65, about nineteen of every twenty are eligible for some benefits. Old age insurance has provided income to a steadily rising portion of the aged population. However, 12 percent of poor elderly families and unrelated individuals report no receipt of social security income. Supplemental Security Income (SSI) is their primary resort.

Individuals must have been insured during their working years in order to receive benefits. Persons who contribute payroll taxes for a minimum of forty quarters (10 years) are permanently insured. The basic benefits payable to a retired or permanently disabled worker are determined by the age at retirement and the level of covered earnings. OASDI has a substantial income redistribution effect: the law provides more generous benefits to workers with lengthy work histories who had very low wages than they would be entitled to on the basis of their earnings history alone.

The benefits of a deceased, insured worker are paid to surviving children under 18 years of age, dependent parents, and dependent widows or widowers. Finally, disability insurance aids adults (aged 18–64) unable to engage in substantial gainful employment. To be eligible for disability insurance payments, the potential recipient must have worked at least twenty of the forty quarters (5 of the 10 years) before becoming disabled; workers disabled before age 31 must have worked half of the quarters (but no fewer than 6) since turning 21. Disability benefits are paid after a five-month waiting period. Medical proof of disability is required, along with a determination that the disability rules out gainful employment.

Retirement Benefits

OASDI redistributes income in two ways. On the one hand, it replaces a significantly higher percentage of lost income for lower-paid workers than for higher-paid workers. In 1994 the ratio of retirement benefits to preretirement earnings differed radically for the hypothetical retirees with lifetime earnings as follows:

Lifetime Earnings Equal to:

45% of average wages	57%
Average earner	42
Maximum taxable social security wage	24

On the other hand, because earnings above a specified amount are not subject to the social security payroll tax, the program's financing places a relatively greater tax burden on low-wage earners. However, by raising the taxable wage Congress has made the payroll tax more proportional. Approximately one-fourth of workers earned more than the 1970 maximum taxable wage of $7,800, compared with about 6 percent who earned more than the $61,200 maximum in 1994. It is only coincidental that the maximum tax paid by a worker to support the OASDI system is now $7,800, the same as the amount on which he would have been taxed a quarter-century ago.

The social security system taxes the employed to support the retired, the disabled, and the survivors of deceased workers. OASDI may be viewed as a kind of compulsory insurance in the sense that it operates on the principle of risk pooling and pays benefits regardless of the recipient's income; however, it differs from commercial insurance by not keeping reserves on hand adequate to meet all potential claims. Under 1983 legislation, OASDI was planned to operate as a partially funded system to provide a trust fund to cover anticipated rising obligations when the post–World War II baby boom generation reaches retirement. Instead, however, the surplus has been used consistently to help cover the federal deficit, though the trust fund is maintained on paper.

Thanks to strong political support from well-organized elderly voters, OASDI benefits are now adequate to raise most but not all recipients above the poverty threshold. In 1996 the average monthly benefit of $722 was sufficient to raise a retired worker over the poverty line by 11 percent, and the benefits of the average retired couple were more than 30 percent above the poverty level (figure 2.3). However, in 1994 about 5.7 percent of OASDI cash beneficiaries aged 65 and over were also eligible for and received means-tested Supplemental Security Income payments because they were either ineligible for or had such low OASDI benefits. To protect the income of retired workers from inflation, the law requires that benefits be adjusted when the cost of living rises. For 1997 the social security system was financed by a 15.3 percent tax (including 2.9% for health insurance) on annual earnings up to $65,400, shared

Figure 2.3. Monthly social security benefits, 1995

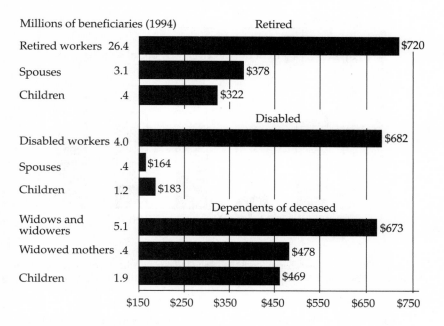

Millions of beneficiaries (1994)

Retired

Retired workers	26.4	$720
Spouses	3.1	$378
Children	.4	$322

Disabled

Disabled workers	4.0	$682
Spouses	.4	$164
Children	1.2	$183

Dependents of deceased

Widows and widowers	5.1	$673
Widowed mothers	.4	$478
Children	1.9	$469

$150 $250 $350 $450 $550 $650 $750

Source: Social Security Bulletin, 1996 annual supplement.

equally by employer and employee. The maximum taxable earnings are adjusted automatically as average earnings rise. For instance, the maximum taxable wage was $61,200 in 1995 and $62,700 in 1996. The employer's contributions are labor costs and are therefore effectively part of the worker's earnings. That being the case, total tax exceeds one-seventh of the employee's cash compensation subject to the payroll tax.

Although not usually considered an antipoverty program, social security significantly diminishes poverty (figure 2.4). One of five poor families and more than a third of poor unrelated individuals receive social security checks. The precise antipoverty effectiveness of social security is difficult to gauge because undoubtedly many elderly individuals would continue to work in the absence of social security benefits. Only 16.8 percent of men aged 65 and over were in the work force in 1994, compared with 54.0 percent in 1930, before the program existed and when private pensions were rare. In 1992 the poverty rate among the population aged 65 and over would

Figure 2.4. Social security's role in reducing poverty, 1992

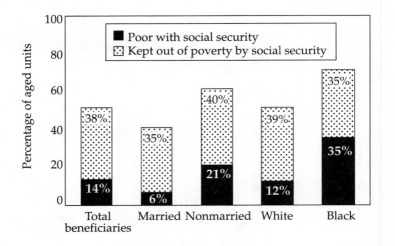

Source: Office of Research and Statistics, Social Security Administration, *Income of the Aged Chartbook* (Washington, D.C.: Government Printing Office, 1992), 10.

have been 52 percent in the absence of social security benefits (assuming no additional work activity) rather than the actual rate of 14 percent for this group.

Generous cost-of-living increases have augmented the antipoverty effectiveness of social security. Between 1965 and 1993 social security cost-of-living increases of 442 percent outpaced inflation (348%) and even average wage increases for men working full-time year-round (405%). Benefit increases combined with higher lifetime earnings have made the retirement program a powerful antipoverty weapon for elderly Americans. Average benefits climbed from half the poverty line when the program began to above the poverty benchmark in 1980, then plateaued. Average retirement benefits as a proportion of the poverty line have been:

	Retired men	Retired couples
1940	41%	50%
1950	47	57
1960	69	81
1970	84	98
1980	116	133
1988	114	137
1996	111	132

Lengthening life spans, an increasing proportion of elderly in the population, and concerns over social security's financial solvency led Congress to prod or encourage more elderly persons to continue working. First, the normal retirement age will gradually be increased from 65 to 67 after the turn of the century. Second, the credit for those delaying retirement has become more generous over time. Third, although 62 will remain the minimum retirement age (60 for widows and widowers), early retirees' benefits will be further reduced after the year 2000. Two-thirds of beneficiaries currently retire prior to age 65. Finally, since 1990, beneficiaries aged 65 to 69 lose only $1 for every $3 earned above a set amount, compared with the $1 reduction for every $2 in earnings in place previously. No reductions are made for any earnings after reaching age 70.

In addressing the future solvency of the system, the 1983 bipartisan compromise on social security financing included major changes in both payroll taxes and benefits. Some of these reforms worked to the detriment of the poor. For example, the more stringent permanent reduction in the benefits of early retirees impacts the poor more harshly because they typically have lower average earnings than workers who retire at age 65 and are frequently forced to retire because of job loss or disability. Further reforms in OASDI will be essential in the near future. A system that promised retirement at age 65 at a time when the average age at death was 59 years cannot cheaply fill that promise, even if the promised age of retirement is delayed to 67, as the average age at death rises to 74 and beyond. Despite the 1996 inflow of $60 billion more than expenditures, the Social Security Administration's midrange projection has outlays exceeding payroll taxes after 2013 and surpassing all OASDI income, including interest, after 2019; the current $500 billion trust fund depleted by 2029; and the system being able to meet only 75 percent of its obligations thereafter.[1]

Concern for the long-term financial viability of the social security system prompted formation of the Advisory Council on Social Security in 1995. A key variable in the system's viability is the dependency ratio, defined as the ratio of the number of social security recipients to current workers. That ratio currently stands at .29 but is projected to be .50 in 2030 and .56 in 2070. A second key ratio is the aggregate replacement rate, the ratio of social security benefits to the taxable wage. Holding the aggregate replacement rate constant at its current level and allowing the forecasted change in dependency to take place implies social security tax rates of 17 percent in 2030 and 19 percent in 2070, compared with the current 12.4

percent, if the system is to remain solvent. A second but related issue is the fact that younger cohorts in the system will likely receive fewer discounted social security benefits relative to discounted tax payments (the money worth ratio) than have older cohorts. The political challenge is obvious: raising social security tax rates or trimming projected benefits will worsen the money worth ratio and threaten the political viability of the system.

In response to these factors at least five alternative policies aimed at improving the economics of social security have been proposed: (1) indexing the normal retirement age to life expectancy; (2) investing part of the trust funds in private bonds and equities rather than investing the trust funds solely in federal debt; (3) partial privatization of the social security system; (4) replacing social security by individually mandated savings; and (5) mandating employer-provided savings.[2] Each option has precedent in the current policies of some other countries. While the issues are complex and deserving of more complete analysis than is possible here, indexing the normal retirement age to life expectancy seems both reasonable and consistent with the underlying philosophy of social security. Investing a portion of the trust funds in the equity market would offer improved discounted benefits at the cost of reasonable increases in assumed risk. Given the relatively short time horizons of our political system, one can be assured that attention will intensify as the time draws nigh and an acceptable (at least short-run) solution to OASDI survival will be found. More relevant to the current discussion, it will be important to be aware of the impact of those alternative changes on the elderly poor. Raising the retirement age would leave them dependent on SSI and other less attractive alternatives longer, and any of the other alternatives would reduce the currently substantial income redistribution effect of the OASDI system.

Disability Benefits

Assistance to the disabled is more fragmented than aid for many other needy groups. Disability is defined under OASDI and SSI as a physical or mental impairment that prevents substantial employment activity and has lasted or probably will last for at least a year or may result in death. Social security disability insurance is the largest program, but it accounts for less than a third of total cash assistance to the handicapped. Other major programs that primarily if not exclusively assist the disabled include programs providing workers' compensation, Supplemental Security Income, and veterans' benefits, as well as various programs for government workers.

Following over two decades of debate, Congress in 1956 added a disability insurance component to the Old Age and Survivors Insurance program. It was originally restricted to workers aged 50 to 64, but in 1960 Congress removed the age barrier. Departing from rules governing old age and survivors insurance, Congress delegated eligibility determination to state governments. The program grew rapidly, partly because state authorities had every incentive to grant eligibility—a rejected applicant would probably otherwise apply, and might qualify for, state assistance. Within a decade and a half the number of disability insurance recipients increased more than fivefold. However, the growth leveled off after 1975, and disabled workers and their dependents constituted 13 percent of social security recipients in 1995.

During the program's first two decades Congress liberalized eligibility criteria. By the late 1970s, however, disability insurance's growing costs and concerns that the program encouraged dependency led to 1980 amendments that lowered benefit levels for future beneficiaries, encouraged recipients to work, and required a review of disability status every three years. As it turned out, the number of disability insurance beneficiaries (disabled workers and their dependents) had already peaked at 4.9 million in May 1978. Perhaps as a consequence of the 1980 law and subsequent administrative restrictions the beneficiary population declined sharply, to 3.8 million by July 1984. The decline in enrollments was not accompanied by any diminution in the pace of applications, which continued to number just over 1 million per year during the 1970s and 1980s. The difference was in the rate of denial, with favorable awards declining from about 45 percent during the 1970s to a low of 29 percent in 1982.

Those critics who argued that disability insurance had created a dependent handicapped population who were capable of work and therefore had contributed to declining rates of work force participation among preretirement-age men were to be disappointed. A General Accounting Office (GAO) study of the denials and terminations during this rigorous enforcement period supported the opposite conclusion that the working-age disabled individuals targeted by the disability insurance program were both numerous and vulnerable to destitution. Two-thirds of those ruled ineligible and terminated during 1981–84 had been returned to the disability benefit roles by 1987. Another 4 percent had become eligible for social security because of advancing age, and 7 percent had died. Only 15 percent of those terminated had returned to work. About 58 percent of those denied benefits in 1984 and still not receiving benefits in

1987 were not working. Two-thirds of them had not worked for more than three years, and 54 percent reported that they did not expect to be able to work ever again. Of those working in 1987, 71 percent reported being limited in the amount and kind of work they could do, and more than 40 percent were earning less than they had at the time of their application and denial. The GAO did not find the health and functional limitations of those denied benefits to be appreciably different from those of persons who had been allowed benefits. Total family income was below the poverty level for 61 percent of persons denied benefits, and 35 percent depended upon government programs other than social security—primarily public assistance—for half or more of their total family income. But then 43 percent of those receiving disability insurance were also below the poverty level. Twenty-nine percent of the working denied benefits and 25 percent of the nonworking denied benefits were without medical insurance.

The experience may have softened the hearts of the enforcers, for thereafter the approval rate climbed gradually until it reached the mid-40s by the early 1990s, with applications rising to 1.4 million per year by 1993. That pace had created a three-month backlog of claim considerations. By January 1995 the total number of disability insurance beneficiaries had risen to 5.9 million—4.2 million disabled workers and their 264,000 spouses and 1.4 million children.[3]

Private Pensions

While not a public program (though encouraged by the tax system), the interaction between social security retirement benefits and private pensions should be noted. Elderly persons who receive only social security benefits are often near or below the poverty threshold. For a growing proportion of retirees, private pension or profit-sharing plans supplement OASDI and ensure a more adequate standard of living. A little more than half (55%) of wage and salary workers over age 24—68 percent of men and 51 percent of women—participated in a pension plan in 1988 (the latest available data); four of five had vested rights in the plan. Coverage ranged from 16 percent of workers in firms employing fewer than twenty-five persons to 73 percent in firms employing more than one thousand workers; 78 percent of unionized employees had pension coverage, but they represented a small and declining proportion of all employment.

Nevertheless, the private pension system has important ramifications for poverty among the elderly. Almost all workers covered under private plans are also covered by social security. Through a combination of the two, a modest majority of recipients are assured of escaping poverty in their "golden years." The passage of the Employees Retirement Investment Security Act (ERISA) in 1974, in addition to safeguarding the integrity of private pension funds, resulted in liberalization of eligibility requirements, increasing the proportion of covered workers ultimately qualifying for retirement benefits. In 1984 Congress amended ERISA, making it easier for women to qualify for pensions and to collect survivors' benefits should their spouses die before retirement—a significant step toward reducing poverty among aged females. However, the impact of the private retirement system on poverty remains limited. In 1987 highly paid workers were more likely to be covered than were low-wage earners:

	Total	Poor	Nonpoor
Elderly households with pension income	41%	8%	47%
Proportion of total income	14	2	14

Public Assistance

In addition to OASDI and unemployment insurance (discussed below), the Social Security Act has provided aid to families with dependent children (AFDC) and assistance to the aged, blind, and disabled through the Supplemental Security Income (SSI) program. In addition, states and localities provide limited general assistance to persons not eligible for federally funded programs. AFDC accounted for two-thirds of the 20.5 million recipients and nearly half of the $42.4 billion (in 1988 dollars) in benefits paid by the three programs in 1993. AFDC has been most frequently identified with "welfare" because it has accounted for most of the increase in means-tested income support during the intervening years (figure 2.5). SSI has generally offered substantially higher benefits than have AFDC and general assistance. Although public assistance lifts many persons out of poverty, more than three-fifths of recipients remain poor.

Aid to Families with Dependent Children

AFDC has been the most controversial public assistance program not only because it has been the costliest but also because its recipients have been primarily female family heads and their children in an era when rising numbers of mothers were joining the work force. In August 1996, in the midst of a presidential and congressional

Figure 2.5. Public assistance payments, 1960–1993 (1988 dollars)

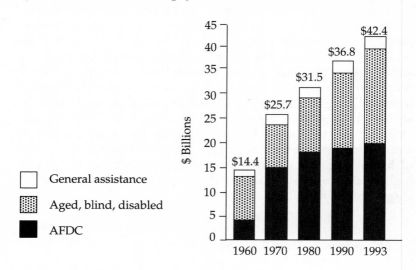

Source: U.S. Department of Health and Human Services.

political campaign, the Congress passed, and President Clinton signed, a "welfare reform" bill ending the 61-year-old entitlement program and substituting a block grant to the states. This newly implemented legislation is described below, but first let us look at how AFDC functioned on the eve of its demise.

In 1995 a monthly average of 13.6 million individuals in 4.9 million families, including 9.3 million children (nearly 1 child in 9), received AFDC benefits totaling $22.0 billion. In 1992, a year of relatively mild recession, AFDC recipients constituted 5.4 percent of the total U.S. population and 14 percent of the nation's children. The federal government paid an average of 55 percent of AFDC costs, states paid 40 percent, and local governments paid the remainder. States with below-average per capita incomes received a higher federal matching share—as much as 80 percent of total AFDC costs. Economic recovery combined with state efforts at welfare reform brought federal AFDC benefit expenditures down from $12.3 billion in 1993 to $11.1 billion in 1996. State expenditures were $10.0 billion in both 1993 and 1995 but as yet unavailable for 1996.

Although the federal government contributed more than half of total AFDC expenditures, it delegated administration of the program to the states within broad federal guidelines. Eligibility required that the household contain at least one child under age 18 and that the household's assets not exceed the levels specified by the program. Income restrictions varied by family size and allowed for some standard deductions from income, such as work expenses and child care. The federal government left it to the states to determine standards of need and benefit levels. Each state's standard of need ostensibly reflected a subsistence budget, but the states differed radically in the standards set and were under no obligation to set welfare payments equal to the needs figures. In twenty-two states and the District of Columbia the payment standard was below the needs standard.

AFDC benefits were calculated as the difference between the state-determined maximum benefit level and net family income. No state paid benefits sufficient to keep an AFDC family out of poverty in the absence of other income or in-kind assistance, and less affluent states tended to pay the lowest benefits (map 1). In 1993 monthly maximum benefits for a mother and two children varied from $923 in Alaska to $120 in Mississippi. The real maximum AFDC benefit fell in every state from 1970 to 1995 (map 2), average monthly payments falling by more than 40 percent. While the 1993 average monthly payment was only 38 percent of the 1993 federal poverty threshold, eight states (all in the South) paid a maximum benefit amounting to less than one-fourth of the poverty threshold (Mississippi's payment was equal to 13% of the poverty threshold, for example). However, the availability of food stamps brightened this bleak picture somewhat. AFDC families were automatically eligible for food stamps, and nearly 90 percent received them. In January 1996 the maximum value of both benefits in the median state was $699 for a family of three—65 percent of the 1996 poverty threshold, the real value of the median state's maximum AFDC benefit having been cut in half since 1970.

The AFDC rolls grew rapidly after World War II, doubling each decade between 1947 and 1967 and again between 1967 and 1972. In the early 1970s the size of the AFDC population stabilized after the proportion of eligible families receiving benefits had leaped from 41 to 85 percent in six years. From 1975 to 1990 the average monthly enrollments fluctuated from 10.3 to 11.3 million recipients. Average monthly recipients climbed to 12.6 million in 1991 and 14.2 million in 1994, before declining to 13.6 million in 1995. A number of factors contributed to the rise in AFDC rolls. More generous benefits, dramatic growth in the number of single mothers, loosened eligibility rules, and less stigma attached to welfare recipiency probably accounted for most of the accelerated caseload growth. With the economic recovery after 1992, the trend pointed down again in many states, and caseloads were declining moderately at the time of the 1996 legislation discussed below.

Federal legislation and Supreme Court decisions also influenced the growth of the welfare population during the 1960s and early 1970s by extending coverage to groups not previously eligible. In 1961 Congress allowed states to grant assistance to poor, two-parent families having a jobless but employable parent. This "unemployed parent" component, which became available in a little more than half the states, covered only those working fewer than one hundred hours per month; those working any more than that were ineligible no matter how meager their earnings. In 1968 the Supreme Court extended AFDC eligibility by striking down the "man in the house" rule, under which many states held a man living in an AFDC household responsible for the children's support even if he was not legally liable. The following year, the court invalidated residency requirements used by numerous states to restrict eligibility for public assistance. During the Reagan years access to AFDC by two-parent families was sharply limited, but in the last year of that administration the 1988 Family Support Act required all states to extend assistance for at least part of the year to qualified two-parent families by October 1990.

While these developments increased the number of persons eligible for assistance, neighborhood legal service agencies, welfare rights organizations, and other groups publicized the availability of AFDC benefits and helped eligible families apply. Through the work of these advocacy groups the stigma of being "on the dole" declined. Improvements in administration further facilitated the expansion of AFDC rolls by shortening delays between application and approval.

Critics have charged that AFDC significantly contributed to the breakdown of the family and undermined the work ethic of the poor. AFDC was a response to economic and social conditions resulting from the increasing number of single-parent families, but the program itself was accused of having induced families to modify their behavior to qualify for benefits. It was thought to encourage the phenomenon to which it was a response by inducing parents to beget children without getting married and without assuming responsibility for supporting their children. Critics contended that because of these negative impacts on families welfare was doing more harm than good.

The evidence that the greater availability of welfare had contributed to marital breakups or reduced the propensity for couples to marry after conception was mostly anecdotal and conjectural. Hard evidence to support these claims remains elusive. Given the low level of benefits and their sharply declining real value, there was little likelihood that AFDC had influenced the increase in single-parent families. Nevertheless, the existence of the income support made the survival of such families possible. In that sense many, perhaps even most, such families would not—could not—have existed without the program. At any rate, while the proportion of children living with a single parent rose from 17 percent to 25 percent between 1975 and 1994, the proportion of all children receiving AFDC rose from 8.8 percent in 1970 to 11.8 percent in 1975, dropped to 10.8 percent in 1982, and then rose persistently to 14 percent in 1992, before dropping back to 13.5 percent in 1995.

Contrary to popular impressions of large welfare "broods," the number of children in AFDC families steadily declined. The proportion of welfare families with four or more children dropped from one-third in 1969 to one-tenth in 1987 and remained at that level in 1993. The average AFDC family size declined from 4 to 2.8 persons by 1995, mirroring the trend for the population as a whole. AFDC families now have fewer children than do families not on AFDC. A formerly married woman who became a family head could expect a substantial drop in her level of economic well-being, even with public assistance. A comparison of states with widely varying welfare payments shows little correlation between the amount of assistance provided and the incidence of single-parent families, out-of-wedlock births, or divorces. It is simply not a lifestyle anyone would rationally choose.

Another charge frequently leveled at AFDC was that the program undermined the work ethic of the poor. The evidence for this claim was more persuasive. Although AFDC cash payments trailed cost-of-living increases from the early 1970s, a significant expansion in corollary programs—food stamps, free school lunches, subsidized housing, medical care, and social services—and the decline in the value of the federal minimum hourly wage increasingly tilted the economic balance in favor of welfare over low-paid jobs. A single mother with three children could receive, on average, roughly the same income from AFDC and food stamps alone as she could earn by working full-time year-round at prevailing minimum-wage rates, and either would leave the family far below the poverty line. However, the AFDC mother was automatically eligible for free medical care, which few minimum-wage employers provided. In addition, she did not face child care and other job-related costs borne by the working mother. Nevertheless, despite the economic incentives

Map 1. Average monthly AFDC payments per person (and per family) in 1993 and maximum three-person benefit as a percentage of the 1993 poverty threshold

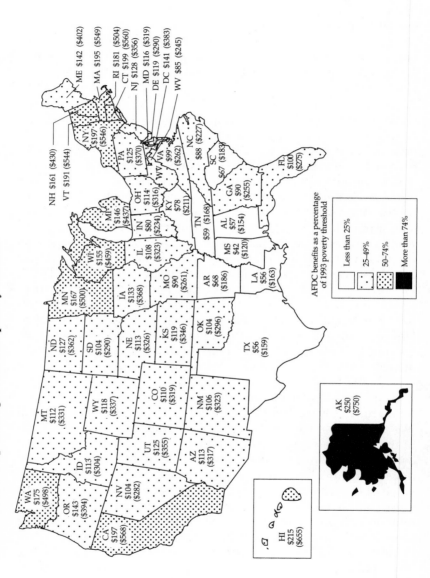

ME $142 ($402)
MA $195 ($549)
RI $181 ($504)
CT $199 ($560)
NJ $128 ($356)
MD $116 ($319)
DE $119 ($290)
DC $141 ($383)
WV $85 ($245)

NH $161 ($430)
VT $191 ($544)

NY $197 ($546)
PA $125 ($370)
VA $99 ($262)
NC $88 ($227)
SC $67 ($183)
FL $100 ($275)

MI $146 ($437)
OH $114 ($316)
KY $78 ($211)
TN $59 ($168)
GA $90 ($255)
AL $57 ($154)
MS $42 ($120)

WI $155 ($459)
IL $108 ($323)
IN $80 ($234)
MO $90 ($261)
AR $68 ($186)
LA $56 ($163)

MN $167 ($500)
IA $133 ($368)
KS $119 ($346)
OK $104 ($296)
TX $56 ($159)

ND $127 ($362)
SD $104 ($290)
NE $113 ($326)
CO $110 ($319)
NM $106 ($323)

MT $112 ($331)
WY $118 ($337)
UT $125 ($355)
AZ $113 ($317)

WA $175 ($498)
OR $143 ($394)
ID $113 ($304)
NV $104 ($282)
CA $197 ($568)

HI $215 ($655)

AK $250 ($750)

AFDC benefits as a percentage of 1993 poverty threshold

Less than 25%
25–49%
50–74%
More than 74%

Source: Social Security Bulletin, 1995 annual supplement.

Map 2. Percentage decrease in state AFDC maximum monthly benefit for a three-person family, 1970–1995 (adjusted for inflation)

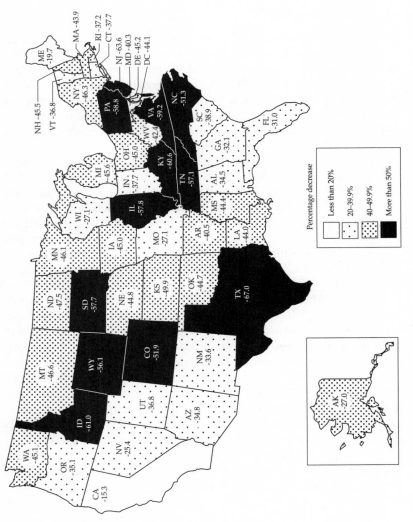

Percentage decrease

Less than 20%

20–39.9%

40–49.9%

More than 50%

Source: Children's Defense Fund, *The State of America's Children, Yearbook 1996* (Washington, D.C., 1996), 4.

75

of welfare, many recipients retained a strong attachment to the work ethic. But the fact that many beneficiaries remained on the rolls for lengthy periods prompted recurrent federal commitments to emphasize work over welfare.

Work with Welfare

The original designers of what was called Aid to Dependent Children (ADC) in the 1930s assumed that the program would aid destitute widows who needed financial support to raise their children. Given the social mores of the times, the female family head was not expected to work but was expected to be fully occupied rearing her children. Moreover, during the Great Depression there was a shortage of jobs for married men, who were considered more deserving of employment than were married women.

The demographic characteristics of AFDC recipients changed radically during the next six decades. By the end, only 2 percent of AFDC mothers were widows and more than half had never married (figure 2.6). The number and proportion of nonwhite mothers on AFDC had vastly increased—though they were still a minority— and the societal views regarding women and work had changed significantly. As more mothers with infants entered the job market, the argument that welfare mothers should earn their living gained broad support.

Prior to 1967 the benefits paid under AFDC were most often calculated as the difference between a client's own income and the maximum payment standard established by a state, although the regulations permitted income deductions for minimal work-connected expenses. Benefits were reduced by whatever amount the family head earned. This "marginal tax rate" or benefit reduction of nearly 100 percent created a disincentive to seek even part-time work. To overcome this disincentive, Congress in 1967 established a different means of treating the earnings of AFDC recipients. Welfare officials were required to disregard the first $30 plus one-third of the remaining monthly wages plus work-related expenses in computing benefits, even if this policy brought a family's total income (earnings combined with welfare) above a state's needs standard. Benefits were reduced by 67¢ for every $1 increase in earned income over allowable deductions, a decrease in the benefit reduction rate from the 100 percent rate referred to above. Under the law in effect at AFDC's legislated abolishment in 1996, the one-third deduction was discontinued after four months, with benefits reduced one to one with earnings—a benefit reduction rate of 100 percent after four months on AFDC. Congress anticipated that these "disre-

Figure 2.6. Number of AFDC families, 1975–1993

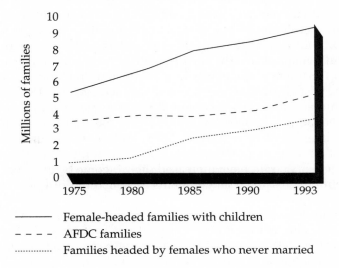

Source: U.S. General Accounting Office, *Welfare to Work: Most AFDC Training Programs Not Emphasizing Job Placement,* GAO/H&HS-95-113 (Washington, D.C., May 1995), 11.

gards" would promote more work effort and enhance self-sufficiency. Yet the earnings level required—assuming jobs were available—to remove a family of three from AFDC was more than most AFDC mothers could command.

To complement the carrot of earnings incentives, Congress in the late 1960s provided a stick requiring all AFDC recipients except those with children under age 6 to participate in a work incentive (WIN) program to gain work experience and to learn job search skills but never appropriated enough money to wield the stick. The Nixon administration contemplated a guaranteed-income family assistance plan (FAP), but congressional conservatives opposed the concept and liberals considered the proposed income level to be too low for consideration. Following the 1970s experience with public service employment, the Carter administration contemplated introducing a job guarantee for welfare recipients but abandoned the notion when a $15 billion per year budgetary cost was projected. Congress made few other work-related changes in the AFDC program until the 1980s, when the Reagan administration inaugurated a series of amendments. The most important was a stricter set of rules for counting a recipient's earned income. Previous administrations treated earned income leniently in order both to encourage welfare recipients to work and to boost the total income of poor families. In contrast, the Reagan administration equated any work with self-sufficiency even if the job provided very low wages. The impact of the 1981 amendments was immediate and dramatic. In the following year, during the worst recession since the Great Depression, the number of families receiving AFDC declined by 8 percent, or 300,000 families. Ironically, the results of the administration's actions demonstrated employed AFDC recipients' commitment to work. Only a small minority quit their jobs to return to welfare even though many could have increased their income by quitting. Subsequent congressional amendments loosened but did not remove the 1981 limitations.

In addition to amendments affecting the earnings of AFDC recipients, Congress used other means to restrict access to the program. After 1981 welfare administrators were required to count the income of stepparents in ascertaining eligibility for AFDC. Three years later Congress also required administrators to count the income of siblings living with a child receiving AFDC. A third change liberalized AFDC by not counting the first $50 the family received in child support payments from an absent father.

Hoping to move a larger segment of the AFDC population toward work and self-sufficiency, the 1988 Family Support Act attempted to impose stricter work requirements. The educational attainment of recipients, although still relatively low, was rising. Studies had shown that AFDC recipients were no less eager to work than the rest of the population, provided their earnings exceeded welfare income. Just as poverty was often transitory, most families did not languish forever on welfare. Many recipients, however, remained on the rolls for years and could benefit, it was thought, by educational, job search, and training assistance. The median continuous length of time spent on AFDC was 2.2 years. However, because many left the rolls for a period and then returned, and because a few remained for a much longer duration, the mean total time per recipient on AFDC rolls at the time of the Family Support Act was 7 years.

Reacting to all of these facts, the Family Support Act required each state to have a job opportunities and basic skills training (JOBS) program in place by 1990 for all able-bodied adult recipients whose youngest child was aged at least 3 years. Aimed at helping recipient families avoid long-term welfare reliance, JOBS included an educational as well as an employment component. But again, bringing AFDC recipients to employability and employment proved more difficult and expensive than politicians assumed. AFDC families have always been predominately female-headed. Fathers, present in fewer than 10 percent of AFDC homes, are often incapacitated and unable to work. Of the 3.6 million AFDC mothers in 1993 only 38 percent were high school graduates, compared with 85 percent of women aged 25 to 34. Only one in eight had any education beyond high school, and 72 percent of those taking the Armed Forces Qualification Test of general problem solving ability scored in the bottom quartile. Young poor mothers averaged two years of work experience, usually only short-term or part-time, compared with their nonpoor counterparts' five years. Those AFDC recipients 18–22 years of age who obtained jobs at the time averaged $6 an hour, which, if they had two children, would have just brought them to the poverty line if they were able to work full-time year-round. Their wages rose at an average annual rate of 1 percent, compared with an average of 4.8 percent for women not dependent on AFDC. Family structure had far more to do with their entry into and departure from welfare than did their earning status:

Reasons for Entering and Departing from AFDC

Entering	*Percentage*
Divorce or separation	45
Unmarried woman gives birth	30
Drop in income	16
Other or unidentified reasons	9
Departing	
Marriage	35
Increased earnings	26
Increase in transfer income other than AFDC	14
Children leave home	11
Other or unidentified reasons	14

Faced with these challenges, JOBS made progress but not enough to placate an increasingly restless political system. The program's ambitions were modest. JOBS called for a minimum participation rate of 7 percent in 1991, 11 percent by 1992–93, and 20 percent in 1995. However, the 1991 participation goal was only reached in election year 1992, by which date "ending welfare as we know it" had superseded such modest expectations. JOBS progress plodded onward behind schedule—10 percent participation by 1995, for instance—but the political die was cast. States failed to provide the matching funding required to draw down the maximum federal assistance available, so that the already limited federal money earmarked for JOBS was partially unspent. At the same time, state programs had difficulty finding or creating the necessary number of job opportunities for those required to participate in the program. Too often employability development was limited to basic education and job search training, with little access to the skill training essential to movement beyond minimum-wage jobs. Some states took advantage of federal encouragement to apply for waivers of federal regulations in order to experiment with state-level reform.

Discouraged by the JOBS program's slow pace and alert to the changing tenor of public attitudes, Congress demanded more drastic remedies during its 1995–96 session. Conflicts in philosophy between the House and the Senate and between Congress and the White House stymied passage of any national welfare reform until just before Congress recessed for 1996 electioneering. The Personal Responsibility and Work Opportunity Reconciliation Act of 1996 did in fact end AFDC, welfare entitlement as it had been known for sixty-one years. Lacking experience, the new act can only be described and subjected to speculation.

Welfare Reform Congressional Style

For more than six decades eligible families were entitled to various financial and other supports, and the federal and state governments had no choice but to come up with sufficient funding to meet those commitments. That entitlement has been replaced by Temporary Assistance to Needy Families (TANF), a block grant to the states. Major provisions of the federal Personal Responsibility and Work Opportunity Reconciliation Act of 1996 are summarized here, followed by some speculation concerning the possible outcomes:

Block granting. For fiscal years 1996 through 2002 the act replaces AFDC, emergency assistance, and JOBS with a single TANF block grant to the states, capped nationally at the fiscal year 1994 level of $16.4 billion per year. Included is a separate allocation for child care. Most states experienced a downward trend in AFDC caseload from the end of the 1992 recession to 1996 and will be able to choose whether the block grant will be at their FY 1994 or their FY 1995 level or at the median level for the years FY 1992–FY 1994. Those states will actually receive more federal money in the short run than they would have received for AFDC. In the longer run, however, cyclical downturns or population growth will inevitably take their toll without means for increasing the federal contribution; at the same time the new work requirements will add to administrative expenses.

Individual entitlement. The sixty-one years of entitlement to family income support guaranteed by the Social Security Act of 1935 is ended. The state must have "objective criteria for delivery of benefits and determining eligibility" and provide for an appeals process for those adversely affected, but there is no provision in the law for enforcement of this requirement. A state can make its own entitlement guarantee if it cares to do so but cannot call down additional federal funds to fulfill it.

Time limits. Families who have been on the welfare rolls for five cumulative years will be ineligible for cash aid. Each state is permitted by the federal law to exempt 20 percent of its caseload from this rule.

Work requirements. States must demonstrate that they will require families to work after two years on assistance, but there is no penalty prescribed for states failing to do so. The state is required to meet a work requirement involving 25 percent of single-parent families in FY 1996, and the percentage will rise to 50 percent by FY 2002. "Work activities" meeting the work requirement include unsubsidized or subsidized employment, on-the-job training, work experience, community service, up to twelve months of vocational training, providing child care services to individuals participating in community service, and up to six weeks of job search. Teenagers can also count secondary school attendance as a work activity.

Waivers. Existing state waivers of AFDC requirements continue until their expiration dates even if they are inconsistent with the new federal law. States can choose to abandon their waivers and return to the federal requirements at any time prior to those expiration dates.

Supplemental funds. The law establishes a $2 billion contingency fund to supplement the TANF block grants to those states impacted by high unemployment or food stamp utilization.

Maintenance of effort. Each state is required to maintain 80 percent of its FY 1994 level of spending on AFDC and related programs, reduced to 75 percent for states meeting the work requirements. One hundred percent maintenance of effort is required during any year in which the state receives extra funding from the contingency fund.

Transfers. States can transfer up to 30 percent of their cash assistance block grant to the child care and Title XX block grants as long as the funds transferred are used to benefit families whose incomes are less than 200 percent of the poverty threshold. Only up to one-third of this total transfer can be used to fund Title XX social services block grant activities.

Penalties. A series of penalties ranging from 1 percent to 21 percent of the block grant may be imposed for state compliance failures, with the penalized states required to substitute state moneys for the withheld federal funds.

Personal responsibility agreement. States are required to make an initial assessment of recipients' skills and have the option to help or require recipients to develop personal responsibility plans.

Teen parent provisions. Unmarried minor parents are required to live with an adult or in an adult-supervised setting and participate in education and training in order to receive assistance.

Supplemental security income. Definitions of disability for the eligibility of children are changed in a number of ways that decrease the number of children eligible for assistance, and cash benefits for institutionalized children are limited.

Child support enforcement. States are required to operate a child support enforcement program meeting federal requirements, including paternity determination and centralized registries of child support orders and enforcement. Recipients must assign rights to child support and cooperate with paternity establishment or suffer reduction of cash assistance. The $50 pass-through of child support payments is no longer required.

Restricting benefits for aliens. Legal aliens except refugees, asylees, veterans, and entrants from Cuba or Haiti are denied Supplemental Security Income and food stamps, and states have the option to deny them income support, Medicaid, Title XX social services, the special supplemental nutrition program for women, infants, and children (WIC) and other child nutrition benefits, and state-funded assistance. The state can choose to continue assistance to aliens who have already been in this country for five years or more or after they have been in the country for five years following the enactment of the federal act.

Child care. Mandatory funding totaling $13.9 million and discretionary funding totaling $7 billion are authorized for fiscal years 1997–2002, with states to receive $1.2 billion each year and the remainder available for state match at the Medicaid rate. States are required to maintain 100 percent of their FY 94 or FY 95 child care expenditures, whichever is greater, to draw down the matching funds. Child care is not guaranteed, but single parents with children under 6 who cannot find child care will not be penalized for failure to engage in work activities.

Food stamps and commodity distribution. Nearly $28 million over six years was cut from the food stamp program. About 70 percent of the cuts impacted families with children through various changes in the way food stamp eligibility is calculated. Two groups share the remainder of the impact: food stamps were denied to legal aliens, but with the above-cited exceptions; and childless, nondisabled individuals will now be eligible for food stamps for only three months (6 months if working at least 20 hours a week) out of each three years.

Child nutrition programs. Approximately $3 billion over three years was cut from child nutrition assistance, primarily to family home day care providers, and to a lesser extent from the summer food program. The states were given the option to deny child nutrition programs to legal aliens. School breakfast and lunch programs were for the most part untouched, as was WIC.

Miscellaneous. Examples of other provisions that might be cited are the Individual Development Accounts, through which recipients of assistance can accumulate savings from earned income without it being charged against their eligibility; competitive Out of Wedlock Reduction Bonuses, limited to five states; and lifetime prohibition of benefits to those convicted of drug crimes.

The impact of the new legislation remains to be seen. Looking at the House version, whose crucial elements were not changed greatly when it was merged with the Senate bill, the Urban Institute estimated that 2.6 million more people, including 1.1 million children, would be pushed into poverty by the legislation.[4] The Urban

Institute also expected the poverty gap to increase by 20 percent and 8.2 families—one out of five U.S. families with children—to see their income fall an average of $1,300. Most of this loss would be from the food stamp cuts, which, along with the denial of services to legal aliens, are the sources of most of the contemplated $55 billion in savings from the legislation. In addition, the Congressional Budget Office estimated that between 2.5 million and 3.5 million children would be affected by the five-year limit once it took effect.[5] In fact, about one-half of the 1996 AFDC population had been enrolled for more than five years, far exceeding the allowable 20 percent. The contingency fund of $2 billion over five years and the population adjustment fund of $800 million over four years must contend with the fact that the 1990–92 recession added $6 billion to AFDC costs. How many states will be able to resist the invitation to maintain only 80 percent of their past effort—a potential cut of $40 billion—also remains to be seen. Conflicts between the work requirements and the available child care funds are also projected. The child nutrition reductions are other matters of concern, as is the deprivation visited upon legal alien families.

The past history of attempted welfare reforms discourages optimism. For the former AFDC population and those hereafter who would otherwise have been eligible, a five-year run at becoming employable and employed, with a 20 percent window for those who do not make it, might seem to be ample time. It is not difficult to imagine a set of circumstances that could make the TANF approach viable:

A sufficient investment in education and training for those who could be prepared for unsubsidized above-poverty employment

Public service employment or subsidized private jobs for those not absorbed by the competitive labor market

Child care support until rising earnings made it affordable

Medical insurance until employer-provided insurance was obtained

Income subsidies through a strengthened EITC or otherwise until an adequate earned income was attained in a secure job

However, there is nothing in past experience or current rhetoric to lead one to expect Congress to "put its money where its mouth is." The last word on welfare reform has not been spoken. The final years of the five-year limit will be crucial decisionmaking times.

One can only hope the experience will not be unduly prolonged for those least able to bear the pain.

Supplemental Security Income

The Supplemental Security Income (SSI) program assists poor people who are aged 65 or older, blind, or disabled. For decades federal public assistance programs for the aged, blind, and disabled operated similarly to AFDC. Although the federal government contributed a share of the cost, state and local governments largely determined eligibility and benefit levels and administered the programs. Benefits were more generous than under AFDC but varied widely from state to state.

Social security amendments passed in 1972 thoroughly revamped this program. The federal government now provides a basic monthly benefit for the aged, blind, and disabled. In 1994 average monthly benefits for individual SSI recipients were $238 for the aged, $358 for the blind, and $376 for the disabled. For couples the average monthly payments were $617, $674, and $612, respectively. By 1996 the federal SSI benefit standard averaged across these groups was $470 a month for an individual and $705 for a couple. Some but not all states supplement these amounts. Disabled and blind recipients generally receive the largest benefits because they are the least likely to receive OASDI benefits or to have other unearned income.

Under the revised SSI program, federal eligibility standards replaced demeaning eligibility criteria required by many states to ensure that only the most destitute received benefits. Requiring applicants to sell their assets and exhaust the proceeds before they qualified on the basis of their income netted little savings for the states but took a heavy toll in recipients' self-respect. However, the federal law retained other stringent standards. Aside from a home, an automobile with a current market value under $4,500, property for self-support, and life insurance policies with a total face value of $1,500 or less, the assets of recipients cannot exceed $2,000 for an individual or $3,000 for a couple. The intent of the law is to protect the taxpayer from the claims of those not in need without debasing the recipients.

The 1972 law also provided that the first $29 per month of social security payments or other unearned income, plus the first $65 of earned income and half of additional earnings, be disregarded in computing SSI eligibility. It is ironic that the law has offered the aged, blind, and disabled—whose ability to work is generally limited—more attractive incentives to work than it has offered recipients of AFDC despite congressional and public anxiety to see the latter working. One explanation is that Congress anticipated a relatively low price tag in approving liberal work incentives for the aged, blind, and disabled, whereas the cost of similar incentives in AFDC was recognized to be far higher.

Congress designed the minimum benefit and work incentives to channel more income to the aged, blind, and disabled. The new program's first-year payments in 1974 were nearly 40 percent more than under the previous system, making more persons eligible to receive benefits. The number of SSI recipients rose from 4 million in 1974 to 6.5 million in 1995, the latter receiving $27.2 million in benefits, $23.5 million from the federal government and the rest from state supplementation. Expanded outreach efforts were also partially responsible for the increase.

SSI benefits, like OASDI benefits, are adjusted for inflation. One of the major differences between the federally administered SSI and a state-run AFDC program is that the latter is not so adjusted. SSI benefits still are not uniform across the nation because all but seven states provide additional payments. Still, nearly 60 percent of 1994 SSI recipients received federal payments only.

Most SSI recipients are old, white, and female. The largest share qualify on the basis of disability:

	65 or older (%)	Female (%)	White (%)
Total	34	58	51
Aged	23	29	21
Blind	1	1	1
Disabled	75	70	77

The number of aged recipients has declined dramatically, a trend generally attributed to rising social security benefits and the greater availability of private pensions. The aged accounted for 58 percent of SSI recipients in 1974, compared with 34 percent in 1994. The proportion of aged SSI recipients who also received OASDI climbed steadily to 71 percent by 1988, declining thereafter to 63 percent in 1994. Only one in six aged SSI recipients lived with a spouse, though ten of every eleven maintained their own households. Only 22 percent had unearned income other than social security benefits, which averaged $77 a month. Their capacity for self-support was meager, which is not at all surprising among a population with more than two of every five recipients above age 80, although 2 percent of those recipients work.

In 1988 nine of every ten blind SSI beneficiaries lived in their own households. About 11 percent were under 18 years of age. Seven percent of blind SSI recipients worked, but a significant proportion had never done so. Many had one or more chronic health problems in addition to blindness.

Federal aid to the disabled began in 1951. As noted above, disability is defined as a physical or mental impairment that prevents substantial employment activity and has lasted or probably will last for at least a year or may result in death. In contrast to the declining ranks of aged SSI recipients, the number of disabled recipients increased steadily to 5.0 million by 1995—77 percent of the caseload, compared with one-third in 1970. The disabled suffer a variety of impediments, both mental and physical, the most common being mental retardation and mental illness, which afflict half of working-age disabled recipients. Nine of every ten disabled adult recipients maintain their own households. The proportion of disabled recipients who are confined to their homes has dropped significantly in recent years. Only a relatively small proportion of disabled recipients also receive vocational rehabilitation.

The aged, blind, and disabled are less capable of self-support and are considered less responsible for their dependency than AFDC recipients. Hence, they are deemed more "deserving" of aid. This public judgment is clearly reflected in notably higher benefits and more humane administration under SSI than under AFDC. Combined with social security and food stamps, federal SSI payments equal 86 percent of the poverty threshold for elderly single recipients and 101 percent for aged couples. State supplements increase these ratios. The more generous SSI benefits reflect the impact of a federal guarantee. A federal minimum AFDC benefit, frequently advocated in the past as part of comprehensive welfare reform proposals, could have been expected to have a similar effect. Contrasted to this relative generosity of SSI is the animosity evident in the 1996 "welfare reform" decision to deny its benefits to most legal aliens.

However, the relative generosity to SSI's disabled may contribute to the next welfare crisis. The number of persons receiving federally administered payments under the SSI disability program grew from 2.9 million in December 1988 to 5.0 million in September 1995, a rise of 2.1 million, or 74 percent, over this time period. While the number of children on SSI disability has been growing rapidly in response to a 1990 Supreme Court ruling allowing them easier eligibility for payments, they still account for only one-fifth of SSI recipients. The typical SSI recipient is in his or her thirties or early forties, and young males are a rising share of the caseload. The lack of a matching requirement has encouraged states to shift AFDC and general assistance cases to SSI. Not surprisingly, SSI disability recipients incur extraordinarily high Medicaid costs ($7,000 per year in 1995) as well. More will be heard from this quarter in the future.

General Assistance

Forty-one states and the District of Columbia provide varying coverage and benefits through general assistance to the needy who do not qualify for federally supported aid; thirty-three of those have statewide programs, and nine have general assistance programs operating only in some counties.[6] Of the forty-two jurisdictions with general assistance programs only twelve provide assistance to all financially needy persons who do not qualify for federally funded cash assistance; the other thirty restrict assistance to certain categories of the needy. All forty-two provide assistance to the disabled, the elderly, and those "otherwise unemployable" who are not eligible for federal assistance. Nineteen programs provide assistance to low-income children or families with children, including women pregnant with their first child. Nine states and a few counties in other states provide some assistance to childless adults considered employable but facing barriers to employment; only four provide assistance to able-bodied employable adults; twenty-one require employable adults, including those with children, to enter work or training programs to maintain benefit eligibility. Seven jurisdictions have durational residency requirements; seven require drug and alcohol abuse treatment if warranted. Twenty-eight states provide cash benefits to all recipients, eleven provide in-kind benefits through either vendor payments or vouchers, and three provide cash payments to the disabled and vendor payments or vouchers to the rest.

Cash benefits average about 40 percent of the poverty threshold, with all but two states paying below 55 percent and one paying 12 percent of poverty. Eighteen have no time limits, fifteen impose time limits on some categories of recipients and not on others, and nine impose time limits on all recipients. Three states and the District of Columbia include general assistance recipients under Medicaid, and twenty-nine states provide medical benefits to some or all under other programs.

General assistance benefit levels have declined in most states since 1992. Eight states have enacted nominal benefit increases, but none has exceeded the rate of inflation. Six states reduced nominal benefits during those years. During those same years, five states eliminated and one further restricted benefits for employable persons without children, one eliminated benefits for those with children, two eliminated benefits for pregnant women, four tightened eligibility rules for the disabled, and three reduced the duration of eligibility for disabled persons.

The following table in 1988 dollars provides insight into trends over time:

	Payments (millions)	Recipients (thousands)	Payment per person (monthly)
1961	$1,408	1,182	$ 99
1966	962	636	126
1971	2,221	1,009	183
1978	2,185	793	230
1984	2,634	1,364	161
1988	2,700	1,115	202
1993	2,647	971	n.a.

Because of rapid turnover, the number of persons receiving general assistance benefits during a year may be twice the number of recipients at any given time. This apparent tattering of the state safety net during these years of devolution from federal to state responsibility for social support programs is worthy of note.

Veterans' Benefits

Income support for veterans and their dependents and survivors predates even the Revolutionary War. Colonial laws mandated public support for men incapacitated in defense of the community. Although present programs do not provide enough support to permit all veterans and their dependents to escape poverty, they go a long way toward providing basic needs, particularly for older veterans and indigent survivors of deceased veterans. In 1995, 26.2 million veterans and 44 million dependents and survivors were eligible for aid. However, most beneficiaries of veterans' assistance are not poor; for example, only 1.5 percent of poor families with children received veterans' benefits in 1988.

In 1996 two types of cash benefits—compensation and pensions—were provided to veterans at a cost to the federal government of $17.9 billion (figure 2.7). The number of recipients has dropped since 1975, but inflation-adjusted expenditures have remained approximately constant owing to the rising costs of providing for an

Figure 2.7. Veterans' income support, 1996

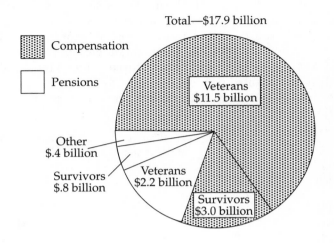

Source: U.S. Department of Veterans Affairs.

aging veteran population and generous congressional appropriations. Compensation is paid to veterans (or their dependents or survivors) for an injury, disability, or death incurred while serving in the armed forces, and pensions are paid to war veterans (or their dependents or survivors) whose annual income is below a specified level and who are permanently and totally disabled or aged 65 and older. In practice, the disability qualifications for a pension are relaxed as the veteran advances in age.

Compensation

About 2.25 million veterans received compensation in 1996 for service-connected disability, at a total budgeted cost to the government of $11.5 billion. Individual annual compensation averaged $5,146, ranging from $1,092 for a 10 percent disability to $22,440 for a total disability in December 1995. Dependents of veterans, and in some cases their impaired spouses, with 30 percent or more disability received supplemental pay, up to $240 per month for a spouse and two children in 1995. Additional special monthly compensation paid to veterans who suffered total blindness, deafness, or loss of limbs may boost the maximum payment to $50,340 annually. More than three hundred thousand survivors of veterans also received a little over $3 billion in compensation in 1996.

Congress has been more generous in raising veteran compensation than in raising pension levels. Whereas pensions are adjusted annually on the basis of increases in the consumer price index, compensation adjustments are made on an ad hoc basis and more often than not exceed the inflation rate. Average annual compensation costs are likely to increase even in the absence of a rise in benefits because service-connected disabilities tend to become aggravated with advancing age. However, the higher mortality rate of injured persons holds total compensation outlays in check. Because America's latest war ended over a quarter of a century ago, the number of individuals receiving compensation has been declining and will continue to do so.

Data are not available on the current income level of veterans receiving service-connected disability compensation. However, a 1971 study found that veterans receiving compensation had lower annual incomes than their nondisabled peers, and many of the disabled would have been counted among the poor had they not received compensation. This is particularly true of the 462,000 (out of a total 2.2 million) in 1988 whose degree of impairment was 50 percent or more. Many of these disabled veterans were probably unable to hold full-time jobs.

A total of $3 billion in survivors' benefits was distributed in 1996 among 303,000 dependents of service persons who died as the result of military service. Dependency and indemnity compensation rates vary with the rank held by the deceased veteran. Annual stipends range from $9,720 for a recruit's widow to $20,688 for a widow of a chief of staff. The basic entitlement is increased for each dependent child, $99 a month per child for a widow who is housebound and $205 per child for a widow who is in need of aid and attendants. Compensation alone barely places widows of low-ranking veterans above the poverty threshold; however, most widows with dependent children and those over 62 years of age are concurrently eligible for social security benefits. Survivors' compensation is not subject to a means test except in the case of qualifying dependent parents. Parents are eligible for support if their income does not exceed $9,381 for a single parent or $12,611 for both parents.

Pensions

A total of 409,000 war veterans received $2.2 billion in pensions in 1996—an annual average of $5,428 per veteran. Pensions are paid under three separate systems. The first two apply only to veterans who qualified for pensions prior to 1979 and continue benefits at that level unless an income cap is exceeded. All veterans qualifying for pensions since 1979 are covered under the third system, which links pensions to total family income and provides inflation-based cost-of-living adjustments. In 1996 the benefit payment was equal to the difference between the veteran's income and the maximum allowable benefit payment of $8,246 for a single veteran and $10,801 for a veteran with a dependent. A single veteran with an annual income of $1,000 was entitled to a $7,246 pension, giving a combined income of $8,246. A veteran with $2,000 of annual income would receive a pension of $6,246, yielding the same combined income as that received by the veteran with only a $1,000 prebenefit income.

Dependents of deceased veterans may qualify for pensions. Benefits are paid to surviving spouses and unmarried children under age 18 (or age 23 if they remain in a VA-approved school) who meet applicable income standards. Veterans' children generally are covered only if they are orphaned and receive no other support from parent or guardian.

Altogether, 334,600 survivors of veterans received $811.6 million through pensions in 1996, with an average benefit of $2,426 per family. Between 1965 and 1980 the number of widows of deceased World War II veterans receiving pensions more than tripled, then dropped to 124,857 by 1996. Only widows of post-Vietnam veterans are likely to have children at home. But with or without children, most veterans' widows would also qualify for social security benefits. Therefore, the combined potential income has significantly reduced the number of poor among veterans' survivors.

In contrast to the public assistance programs, veterans' benefits are administered with maximum consideration of the recipients' dignity and self-respect. Any veteran who can prove eligibility has only to file a simple form in order to qualify. Thereafter the veteran is required to submit annually only the information needed by the Department of Veterans Affairs to keep the claim current and active. The annual data are filed on a simple form supplied to the veteran or dependent. The form elicits information about the beneficiary's assets and income needed to determine continuing eligibility.

Once eligibility is established, the Department of Veterans Affairs makes only a cursory check on claims. Although the GAO has criticized these methods of certification, the department has insisted that the trust is justified since spot checks made with the Internal Revenue Service in cases of questionable claims show that the incidence of false claims is small. Assistance of veterans and their surviving dependents continues to be delivered with a minimum of delay. The system is worthy of emulation by other public assistance programs, in which onerous and costly needs tests are made at the expense of services to the needy and at little savings to the taxpayer.

Unemployment Insurance

Unemployment insurance (UI) was not designed as an antipoverty program but rather to help tide over the unemployed during spells of forced idleness. Because eligibility and benefits are based on past earnings and work experience, and not on need, often the poor are excluded or receive meager benefits. One of twelve poor families with children received UI benefits in 1986, the latest year for which data could be identified. In 1994 the program spent $22.7 billion to assist 6.8 million jobless individuals, who received on average $177 a week for 15.9 weeks.

UI was established along with the other social insurance programs under the Social Security Act of 1935. However, it was given a unique administrative structure to avoid constitutional challenges. The law imposed a payroll tax on employers. The tax rate is currently 6.2 percent of the first $7,000 of an employee's annual earnings, 87 percent of which (5.4% of applicable earnings) is returned to the states to fund state UI benefits, the principal part of the program. The federal portion of UI tax revenues is earmarked to cover the administrative costs of the program and the federal-state extended benefit program, which is triggered primarily during recessions.

Federal regulations subject state programs to only a few standards that specify covered industries and workers. States determine the duration and amount of benefits, the eligibility of the covered worker, and the amount of the employer's contribution through a system that reduces the tax burdens of employers whose workers have a low unemployment experience. Not surprisingly, employers encourage states to erect barriers to qualification. As a result, individual state programs vary widely even though the tax is universal. Three additional UI programs are administered by the federal government for veterans, railroad workers, and federal employees.

About 98 percent of all wage and salary workers (85% of the entire work force) are potentially covered under the UI provisions of the Social Security Act or one of the three separate federal programs. Most of the excluded workers are self-employed or farm or domestic workers. The last two groups commonly face low-income and intermittent employment, leaving them particularly vulnerable to poverty. In order to establish eligibility for unemployment benefits, a worker forced into idleness must meet the state's employment and earnings tests, be available for work, and register with the local employment service office. The unemployed are also required to report periodically on their job search efforts. However, the increasing computerization of employment service functions and remote access by computer kiosk or telephone are increasingly making these reports pro forma.

States have enacted additional eligibility rules that may exclude the poor from unemployment compensation. The covered worker typically must have been employed during two of the four quarters in the qualifying year and must have earned from $130 to $5,400 in that year (depending upon the state) to receive the minimum benefit. These minimum earnings requirements force low-wage earners, who are most susceptible to unemployment, to work longer than high-wage earners in order to qualify for unemployment benefits. For instance, a person working half-time at the federal minimum wage for a full year would be ineligible in eight states, and a person working half-time for only twenty-six weeks during a year at less than $6 an hour would be ineligible in fifteen states.[7] Also excluded are those unemployed who are just entering or reentering the work force and those who either have been terminated for misconduct or have quit voluntarily. As the result of this combination of factors, whereas 81 percent of the unemployed received unemployment compensation in April 1975, only 26 percent did so in October of 1987; in 1995 the figure was 36 percent.

A related problem (and one that is most significant to the poor) concerns the availability of unemployment benefits to those who leave the work force to enroll in employment and training programs. In most states the unemployed are ineligible for UI benefits if they are undergoing training because they are not immediately available and looking for work. Federal law prohibits states from denying benefits to the jobless who are enrolled in the relatively small dislocated worker program, although some states apparently have ignored this law.

Weekly UI benefit amounts vary widely among states. Most states compute benefits as a fraction of the worker's weekly or quarterly earnings but establish a maximum payment defined as a set dollar amount of a fixed proportion of the state's average weekly wage. Eleven states pay additional allowances for dependents. In 1995 maximum benefits ranged from $133 to $487 per week (for a claimant with dependents) and minimum benefit levels ranged from $5 to $68 per week.

The duration of benefits is often as crucial to recipients as the weekly payment amount. Until the early 1970s the maximum duration of payments was normally twenty-six weeks. As a cushion during periods of rising unemployment, Congress in 1970 authorized an additional thirteen weeks of benefits in all states when the national seasonally adjusted insured unemployment rate (IUR) exceeded 4.5 percent for three consecutive months. The 1981 Omnibus Budget Reconciliation Act repealed this national trigger. Under this revised legislation individual states are permitted to extend benefits for a thirteen-week period when their IUR exceeds 6 percent or when it is at least 5 percent and also 20 percent higher than the average IUR for the preceding two years. This change in the law limits the availability of extended benefits for the long-term unemployed, many of whom are poor. In 1989 extended benefits were not available at all, although four states experienced 8 percent or higher unemployment. Yet extended benefits became available in several states the following year, with the result that the yearly average exceeded 50 percent in 1992 for the first time since 1980.

Although few of the poor receive UI, it serves as a preventive antipoverty measure. Unlike welfare benefits, UI eligibility or benefits are not affected by the income of other family members. Without the protection of UI, low-wage earners who become jobless are likely to become impoverished. Both the value and the scope of UI have declined in recent years; real weekly benefits climbed steadily, reaching $159 in 1971 (1988 dollars), but have since dropped by 12 percent, to $136 in 1994 (1988 dollars). Although the coverage of the program has expanded, considerable concern was generated when, as noted above, fewer than a third of the unemployed in 1987 actually received benefits—a record low since such data became available in 1955. Factors such as increases in base-period earnings requirements, tightening of nonmonetary eligibility requirements in state program characteristics, declines in the proportion of the unemployed from manufacturing industries, and changes in unemployment as measured by the current population survey contributed to this decline. In 1992, 51 percent of the unemployed received UI benefits, but the increase from 1987 was primarily due to the emergency unemployment compensation program authorized in 1991 and actuated in the recession of that time period. As noted, the recipiency proportion had dropped back to 36 percent by 1995. But that national average hid the fact that the proportion of the unemployed who received unemployment compensation in 1995 varied from 65.0 percent in Rhode Island to 17.6 percent in Virginia.[8] In general, the more rural and the less manufacturing-oriented a state, the lower the proportion of UI recipients.

The weakening of the program dramatically lessened its antipoverty effectiveness. Although unemployment was more severe in 1982 than in 1975 (the peak unemployment years associated with the two deepest post–World War II recessions), total UI benefit payments dropped from $41.0 billion to $31.2 billion (1988 dollars). They were $37.1 billion in the next, more modest peak recession year, 1992, despite the increase in coverage from 86.3 million workers in 1983 to 105 million in 1992. For each of those three recession years, extended compensation was added to the regular benefits, which were $20.8 billion in 1983 and $25.6 billion in 1992. The average weekly benefit per unemployed person rose from $120 in 1983 to $182 in 1995 but in constant 1994 dollars continued at an approximately level rate of $177.

The UI program's benefits and financing are a hybrid of progressive and regressive features. Although many eligibility rules deny or restrict benefits for the working poor, benefit formulas typically replace a higher proportion of lost earnings for workers with low wages. States historically have paid benefits of between 50 percent and 70 percent of previous earnings up to a maximum amount. In 1994 a jobless individual who worked full-time year-round at the minimum wage during the base period qualified for benefits ranging from $77 to $176, depending upon the state. The national average weekly benefit was 37 percent of the average covered weekly wage in 1993. The system's financing structure has become increasingly regressive. The minimum federal taxable wage base (currently $7,000) dropped from more than 90 percent of total wages in 1940 to less than 29 percent in 1992. With an average weekly benefit of $173 and an average benefit duration of 15.6 weeks, the average total jobless benefit in 1993 was $2,699.

Clearly, UI's ability to stave off poverty "ain't what it used to be." Nevertheless, many of the 9.4 million 1995 recipients would have fallen into poverty in its absence.

Workers' Compensation

Workers' compensation, similar to unemployment insurance, is designed to protect individuals and families during a period when wages are reduced or interrupted, though by workplace accident or disease rather than inability to find a job. Therefore, its antipoverty role is to help prevent falling into poverty as a result of a work interruption rather than to boost out of poverty a family already mired in it. In addition to cash benefits, workers' compensation provides medical care and limited rehabilitation services for work-connected injuries and compensates survivors in the event of fatal injuries.

Workers' compensation, the nation's first social insurance program, dates back to the second decade of this century. The program is similar to UI in that each state has broad discretion over its own compensation program. Unlike in the case of UI, however, there are no federal standards, and the states oversee but usually do not administer workers' compensation programs. Cash compensation has increased more than tenfold (in 1988 dollars) since 1950:

| | *Cash compensation* |
	(1988 $ billions)
1940	$ 1.4
1950	2.0
1960	3.4
1970	6.0
1980	13.8
1986	17.8
1990	20.6
1993	25.4

In contrast with other cash assistance programs, workers' compensation made larger payments during the 1980s. However, this was not necessarily to the advantage of the worker, who received reimbursement for only a portion of lost income, the bulk of the payment going to cover the costs of medical treatment. In 1993 employer costs per protected worker were $590, compared with $296 in 1982. Costs per $100 of payroll increased from $1.75 in 1982 to $2.30 in 1993. No information is available on the number of beneficiaries, but increasing payments may indicate broader coverage, more generous awards, or both.

Widespread dissatisfaction with state workers' compensation programs prompted movements in the late 1930s and early 1940s and again in the early 1970s to establish minimal federal standards or even to federalize the program. In response to the inadequacies of workers' compensation, Congress enacted the 1970 Occupational Safety and Health Act, which established the National Commission on State Workmen's Compensation Laws. In 1972 the commission adopted recommendations relating to benefit, coverage, and rehabilitation standards. Possibly to avoid a federal takeover, the states significantly improved their programs. The number of states that paid maximum weekly benefits equal to two-thirds of the state's average wage increased from six to thirty-one in the decade following the commission report and now stands at forty states.

State laws generally specify a reimbursement rate of two-thirds of the injured worker's previous wage, although the widespread existence of minimum and maximum benefits and the absence of data on average weekly payments make unclear how strictly the states adhere to the two-thirds wage replacement benchmark. The median state's maximum payment for a total disability was $465 in 1996, ranging from $264 in Mississippi to $760 in Illinois. Unlike other social programs, state workers' compensation minimum benefits do not provide a floor for low-wage earners. Rather, twenty-eight states pay the lesser between the minimum benefit and two-thirds of the previous wage. The maximum payment for specified injuries differs radically: benefits for the loss of an arm ranged in 1996 from $25,000 in Massachusetts to $228,000 in Illinois. A weakness of the present system is that temporarily disabled persons get about the same benefits as do the totally and permanently disabled. Phasing down benefits to the temporarily disabled would induce them to resume work as soon as they were able.

Workers' compensation laws covered approximately 96.1 million workers in 1993, 87 percent of wage and salary workers—basically unchanged since 1973. Most farm and domestic workers and other low-earning casual workers are excluded from coverage in many states. Injured workers requiring medical rehabilitation receive scant attention. When available, vocational services received by disabled workers are most often the results of efforts by employers and insurance carriers, who have a vested interest in restoring injured workers' productivity.

Occupational illnesses are a weak link in workers' compensation programs. Unlike injuries, illnesses are difficult to trace to a specific employer because the impairment may not appear for decades, it may be caused by a similar type of work for several firms, and many illnesses are attributable to both occupational and nonoccupational factors. Most states only pay benefits for occupational illnesses that appear within several years after the worker leaves the firm, and claims often must be filed soon after the onset of the disease.

Although Congress left the administration of workers' compensation to the states, in 1969 it created the federal black lung benefit program because it found that coal mining clearly caused the ailment. In FY 1996 more than 90,000 claimants received $500 million in total payments. Beneficiaries receive a flat payment equal to 37.5 percent of the monthly pay for a federal employee at a grade 2 level. In 1996 this amount was $435 monthly. Dependents receive additional payments. Congress has not extended the principle of the black lung program to other occupational illnesses.

The generally accelerating costs of medical care, the tendency of doctors and hospitals to multiply their fees under workers' compensation, the efforts of lawyers to leverage work injuries out of the no-fault realm of workers' compensation insurance into the more profitable realm of tort litigation, and the new and unfamiliar emergence of stress-related and soft tissue injuries have motivated employer and insurance company reforms. As important as that is, the poverty prevention contribution of workers' compensation should not be forgotten.

Taxing the Poor

Several income tax provisions are intended primarily to diminish the federal tax burden of the poor and can be viewed as indirect income payments. Of particular importance to the poor is the earned income tax credit. In FY 1996 the following measures accounted for an estimated one-fifth of the total personal income tax revenues forgone by the federal government:

	Billions
Exclusion of social security benefits	$23.1
EITC	23.1
Additional deduction for the aged and blind	2.0
Exclusion of veterans' benefits (1990)	1.4
Exclusion of public assistance and SSI benefits	0.5
Exclusion of Medicare benefits	15.3

Taxing the poor began, ironically, during Franklin Roosevelt's administration, when the federal government was laying the foundation of the welfare system. Social security payroll taxes instituted in 1935 were levied on the very first dollar of earnings. The Roosevelt administration also significantly lowered income tax thresholds to finance World War II, although this tax probably did not affect the poor until the 1950s. In 1959 the federal income tax threshold for a family of four was 10 percent below the poverty line, and social security taxes amounted to 2.5 percent of earnings. Despite other efforts of the Great Society, by 1969 the income tax threshold was 20 percent below the poverty line and payroll taxes had nearly doubled, to 4.8 percent.

During the 1970s the anomaly of the poor's paying taxes while

Table 2.1. Earned Income Tax Credit Returns, 1996 ($ millions)

Income Class	Joint Returns		Single Returns		All Returns	
	Number	Amount	Number	Amount	Number	Amount
$0–10	970	$1,164	4,480	$4,259	5,540	$5,423
$10–20	1,780	3,796	4,237	7,824	6,017	11,620
$20–30	2,438	3,162	2,950	3,398	5,388	6,560
$30–40	970	727	700	584	1,670	1,312
$40–50	114	92	16	13	129	105
$50–75	33	31	3	6	36	37
Total[a]	6,305	8,974	12,387	16,084	18,692	25,058
Percent distribution by type of return	33.7%	35.8%	66.3%	64.2%	100%	100%

[a]Columns may not add up to totals because of minor income class amounts above $75.

Source: House Committee on Ways and Means, *1996 Green Book: Background Material and Data on Programs within the Jurisdiction of the Committee on Ways and Means* (Washington, D.C.: U.S. Government Printing Office, 4 November 1996), app. K.

federal policy sought to raise their income prompted revisions in the federal income tax structure. Congress raised the standard deduction and personal exemption to ensure that most poor families were relieved of paying federal income taxes and enacted the EITC in 1975 to offset rising payroll deductions for low-wage earners with children. However, because the above tax breaks were not adjusted for inflation their value eroded over time. By the mid-1980s a family of four earning a poverty-level income paid a combined income and payroll tax rate of 10.4 percent.

Congress has since taken several steps to lower the tax burden on the poor by indexing the standard deduction and the EITC for inflation. The 1986 Tax Reform Act implemented the long-term goal of ensuring that poor families with children will be exempt from the federal income tax. For instance, in 1995 a married couple with two children incurred no tax until their income reached $16,550.

However, of greater importance as an antipoverty measure was the 1993 expansion of the EITC. Tax credits directly reduce liability and are therefore worth more than tax exemptions or deductions, which reduce taxable income. The EITC is in fact a negative income tax. Low-wage earners with dependent children whose tax credit exceeds their tax liability receive a rebate, which varies with the number of dependent children. The EITC only applies to working parents, and it attempts to encourage the work ethic by denying eligibility to parents dependent on welfare. In 1994 for a family with two children the credit was worth 30 percent of an eligible taxpayer's first $8,425 in earned income, up to a maximum of $2,538. This maximum credit remained in effect for adjusted gross earnings of $8,425 to $11,000. For every subsequent dollar earned the credit was reduced by 10¢, effectively eliminating the credit for parents earning more than $25,300. In 1993 an estimated 14 million families received tax credits, the average credit being $945. The credit cost $13.2 billion during that year, of which 90 percent was refunded as a transfer payment, either in a lump sum at the next annual tax filing time or previously as an addition to the worker's paychecks. The remainder went to offset tax liability.

A family may claim a tax credit, which diminishes as family income rises to $28,525; in 1996 the tax credit for that amount was $3,560 for a family with two or more children and $2,094 for a family with one child. In 1996, 18.7 million families were expected to claim a total of $25.1 million. As table 2.1 shows, two-thirds of the tax relief or direct spending from the EITC accrues to single-parent households, a prime target of antipoverty policy.

Social security payroll taxes had become a much greater burden than income taxes for low-income families. However, the expanding EITC approach not only offsets the costs of social security taxes to a substantial degree, it offers an approach to income supplementation to families who have demonstrated their commitment to work. Its possibilities as an adjunct to the welfare reform begun in 1996 are obvious. That seven states have introduced their own versions of the EITC is another indicator of its promise.

A dependent care tax credit offers a nonrefundable credit of up to 30 percent against income tax liability for expenditures of up to $4,800 for dependent care enabling a householder to work. More than 6 million taxpayers in 1994 claimed an average credit of $435, amounting in aggregate to $2.7 million, about 15 percent of which went to families with adjusted gross incomes below $20,000. Exclusions of workers' compensation and disabled mine workers' benefits, tax credits for the elderly and disabled, and additional standard deductions for the elderly and blind are other examples of aid to the poor through the federal tax structure. Poor families also face generally regressive state and local taxes, which are not documented here.

Income Maintenance Proposals

Administrative problems, low benefit levels in some states, gaps in coverage, rising costs, and the persistence of mass poverty occasionally generate speculation about possible alternatives to existing income maintenance programs. Among the alternatives discussed are guaranteed incomes, children's allowances, employment guarantees, and wage subsidies. The EITC as an approach to wage supplementation has already been discussed in this chapter. Public employment as a form of job guarantee and minimum-wage provisions as an effort to enhance earning levels are covered in chapter 5. The negative income tax as a form of income guarantee and the family allowances prevalent in Europe merit a few words, though their unlikely acceptability in the American political system discourages extensive exploration.

The most straightforward method of eliminating poverty would be simply to guarantee a predetermined, socially acceptable minimum income. For example, in order to lift its total income to the official poverty threshold ($15,569 in 1995) a family of four with an income of $10,000 a year could receive a grant of $5,569. If the family had no income, it would receive the full $15,569. Such a program to fill in the poverty gap would require an annual outlay of about $80 billion, assuming that its availability did not cause the poor and near poor to decrease their earnings and rely on the guarantee—a heroic assumption. A simple income guarantee would reduce work incentives for millions of people because they would be assured a poverty-level income whether or not they held jobs. Acknowledging that any workable plan should ensure that work would provide more income than welfare, a negative income tax provides an alternative approach that would allow low-wage earners to keep a portion of their earned income yet end the taxpayer subsidy at some prescribed level. For instance, a possibility would be to exempt half the earnings of low-income families in determining payments. Thus, a family of four earning $10,000 would count only $5,000 for negative tax purposes and would be able to claim $10,569, for a total income of $20,569, compared with the $15,569 maximum paid to a family without a wage earner. Such provisions would, of course, increase the cost of the program beyond the amount needed simply to bring all poor people up to the poverty threshold. The magnitude of the increase would depend on the level of work incentive offered by the plan. However, it is reasonable to suppose that the annual cost of the plan might rise to at least double the amount needed to bring every family's income to the poverty threshold. That such a sum would be about one-third what is currently spent to support the vote-intensive elderly says something about its desirability and likelihood.

A crucial problem for guaranteed income and negative income tax proposals would be selection of the minimum benefit and the "marginal tax rate," or the formula by which payments would be reduced as earnings rise. Benefits must be adequate for those who cannot provide for themselves, and incentives must be attractive enough to induce the able-bodied to contribute to their own support. A low tax rate is of no help to those who cannot work, whereas a high benefit level may draw able-bodied workers out of the labor market. The availability of earned benefits may decrease the earnings differential between skilled and unskilled workers and may dampen the incentive to acquire skills. Combining a high benefit level with a low tax rate could qualify many middle-income families. Ever present as a constraint on benefits and incentives is the cost of such a program. Taxpayer backlash at the high cost of welfare keeps benefits low. The trade-off between benefits, incentives, and costs is part of any public assistance system. Since a guaranteed income is beyond political feasibility, neither debate about its desirability nor answers to all or any of the administrative complexities are necessary. Still, the success of the EITC in providing income supplements without destroying work incentives justifies keeping the idea in the intellectual tool kit.

The European practice of paying families with children an allowance or income supplement to meet a portion of child rearing costs is another method of providing cash assistance to the poor. This alternative recognizes that the wage system alone distributes income inadequately because wages are based on productivity or tradition rather than on need. While the principle of equal pay for equal work is desirable as a means of eliminating discrimination based on color, age, or sex, it ignores the differing needs of families and tends to deprive children in large families of basic necessities. The underlying justification for family allowances is that a child's well-being should concern society as a whole.

Family allowance policies developed in Europe out of concern over declining birth rates earlier in the century, a development not faced by the United States until very recently and one that has generated no anxiety. Other advanced industrial nations annually spend roughly 1 percent to 3 percent of their gross domestic product on cash family benefits, equivalent in the United States to about $70 billion to $200 billion. Family allowances in other nations vary widely in benefit patterns, adequacy, and financing. In some countries eligibility is universal; in others no benefits are paid for the first or second child. Benefits are usually paid up to the age at which children normally leave school, but they may be extended to cover further full-time schooling, training, or apprenticeship. The allowance per child also varies widely.

Family allowance programs are not in Europe, and could not be in the United States, a complete alternative to other forms of public assistance and would be no substitute for existing welfare assistance to the aged or to others without dependent children. One-fifth of the poor live outside families, and one-fifth of poor families have no minor children. An alternative way to meet this need would involve a "demogrant," or payment to each person regardless of family status. Instead of the fragmented AFDC program, operated by each state independently with federal contributions, the federal government would establish a uniform minimum benefit schedule. Proposed benefit levels have ranged from half of the poverty threshold to 50 percent above it. Even the lower level of support would increase AFDC payments in more than half the states. The states, however, would not be prevented from supplementing the federal payments. In some versions the payment is solely a transfer, but in other versions public service jobs would be available at low rates of pay to supplement low base payments. Determining who is employable and which measures to take in order to induce the employable to work are other stumbling blocks. The most lenient proposals have rejected coercion and relied upon attractive incentives to work, permitting recipients to keep up to two-thirds of their earnings. Others have urged that recipients be required to find employment, take make-work jobs, or undergo training and have included modest work incentives such as keeping as little as one-third of earnings—the negative income tax again.

But because family size is so closely correlated with poverty, significant family allowances would lift many adults out of poverty along with their children. Universal family allowances have several advantages over other forms of income maintenance. There is no need for an income test; thus administrative costs would be reduced. Because the program distributes benefits to all children, politically it might become more acceptable than other alternatives, but nothing like that is on the horizon at present.

Meshing cash assistance with existing in-kind programs such as food stamps, Medicaid, and housing subsidies adds other thorny problems. Each program reduces benefits as earnings increase. These reductions are not coordinated, however, so that cumulative "marginal tax rates" for several programs sometimes approach or even exceed 100 percent. In such cases recipients lose economic benefits by working more. This phenomenon is known as the "notch" effect. For example, a minor increase in income may disqualify recipients from obtaining certain in-kind benefits that exceed the value of the increased cash income.

But all of this is idle speculation. Much more thought has recently been given to ending welfare as we know it than to devising an acceptable alternative to protect the poor while maximizing their self-reliance.

Notes

1. Olivia Mitchell and Joseph Quinn, "The Hard Facts about Social Security," *Challenge: The Magazine of Economic Affairs,* November–December 1996, 16–17.

2. Peter A. Diamond, "Proposals to Restructure Social Security," *Journal of Economic Perspectives* 10 (summer 1996): 67–88.

3. House Committee on Ways and Means, *Overview of Entitlement Programs: 1994 Green Book, Background Material and Data on Programs within the Jurisdiction of the Committee on Ways and Means* (Washington, D.C.: U.S. Government Printing Office, 15 July 1994), 59–61.

4. Quoted in David A. Super et al., *The New Welfare Law* (Washington, D.C.: Center on Budget and Policy Priorities, August 1996), 3.

5. Ibid., 2, 13–14.

6. Cori E. Ucello and L. Jerome Gallagher, "General Assistance Programs: The State-Based Part of the Safety Net," in *New Federalism: Issues and Options for the States* (Washington, D.C.: Urban Institute, January 1997), 1–5.

7. Advisory Council on Unemployment Compensation, *Unemployment Insurance in the United States: Benefits, Financing, and Coverage,* A Report to the President and Congress (Washington, D.C., February 1995), 95.

8. Advisory Council on Unemployment Compensation, *Defining Federal and State Roles in Unemployment Insurance,* A Report to the President and Congress (Washington, D.C., January 1996), 46.

3. Provision of Services and Goods

For I was hungry and you gave me food, I was thirsty and you gave me
drink, I was a stranger and you welcomed me, I was naked and you
clothed me, I was sick and you visited me, I was in prison and you came
to me.

Matthew 25:35–36

The provision of goods and services complements cash assistance
to the poor. Although income support programs grew rapidly in the
late 1960s and early 1970s, subsequent efforts on behalf of the poor
have been dominated by in-kind assistance. Goods and services
now account for more than 80 percent of total government outlays
in aid of the poor, compared with half in 1968 after rising from 15
percent in 1960 (figure 3.1). As a result, the welfare system has assumed unprecedented scope and diversity, providing both necessities—such as medical care, food, and shelter—and supportive services designed to improve the quality of life of poor people.

The heavy reliance on goods and services in antipoverty programs can be traced to a deep and longstanding public skepticism
concerning the moral character and reliability of poor people. In its
most cynical form this skepticism is expressed in a view of the poor
as indolent, beating the system and thriving on government handouts. Those less suspicious often question the ability of the poor to
manage their own resources responsibly and prefer providing
goods and services that meet needs directly over giving cash, which
might be squandered. Such perceptions of the poor enhance the political acceptability of in-kind assistance minimizing the risk of
fraud or waste. But even those who favor maximum flexibility of aid
through direct income support find that in the absence of government intervention needed services and facilities often are not available to the poor either because of their isolation or because of shortcomings in market mechanisms.

The relative merits of cash and in-kind assistance can be debat-
ed at length, but it is important to note that the federal provision of
goods and services does offer a measure of flexibility for the poor.
While some services (e.g., compensatory education) are provided
directly by the government, many others are offered through a system of payments and reimbursements that utilizes a broad range of

Figure 3.1. Federal per capita cash and in-kind assistance for the poor (1992 dollars)

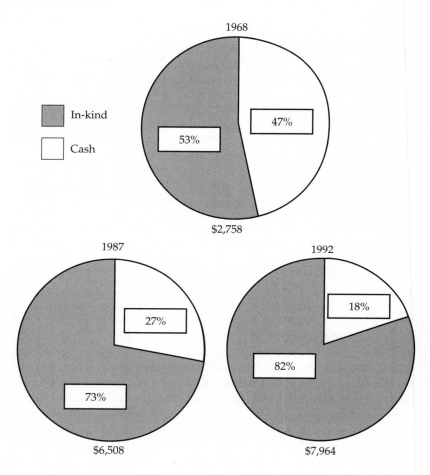

Source: U.S. Congressional Research Service.

service providers. Most health care for the poor is provided through the private sector, with all three levels of government sharing the cost and with some opportunity for the poor to choose their own physicians. These payments differ significantly from general income supplements in that they cover the cost of specific needs and services yet allow more freedom of choice than does direct government provision of basic necessities.

This chapter focuses primarily on goods and services funded by the federal government on the basis of need. A broader study would show that the federal role in the provision of goods and services extends far beyond these antipoverty efforts. The bulk of federal in-kind assistance is dispensed without regard to the recipients' level of income, at a cost far higher than federal expenditures expressly designed for the poor. For example, federal contributions to educating the nation's children and young adults alone cost twice as much as all federal programs targeted directly at the poor. The magnitude of aid to the nonpoor is illustrated even more clearly by the revenue system, which, for example, allows homeowners to deduct interest on home mortgages or the value of health insurance from taxable income. Therefore, even in the context of a discussion of goods and services directed to the poor it should be recognized that many direct public services—as well as "fiscal welfare" provisions—tend to favor the affluent members of society over the poor. One analyst referred to these tax provisions as the "iceberg phenomenon of social welfare."

Health Services

The linkage between poverty and poor health has long been recognized, and health services are now considered to be an essential ingredient of even a minimum standard of living. Health insurance enables most Americans—rich and poor—to obtain and afford medical care. Private insurance, usually obtained through employment, covers about three-quarters of the nonelderly population but a much smaller proportion of the poor. Only one in five poor, nonelderly Americans and one in two of the near poor are covered by private insurance.

Since the passage of Medicare and Medicaid in 1965 the federal government has assumed the major responsibility for providing health care for the aged and the poor. In 1996 the federal government spent over $290 billion on health care for the poor and nonpoor.

	Billions
Total	$292.0[*]
Medicare	186.0
Medicaid	86.3
Community health centers	.7
Veterans	16.1
Maternal and child health	.7
Native Americans	2.2

[*]The total figure differs from others cited in the text because of different sources and methods of estimating the data. No exact figures are available.

Despite massive and increasing public expenditures, the deficit in health care for the needy remains startling whether it is measured in life expectancy, infant mortality rates, or numbers of visits to physicians and dentists. What accounts for this paradox of poor outcomes in the face of rising expenditures? Several factors figure prominently:

1. The value of the health care dollar is shrinking. Medical inflation has outpaced general inflation for decades, and the gap widened significantly during the 1980s and 1990s.

2. The poor, on average, experience more health problems than the general population. The very infirmities that keep people out of the work force reduce them to poverty. This may reflect the inadequacy of preventive health services available to the impoverished; the cumulative effect of deprivation; or behavior deleterious to health (smoking, alcohol or drug abuse), which disproportionately afflicts the poor.

3. The delivery system for health services, generally inefficient in the United States, is particularly disorganized and inadequate in serving the poor. Hospital closings, shortages of medical and allied health personnel, and AIDS and violent crime disproportionately affect communities subject to the most severe economic distress.

Medicare and Medicaid

The federal government's most important health care programs are Medicare and Medicaid, both added to the Social Security Act in 1965. More than 62 million people, or 13.5 percent of the total U.S. civilian population, received services paid for by either Medicare or Medicaid in 1996, compared with 10.2 percent in 1990. In 1996 Medicare and Medicaid expenditures by the Health Care Financing Administration were $272.5 billion, 15.5 percent of the federal budget, compared with 9.8 percent in 1980.

Medicare, a universal program covering all elderly regardless of income, covers most hospital and medical costs for persons 65 years of age and older as well as for disabled social security beneficiaries. Medicare coverage increased from 19.6 million people in 1967 to 38.1 million in 1996, a 95 percent increase. Eleven percent of Medicare enrollees are poor, and another 25 percent have incomes less than double the poverty threshold. No doubt Medicare has kept many near-poor elderly out of poverty and has eased the anxieties of elderly persons whose life savings would have been wiped out by a major illness. In 1994 an average 65-year-old enrollee could have expected an annual lifetime Medicare subsidy of $3,993.

Of more direct benefit to the poor is Medicaid, which provides health care coverage to persons receiving federally supported public assistance. Thirty-five states, three territories, and the District of Columbia also extend Medicaid eligibility to persons who do not qualify for public assistance but whose incomes are sufficiently low to qualify them as "medically needy."

Medicare offers elderly and disabled Americans both basic hospital insurance (Part A) and optional supplementary medical insurance (Part B). In FY 1996 Medicare benefit payments totaled $121 billion under Part A and $65 billion under Part B. Hospital insurance pays a major part of costs and also pays for posthospital extended care and home health services for all social security and railroad retirement recipients, employees of federal and state governments, and some people who are permanently disabled or in need of kidney transplantation or dialysis. All individuals eligible for Part A are assessed an annual, income-related supplemental premium to offset the cost of a new acute-care catastrophic benefit. Men and women eligible for Part A can also choose to participate in the Part B program, which helps pay the cost of physicians' fees, diagnostic tests, medical supplies, and prescription drugs. Those enrolled in the supplementary program pay an annually adjusted monthly premium ($42.50 in 1996) that is matched by the federal government. In 1996, 32.8 million aged and 4.7 million disabled persons were covered by hospital insurance, and about 8.3 million received reimbursed services under Part A, while 32.8 million elderly and 4.7 million disabled persons, 85 percent of whom used reimbursed services, were enrolled in the supplementary program.

Medicaid, also launched in 1965, replaced a fragmented and grossly inadequate system of medical assistance to recipients of public assistance programs. In contrast to Medicare, which offers the elderly subsidized health insurance similar to that found in the private market, Medicaid provides federal grants to states. The grants help finance health care for low-income persons, 74 percent of whom are recipients of either public assistance or Supplemental Security Income. The federal share of expenses ranges from 50 percent to 83 percent, depending upon the state's per capita income. Each state operates its own program and establishes its own rules within the confines of federal guidelines and regulations. Federal regulations specify the basic health services that must be offered to the categorically eligible in any state program. Other services are optional; the state may or may not elect to include these in its program. States also exercise wide discretion over the duration of services. In 1996 the federal government spent an estimated $86 billion (57% of total Medicaid expenditures) on grants to the states. States spent another $66 billion (43% of total Medicaid expenditures on health care). While precise data are not available, about nine of every ten Medicaid dollars are spent in aid to the poor. Nevertheless, only 43 percent of the poor are covered by Medicaid. Approximately 16 percent have private coverage or are insured by the military's program, and 12.5 percent are covered by Medicare. However, nearly 29 percent of the poor and 28 percent of the near poor have no health care insurance of any kind.[1]

Single mothers and their children receiving AFDC are automatically eligible for Medicaid and make up the bulk of beneficiaries, but blind and disabled persons receive a larger portion of Medicaid funds than any other recipient group (figures 3.2 and 3.3). Medicaid operates as a vendor payment system, with payments made directly to the service provider. Medicaid also pays for custodial nursing home care of the impoverished. Elderly individuals receiving Supplemental Security Income are also automatically eligible for Medicaid assistance, and others may qualify by depleting their assets—often called "spending down"—to the income eligibility level. With annual nursing home costs increasing dramatically, Medicaid payments for nursing home care account for most of the program's spending on the elderly. In fact, Medicaid is the largest insurer of long-term care in the United States, covering 68 percent of nursing home residents and over 50 percent of nursing home costs—an example of the extent to which Medicaid's tie to federally funded income maintenance program eligibility has weakened over time. Legislative change has increased Medicaid access for low-income individuals not qualified for any other specific program.

The dominant theme in the development of both Medicare and Medicaid as well as other in-kind assistance programs—shelter, food, and social services—has been the attempt to contain program costs. In the early stages of these programs, efforts to improve the quality of medical services for the elderly and poor led to federal requirements that states set standards for the reimbursement of hospitals and physicians at prevailing local rates. In order to allay fears of "socialized medicine," however, no provision was made for federal regulation of reimbursements, and charges of program fraud haunted both Medicare and Medicaid. In the early 1970s, Congress responded by directing federal program administrators to spell out standards controlling the reimbursement of hospitals and physicians under Medicare, Medicaid, and maternal and child health

Figure 3.2. Medicaid users and Medicaid payments, by eligibility group, 1984–1993

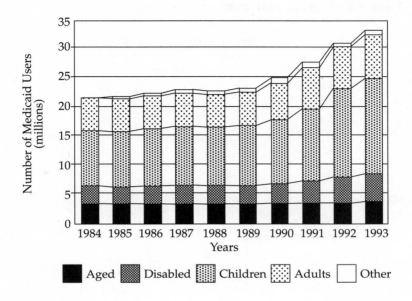

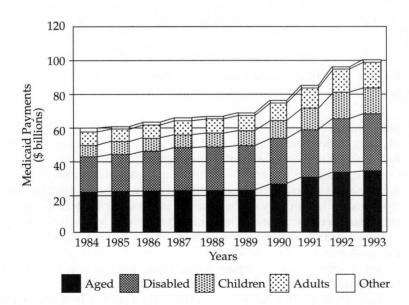

Source: U.S. Health Care Financing Administration, *Health Care Financing Review: Medicare and Medicaid Statistical Supplement, 1995* (Baltimore: HCFA Office of Research and Demonstrations, 1995), 359, 387.

Note: Dollar amounts are in 1993 dollars, adjusted using a personal-consumption expenditure index for medical services provided by the U.S. Department of Commerce, Bureau of Economic Analysis.

Figure 3.3. Medicaid, 1994–1995

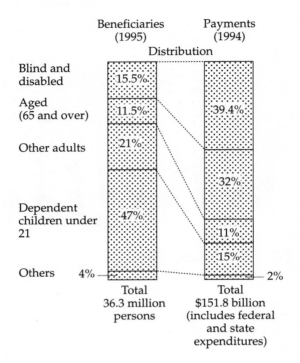

Source: U.S. Health Care Financing Administration.

Note: Payments include federal and state expenditures.

programs. The late 1970s and early 1980s brought the introduction of peer review boards, made up of local medical personnel, in an effort to weed out unnecessary or inept care.

Rising medical expenditures and a growing elderly population have made Medicare the second most costly federal domestic program, exceeded only by social security income support. At the same time, earlier retirement and lower birth rates will leave fewer workers to support the program through income and payroll taxes in the future. Analysts now predict that barring significant changes in revenues or expenditures, the hospital insurance (Part A) trust fund will become insolvent about 2002.

This situation is reminiscent of the early 1980s, when Medicare administrators concluded that the program's trust funds were approaching insolvency. One reaction to this was to introduce the prospective payment system, the most sweeping structural reform to date. Enacted as part of the social security amendments of 1983, the prospective payment system changed the way Medicare reimburses hospitals for services rendered under Part A. An illness or injury is assigned to one of several hundred diagnosis-related groups (DRGs). Medicare pays a fee based on the diagnosis rather than on the services provided to treat it, with one national payment standard for each DRG. While DRGs have helped stabilize inpatient hospital costs, outlays for outpatient services under Medicare (Part B) have not stabilized. In 1989 the Physician Payment Review Commission (PPRC), established by Congress in 1986 to address this problem, proposed that Medicare adopt a national fee schedule for Part B payments that would specify a predetermined amount for a specific service. In addition, because overall health care expenses are dependent upon the volume of health services rendered as well as their price, the PPRC also proposed setting a ceiling on overall expenses to control volume.

The Medicare Catastrophic Coverage Act of 1988 would have expanded the program to include insurance against major bills for acute care. The act removed the limit on the number of hospital or hospice days covered under Medicare and expanded skilled nursing facility coverage; limited liability of beneficiaries to one hospital deductible payment per year and eliminated hospital coinsurance; extended Part B coverage to include mammography and respite care; and introduced a prescription drug benefit. Two features directly addressed problems of the impoverished elderly. First, after 1992 state Medicaid programs would have been required to pay supplemental medical insurance premiums and copayments of the aged poor. Second, the rules governing the assets of married couples would have changed to prevent the impoverishment of one spouse when the other qualified for Medicaid nursing home assistance.

The Medicare Catastrophic Coverage Act was expected to cost some $31 billion during its first five years. In a new approach to Medicare financing, Congress mandated that the potential beneficiaries pay for these new benefits. Approximately one-third of the funding would have come from a fixed monthly supplement ($4 in 1989) to the Part B premium; the remaining two-thirds was to be collected through an income-related surcharge on all those eligible for Part A. Enrollees with less than $150 in annual tax liability—an estimated 64 percent of the elderly—would have paid nothing, while others would have been taxed up to $800 ($1,600 for a couple). However, strong opposition by elderly groups moved Congress to repeal the act.

In contrast to Medicare, Medicaid never has been a universal program for the poor. The number of Medicaid beneficiaries reached 22.8 million in 1977. Both federal and state governments reduced eligibility during the Carter administration and the early years of the Reagan administration. Recent concern about health care for the poor has reversed the retrenchments. In 1995 Medicaid served 36.6 million beneficiaries (13.8% of the U.S. population), including 18.7 million children (1 out of every 5 children in the United States and 1 out of every 3 babies born in the United States), 7.6 million adults caring for these children, 4.4 million elderly Americans, and 5.9 million blind and disabled individuals. While the number of elderly beneficiaries increased from 3.1 million in 1985 to 4.4 million in 1995, payments more than doubled. For the blind and disabled, while the number of beneficiaries grew from 3 million to 6 million over the decade, payments to beneficiaries increased from $13 billion in 1985 to $49 billion in 1995. States and the federal government combined spent an average of $3,700 per Medicaid-eligible individual in 1995. Medicaid accounts for 86 percent of the total federal spending on means-tested medical care, veteran care for 10 percent, and six other programs for the remaining 4 percent.

Three factors account for the limited Medicaid coverage of the poor. First, loose federal guidelines result in wide disparity among state programs. In 1994 income eligibility levels for AFDC—which also determine eligibility for Medicaid—ranged from 13 percent of the poverty threshold in Mississippi to over 75 percent in Alaska. Second, no matter how low their income, some are excluded from Medicaid eligibility: originally single adults who are not elderly, disabled, or pregnant; married couples who do not have dependent children; and older children living in impoverished families. Third, roughly one-quarter of poor individuals have private insurance, Medicare, or some other form of insurance.

In 1984 federal legislation expanded access to Medicaid, requiring states to cover all pregnant women and, on a phased-in basis, children under age 7 who meet state income assistance guidelines, whether or not they actually receive financial aid. If the 1988 Medicare Catastrophic Coverage Act had not been repealed, it would have expanded family coverage further, requiring Medicaid eligibility for all impoverished women and young children, allowing states to cover those with incomes up to 185 percent of the poverty line. Provisions of the 1988 Family Support Act required states to operate AFDC programs for two-parent poor families and to extend Medicaid eligibility for a twelve-month transition period to families earning their way off welfare. The 1996 welfare reform legislation that eliminated AFDC as an entitlement continued access to Medicaid for those who would have been eligible under AFDC, with one exception: most new legal immigrants are denied all but emergency services for their first five years in the country, and the states have the option to continue denying them thereafter.

The architects of Medicare and Medicaid did not foresee rampant inflation of health care costs. In the rush to pass the original legislation "while the iron was hot" and to neutralize opposition by organized physicians and their allies, the drafters did not include measures to restrain costs. The introduction of the prospective payment system, greater cost sharing, and other measures has slowed but not arrested the upward spiral of expenditures for federal health care programs. Some policymakers and advocacy groups favor expanding Medicare to include long-term care and expanding Medicaid to cover uninsured workers. Outside the confines of political campaigns the need to limit Medicare and Medicaid costs is generally recognized, but the known options are unattractive. Managed care appears to be generating less savings than anticipated. How to retain both availability and quality of care while lowering costs is a mystery. The search for an appropriate balance between access to Medicare and Medicaid and cost undoubtedly will continue into the next century.

Community, Maternal, and Child Health

In addition to health insurance for the poor, federal programs have sought to improve the quality and efficiency of health care services provided directly to the poor. The creation of community health centers in low-income areas reflected the Great Society belief that improving the health of the poor required a major restructuring of the health care delivery system. These federally funded neighborhood health centers were established to fulfill four objectives: (1) to provide a full range of ambulatory health services; (2) to maintain a liaison with other community services; (3) to develop a close working relationship with a hospital (preferably one with a medical school affiliation); and (4) to foster the participation of the indigenous population in decision making and to provide them employment in the centers. By restructuring the health care system in poor neighborhoods and supplementing the services of private physicians, the neighborhood health care centers have provided an essential complement to federal health care coverage. Federal support for community health has continued long after the dismantling of the Office of Economic Opportunity, the antipoverty agency that initially funded the centers. Despite the Reagan administration's efforts to consolidate federal health care programs in 1981, Congress ensured that funding for the health centers would be preserved by creating a separate block grant to states for primary health care provided through community health centers. However, outlays for health centers have not kept pace with other government contributions to medical services for the poor. In 1996 the federal government spent approximately $700 million to support 550 primary care facilities. Each year the centers serve more than 5 million patients, 60 percent of whom claim to be poor.

During the 1970s Congress launched additional categorical programs to bolster maternal and child health in low-income families. These diverse initiatives were also consolidated into a single block grant to states in 1981 at reduced funding levels. As a result, most states curtailed prenatal and delivery services to low-income women in the early 1980s. In 1996 an estimated $674 million in federal maternal and child health block grant funds reached the states. Extension of Medicaid coverage to larger numbers of impoverished women and children has enabled more to obtain free or low-cost medical care, but many uninsured near-poor women and children still have nowhere to turn for primary health care.

Veterans

A variety of other federal programs support health care for the poor, most of them concentrating on veterans, Native Americans, migrants, or handicapped children. The most extensive of these are the medical programs for veterans.

The Department of Veterans Affairs (DVA) health care system, originally designed to care for the war-wounded, currently provides care on a broad scale to aged and indigent veterans whether or not their health care needs are related to military service. The department spent $16.7 billion on medical care for approximately 2.8 million qualified patients in 1996. The system operates 173 hospitals, 131 nursing homes, 39 domiciliaries, and 391 outpatient clinics. The DVA also contributes to the cost of care received by veterans in state-run domiciliaries and nursing homes.

America's veteran population is shrinking; it was estimated at 26.2 million in 1995. With the World War II and Korean War cohorts being much larger than the Vietnam War and Persian Gulf cohorts, the veteran population is also aging. In 1990 more than 7 million veterans were 65 years of age or older. This demographic reality, combined with the strictures of the federal budget deficit, led Congress in 1986 to establish a means test, albeit a liberal one, for veterans' health services. All who have served in the armed forces remain eligible for VA care, but the law distinguishes between mandatory and discretionary patients for purposes of access and payment. Mandatory veteran patients have the highest priority, and the DVA must provide them with free medical care. Mandatory patients include veterans with service-connected injuries or income below a specified level ($21,001 for a single veteran and $25,204 for a married veteran or a veteran with one dependent in 1996, the maximum figure increasing by $1,404 for each additional dependent), former prisoners of war, pre–World War II veterans, and those exposed to radiation or toxics during service. Discretionary patients are veterans with non-service-connected ailments but with higher incomes. Care is provided to discretionary patients when space and resources permit. Discretionary patients must agree to pay an amount equal to what would be paid under Medicare and a copayment. The DVA bills any insurance company with which the discretionary veteran patient may have coverage.

The relatively liberal income guidelines, adjusted annually for inflation, place the DVA medical system outside the traditional confines of poverty programs. In practice, however, the DVA serves a disproportionate number of poor and near-poor veterans, as well as those with no other source of medical coverage. In a typical year mandatory veteran patients account for 90–95 percent of the some 28 million DVA outpatient visits and over 1 million individuals cared for in DVA-supported hospitals and nursing homes.

The acute and chronic care needs of elderly veterans will place growing demands on the DVA medical system in years to come. Unless national priorities shift in favor of vastly increased funding, the system will have to continue limiting access and/or charge a larger share of costs to veterans treated for non-service-connected ailments, though the 1986 guidelines shield impoverished and service-disabled veterans from the harshest of budget cuts.

Native Americans

American Indians living on reservations and Alaskan natives are perhaps the most poverty-stricken minorities in the country. Yet because of their geographic isolation and widespread poverty, Native Americans receive only limited health care. About one-third of all Native Americans live on isolated reservations, tribal lands, or other established Indian areas, and most native Alaskans reside in inland villages. Such geographic and economic settings rarely attract private health facilities. Poor roads and inadequate transportation and communication heighten barriers to health care, creating serious problems for individuals hampered by illness.

In this context, it is clear that both isolation and poverty take their toll. The incidence of tuberculosis is more than four times as great among Native Americans as among the white population, and Native Americans also suffer disproportionately from streptococcal infections, nutritional and dental deficiencies, and poor mental health and attendant disorders. Alaskan natives fare only slightly better in major health indices. To alleviate the debilitating health consequences of isolation and dire poverty among Native Americans and Alaskan natives, in 1955 the federal government mandated special health services, currently operated under the auspices of the U.S. Department of Health and Human Services.

The Indian Health Service (IHS) employs 15,800 health service personnel in its 37 hospitals, 64 health centers, and 89 smaller health stations and satellite clinics. In addition, tribes operate 12 hospitals and more than 300 outpatient facilities under contract with the IHS, and IHS also maintains contracts with nonfederal facilities that provide health services to the agency's clientele. In 1996 IHS annual appropriations stood at $2.2 billion, with expenditures for maintaining facilities and providing services amounting to well over $1 billion. In addition to health services provided on or near reservations, $369 million in medical care was purchased from local providers in 1996 in areas not serviced by IHS facilities.

Measured in terms of progress in lessening the tremendous health deficit of Native Americans, IHS efforts have attained significant results. According to the IHS, since 1955 the average life expectancy of American Indians and Alaskan natives has increased by approximately ten years. Moreover, their death rate from influenza and pneumonia has decreased 76 percent, the maternal death rate has declined 90 percent, and death from tuberculosis has dropped 96 percent. The infant mortality rate also has declined, from 63 to 10 deaths per 1,000 live births. Family planning services are supplied to a growing portion of the population, contributing to a drop in fertility. Although greatly reduced, the annual birth rate of 28 per 1,000 women aged 15 to 44 is still nearly double the rate among the population that arrived after Columbus. Despite these improvements, Native American access to medical care has worsened in recent years. For example, Native American access to physicians was 89.8 physicians per 100,000 population in 1994, compared with 99.7 per 100,000 in 1982. In 1995 Native American per capita expenditure on health care was $1,153, or 40 percent of the $2,912 per capita expenditure for Americans as a whole. Recent developments in government budgeting and welfare reform threaten past progress further. For example, in recent budget reduction discussions the Bureau of Indian Affairs was slated to absorb 45 percent of Department of Interior budget cuts even though it constituted only 26 percent of the department's budget.

Despite the progress achieved by the IHS, facilities remain primitive compared with modern city hospitals, and adequate and experienced personnel are lacking. In order to alleviate shortages of physicians and other health care personnel, as well as to eliminate the cultural gaps between the health workers and the target population, IHS has pushed for more extensive training of its health personnel. The program actively recruits Indians to pursue health careers and offers professional scholarships to those who choose to study in the health field. In order to improve the health of the Native American population, underlying deficiencies in housing, nutrition, and health education also need correction.

Shelter

Given the high and rising cost of shelter, both old and new poor families are faced with grim choices: they can live in substandard units, they can crowd into better dwellings, or they can use a disproportionate share of their meager incomes for housing. Two out of three poor and near-poor households experience at least one of these bleak alternatives, and many must cope with all three conditions. Median shelter costs—including mortgage payments, real estate taxes, property insurance, rent, and utilities—account for nearly 20 percent of the average nonpoor household's income. For poor households the median expenditure is 60 percent of household income.

Since the 1930s various federal programs have mitigated the housing problems of low-income households by providing subsidies for construction, rental, leasing, purchase, and operation of apartments and houses. Some sixteen different federal programs provide housing assistance to low-income individuals, with expenditures of over $22 billion in 1992. In 1994 the Department of Housing and Urban Development (HUD) and the Farmers Home Administration, the two primary federal agencies handling housing programs, assisted 5.0 million low-income renters and 750,000 low-income homeowners. The bulk of this assistance is provided by HUD through its low-rent public housing (23% of total means-tested housing assistance funds) and Section 8 low-income housing assistance programs (55%). In addition to housing programs for the poor, federal loan programs and tax expenditures also provide broader assistance to middle- and upper-income Americans for housing construction and purchases, thereby enhancing the nation's overall housing stock.

Since the late 1970s newly subsidized low-income housing units have become increasingly scarce. This shortage is a result of increased demand for low-income housing brought about by increasing numbers of poor families with declining incomes and cutbacks in government housing assistance for the poor. Overall, assistance provided by HUD to add new units to the stock of low-income housing declined from about $71.5 billion in 1978 (in 1994 dollars) to $19.4 billion in 1994. In addition to a decline in the number of newly assisted households, the decline reflects a shift to less expensive assistance through existing housing and a reduction in the average length of commitments undertaken. From 1977 to 1982 commitments for new construction constituted 53 percent and substantial rehabilitation constituted 73 percent of total commitments. Since 1982 these percentages have fallen to 28 percent and 40 percent, respectively, due to movement to lower-cost existing housing and housing vouchers. The proportion of assisted households receiving homeownership declined from 34 percent in 1977 to 13 percent in 1994.

At the same time that spending for low-income housing decreased during the 1980s and early 1990s, the federal government provided generous subsidies to nonpoor homeowners in general by allowing them to deduct mortgage interest and property taxes from their taxable income. In 1995, for example, the federal government provided $52 million in indirect tax subsidies to homeowners by exempting mortgage interest from income taxes. Two-thirds of this tax expenditure benefited homeowners earning more than $75,000 per year, and 16.5 percent went to those earning more than $200,000 per year.

Public Housing

Initiated in 1937 and currently serving approximately 1.3 million households through some 3,300 local housing authorities, public housing is the oldest housing assistance program for the poor. It is estimated that the federal government has invested more than $90 billion in the federal housing inventory. The public housing program provides federal subsidies for the amortization of construction costs on units built, owned, and operated by local public housing authorities (PHAs). The units are reserved for families with incomes not exceeding 80 percent of the median income level in the locality. For the most part, however, locally established criteria limit eligibility to households with annual incomes below 50 percent

Table 3.1. New Federal Housing Commitments, 1978–1994

Fiscal Year	New Commitments for Renters		New Commitments for Homebuyers	Total New Commitments
	Existing Housing	New Constructions		
1978	126,472	214,503	112,214	453,189
1980	58,402	155,001	140,564	353,967
1982	38,372	47,618	66,711	152,701
1984	78,726	36,719	44,409	159,854
1986	85,476	34,375	25,479	145,330
1988	65,295	36,456	26,200	127,951
1990	61,309	23,491	24,968	109,768
1994	64,791	35,861	42,430	142,882

Sources: U.S. Congressional Budget Office; U.S. Department of Housing and Urban Development.

Note: Figures for 1994 are estimates.

of the median income; fewer than 25 percent of the units are available to households with incomes between 50 percent and 80 percent of the area median. The average income of families in public housing units is approximately 17 percent of the average area median income, or roughly $6,100.

Originally the federal public housing subsidy covered only capital costs; rents were expected to pay for operating expenses. As operating costs continued to rise, however, poor households could not afford to cover operating costs fully. Consequently, in 1969 federal law authorized subsidies to make up the difference between operating costs and 25 percent of an adjusted household income (it was later raised to 30 percent).

For three decades after the inception of direct federal housing aid during the 1930s public housing was the mainstay shelter program for the poor. Often working in tandem with other public assistance programs, public housing brought highly targeted assistance to the poor. About two households in five occupying publicly subsidized housing receive some form of welfare income. About 40 percent of households are minority households—30 percent black and 10 percent Hispanic. Some 45 percent of these households are families with children, 35 percent are elderly, and 10 percent are people with disabilities.

The greatest strength of public housing—its highly targeted aid to the poor—has also generated the program's greatest political liability. Public housing has been plagued by increasing difficulties that were exacerbated during the half-century after the program was first enacted. To save costs and to avoid political opposition, many public housing units were located in high-rise, inner-city projects. For example, the General Accounting Office has estimated that 23 percent of public housing residents live in high-poverty neighborhoods, compared with fewer than 10 percent of Section 8 recipients. The concentration of poor families in deteriorating neighborhoods often led to problems of vandalism, crime, drug abuse, and general malaise among tenants. Many inner-city housing authorities proved unable to maintain their units in the face of such widespread problems, and public opposition frequently forestalled the initiation of new projects. Finally, rising construction and operating costs undermined political support for public housing, causing federal investment to decline. During the 1980s federal priorities shifted toward greater reliance on the stock of existing housing to meet public housing needs and away from investment in more costly new construction projects. Long waiting lists for public housing projects reflect declining federal funding and attest that the poor often have few alternatives.

Additions to the pool of public housing declined substantially during the 1980s. In 1989, 6,947 units of public housing were added, compared with 36,727 newly added units in 1980. Budget authority for public housing, which reflects funding for additional commitments to the pool of existing housing plus funds carried over from previous years, declined from $6.5 billion in 1980 to an estimated $2.2 billion in 1989. Adjusted for inflation, the decline exceeded 75 percent. Public housing's 1996 appropriation remained at approximately its 1989 level, $2.3 billion. Increased rents require larger federal subsidies per household, with the result that fewer tenants qualify for assistance over time. Because assistance has been aimed at the poorest households, public housing has become less accessible to the working poor.

Subsidized Housing

In the 1960s the Great Society championed new approaches for expanding housing options for the poor. The new strategies involved leasing of private units by local housing authorities or direct payments of rent supplements to low-income families. In experimenting with these subsidy and incentive programs, critics of public housing hoped to disperse low-income families beyond the confines of neighborhoods with a high concentration of poverty and to contain federal housing costs by relying on existing housing stock.

Neither approach yielded much success in dispersing low-income families. Because of widespread opposition by residents in affluent neighborhoods, the overwhelming majority of leased units remain in low-income neighborhoods. Rent supplements may have had more potential for promoting dispersal, but the rising operating costs of other federally assisted housing have forced piggybacking of rent supplements with other housing subsidies to keep rent levels within the reach of low-income households. Most rent supplements covered units in completely rent-supplemented projects or were used along with other subsidy programs to reach an even lower-income clientele. Thus, rent supplements received only $57 million in 1996, while Section 236 rental housing assistance received $66.3 million out of total subsidized housing outlays of $21 billion.

Section 8 of the Housing and Community Development Act established the most significant rent supplement program. The law has offered communities flexibility in adapting federal block grants to local conditions and needs, and it has provided recipients of rent subsidies a choice of location and housing type in publicly or privately owned units. Section 8 provides no direct assistance for either construction or permanent financing, but state housing finance agencies or local public housing authorities may obtain indirect aid. Net new commitments for Section 8 housing declined from 169,000 units in 1980 to an estimated 78,000 units in 1993. Although net new commitments declined during the 1980s, Section 8 still required larger federal subsidies because of rising rents, the targeting of assistance to very low-income households, and the growth in the number of households in newly constructed Section 8 units, which cost more to build than similar units built in the 1970s. Consequently, Section 8 outlays increased twofold between 1977 and 1994, and were $15.8 billion in 1996.

Households with incomes below 80 percent of the area median are eligible for Section 8 assistance, but local administrators are required to allocate 95 percent of all new Section 8 assistance to households with incomes below 50 percent of the area median. Rent for most tenants in Section 8 housing is equal to 30 percent of adjusted income; the federal government pays the difference between the tenant's payment and the actual rent.

Subsidized housing grew rapidly under Section 8 during the late 1970s, reaching a peak when one-fourth of all renters below the poverty line lived in subsidized housing. In the 1980s the Section 8 program overtook public housing as the major federal program offering housing assistance to the poor. In 1996 public housing received only $4.5 billion, compared to Section 8's $15.8 billion. In

1992 Section 8 assisted some 2.8 million families on expenditures of $12.3 billion. At the same time, however, the federal government has substantially reduced its commitment to supporting construction of lower-income housing. As a consequence, in many communities low-income families, though eligible, may remain on the waiting list for subsidized housing for as long as five years.

Low-Income Rental Housing Tax Credit

Assistance to low-income renters is also provided indirectly through the low-income rental housing (LIRH) tax credit. As part of the Tax Reform Act of 1986, Congress created the credit to encourage developers and corporations to invest in low-income rental housing. Rental projects are eligible for the credit if either 20 percent of the units in a project are set aside for persons with incomes below half of the area's median income or 40 percent of the units are set aside for persons with below 60 percent of the area's median income. Between 1990 and 1994 the program added approximately 247,000 rental units to the U.S. housing stock, 224,500 of them low-income units. The LIRH tax credit dispenses more than $3 billion in annual budget authority.

Varying Levels of Federal Support

The 1974 Housing and Community Development Act signaled a departure from the goal of establishing a national housing policy. By stressing community block grants that could be spent by local officials according to broad guidelines, Congress substituted local discretion for a strong federal role in providing housing for the poor. Although the 1949 pledge of "a decent home and suitable living environment for every American family" has not been formally abandoned, inflationary trends, a weakened commitment, and rising housing costs have reversed earlier gains of federal housing policy. The emphasis in housing—as in other social action areas—is on returning the strategy initiative to the local level. Some states and localities have integrated other social services with housing programs, promoted tenant management of public housing projects, and introduced other innovative programs. However, federal retrenchment has left the poor with diminished housing assistance in recent years.

The sharp decline in federal support of housing programs for low-income households set the stage for a housing crunch. Beginning at the end of the 1970s and continuing through the 1980s, HUD reduced drastically the supply of new housing units for the poor. Awards for new construction and rehabilitation as well as total Section 8 subsidized units declined from 453,189 in 1978 to 353,967 in 1980, 152,701 in 1982, and 134,322 in 1988. Meanwhile, existing commitments are nearing their end. HUD's agreements with housing developers obliged the developers to allocate a portion of new units for low-income housing for twenty to forty years; Section 8 certificates and vouchers remain valid for five to fifteen years. Between 1990 and 1994 commitments for 900,000 low-income units expired—far more than can be replaced at current funding levels.

The 1990 Housing Act included two new initiatives. The first, the HOME investment partnership block grant program, seeks to increase the supply of affordable low-income housing through grants to state and local governments for tenant-based rental assistance or rehabilitation of rental housing. The second, HOPE (Home Ownership and Opportunity for People Everywhere), enables low-income individuals to own units in properties owned by or where the mortgages are held by the federal government or the Resolution Trust Corporation. The initiative also includes the Homeownership Trust Demonstration, which lowers home ownership costs for low-income families by using a trust fund to buy first-time mortgages down to a 6 percent rate. Under HOPE grants $1.4 billion has been expended in redesigning eighty-five public housing developments nationwide during the Clinton administration. The trend has been to replace high-rise buildings with townhouse and garden apartment configurations that allow more private responsibility and greater safety. Some 24,000 units of poor public housing were demolished during the first Clinton term.

The federal government continues to provide broad incentives and financial support to promote the construction of new homes for middle-income families, hoping thereby to expand "hand-me-down" vacancies for lower-income renters and homebuyers. One of every four mortgage loans for private homes is guaranteed by the Federal Housing Administration, the Department of Veterans Affairs, and the Farmers Home Administration. In 1995, as noted, federal tax policy subsidized homeowners through mortgage interest deductions of $52 billion. The deductibility of mortgage interest and property taxes on rental property, as well as owner-occupied homes, along with the deferral of capital gains on home sales, the one-time exclusion of capital gains for home sellers aged 55 and over, and accelerated depreciation of rental housing accounted for probable reduced federal tax revenues of that much more. All these forms of assistance stimulate housing construction. The poor receive only a minor proportion of this aid, and the hope that the benefits may "trickle down" to them remains just that.

Aside from assuming a direct financial burden, Congress has taken legislative action beyond the open housing laws in attempting to alter the structural elements of the housing market itself. Although unwilling to outlaw "redlining," the practice of denying loans in certain urban neighborhoods regardless of the applicant's creditworthiness, legislation in 1975 attempted to discourage the practice of requiring lending institutions to disclose the amounts of mortgage money they lend in different neighborhoods of a city. During the Carter administration, HUD also adopted a more aggressive role by challenging in the courts the exclusionary zoning policies of affluent communities, as well as by monitoring local compliance with federal equal opportunity housing statutes as a condition for receipt of federal community development and recreation funds. The Reagan administration reverted to a passive role of processing individual housing discrimination complaints while opposing broader initiatives. However, a 1988 wide-ranging fair housing law prohibits housing discrimination against the disabled and families with children, and it gives HUD authority to penalize violators.

The number of American households has been growing rapidly as a result of delayed marriage, family breakup, and the maturing of the post–World War II baby boom generation. Drastically rising shelter costs have consistently outpaced increases in the overall cost of living. For young families with moderate incomes the high cost of shelter means forgoing home ownership; for the poorest, it may mean homelessness. Making safe, affordable housing available to all citizens will remain a major challenge beyond the 1990s.

Homelessness

Since the early 1980s, homelessness has become a more visible problem, particularly in urban areas. In a study of homelessness based on a sample of twenty cities, the Urban Institute estimated that the total U.S. homeless population doubled to an estimated 500,000 to 600,000 between 1983 and 1987. There is little reason to believe that the trend has slowed since then. A 1995 estimate included a lower-bounds point-in-time estimate of 700,000 homeless, amounting to a total of 2–3 million homeless during the course of a year.[2]

Although the homeless are a heterogeneous population, the vast majority of those using shelters or soup kitchens are single men. Only about 10 percent of the homeless population are families, but this proportion is persistently rising; the majority of homeless families are headed by women. Nearly one-half of homeless adults lack a high school education and have been unemployed for nearly two

years. Many homeless adults have a history of mental hospitaliza-
tion, alcoholism, or drug addiction, and one in four has been in a
state or federal prison. Compared with the homeless population as
a whole, homeless families appear less likely to suffer from personal
instability.

Deinstitutionalization of psychiatric hospitals and a shortage of
low-cost housing, combined with meager financial resources, have
contributed to the rise of homelessness. In response to this problem,
Congress passed the Stewart B. McKinney Homeless Assistance Act
of 1987 to meet the diverse needs of the homeless population. The
program funds a wide variety of services, including emergency food
and shelter, health services, job training, education, and other support services. In fiscal year 1996 Congress appropriated a total of
$785 million, enough to provide for only a small fraction of the
housing and support needs of the homeless population.

Household Energy

Fuel and weatherization assistance for low-income households
represents another extension of the welfare system. Policies designed to help the poor heat their homes were initiated in response
to rising fuel costs and reflect an expanded concept of basic needs.
During the first decade following the initial OPEC cartel boost of oil
prices in 1973 the real cost of fuel nearly quintupled. Prior to the
OPEC oil embargo in 1973, home energy costs accounted for 9 percent of the entire income of low-income households and about 3
percent of the income of the average American household. By the
mid-1980s, home energy costs for low-income households represented about one-quarter of their income—about three times the
share paid by the average American household.

The Low-Income Home Energy Assistance Program (LIHEAP)
was initiated in 1978 as an experimental effort and made permanent
in 1980. Administered by the Department of Health and Human Services, the program allocates block grants to the states based on the
climate and the number of low-income households. Funds are used
to cover the residential heating or cooling costs of the poor and near
poor, to purchase or install low-cost weatherization materials, and
to help households with energy-related emergency situations.
States may unilaterally use a maximum of 15 percent of their funds
for weatherization activities, and up to 25 percent through federal
acceptance of a waiver request. States may grant LIHEAP eligibility to households receiving AFDC, SSI, or certain veterans' assistance or to any household that has an income below either 150 per-

cent of the poverty line or 60 percent of a state's standard of need, whichever is higher. Within these guidelines, states retain wide discretion concerning eligibility and provision of assistance. LIHEAP allotments to states peaked at $2.3 billion in 1990, but funding has fallen since then. The federal government allotted $1.7 billion in LIHEAP grants in 1994 and $1.3 billion in 1996. In 1993 heating assistance benefits of $954 million were given to 5.4 million households, an average benefit of $176.

Since 1975 federal programs have also helped low-income households conserve energy. Families with incomes below 125 percent of the poverty threshold or who received AFDC, SSI, or general assistance within the last twelve months are eligible for assistance. The Department of Energy allocates weatherization funds to the states based on a formula that considers local temperatures and heating requirements along with estimated numbers of low-income households. Weatherization assistance was funded at $174 million in 1992 and served 87,000 household units.

Food

The federal government began providing food to the poor during the Great Depression, when it launched the precursors to the current food stamp and school lunch programs. These programs acted as farm support programs. They relieved farmers of surplus agricultural commodities, which were redistributed to needy persons and schoolchildren. In the 1960s the government revived these programs and established other child nutrition programs. After a slow beginning in the 1960s, federal spending for food assistance to the poor grew rapidly. In 1992 food and nutrition assistance exceeded $34 billion. Eleven different programs provide food assistance to low-income populations with funding provided almost entirely by the federal government. The major components of the program include food stamps, child and elderly nutrition, and distribution of surplus food (figure 3.4).

The dramatic expansion of food programs was the result of a highly diverse political coalition with widely varying interests and concerns. Some saw food programs as a way of getting more for the poor by raising the cry of "hunger in America." Others favored food distribution because they were concerned that the poor would use cash grants unwisely. Still others sought to sustain the demand for certain agricultural products. Whatever the reasons, the results were a strong and sustained public policy preference for providing food directly to the poor instead of allocating a portion of cash as-

Figure 3.4. Food assistance, 1980, 1989, and 1996 (1996 $ billions)

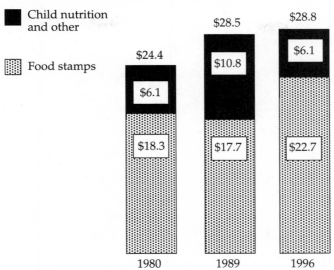

Source: U.S. Office of Management and Budget, *Budget of the United States Government* (Washington, D.C.: U.S. Government Printing Office, 1979, 1988, 1995).

sistance to food and a corresponding growth in the federal network of in-kind assistance programs. More than 90 percent of all benefits under these food programs are distributed on the basis of need, and perhaps more than in any other in-kind program, the poor—including the working poor—receive an overwhelming share of this federal assistance.

Food Stamps

By far the largest of federal food subsidies (constituting 72% of all federal food and nutrition assistance), the food stamp program is designed to ensure that the poor can obtain basic food needs. In 1996, 25.8 million people in 10.7 million households received food stamps during an average month, down from a high of 27.5 million in 1994. Food stamp benefits in 1996 were $22.7 billion (figure 3.5), with more than 50 percent of food stamp recipients children, approximately 40 percent nonelderly adults (two-thirds of them women), and 7 percent elderly adults. Approximately 25 percent of the households receiving food stamps had some earned income.

Figure 3.5. Food stamp benefit costs and participants, 1969–1996

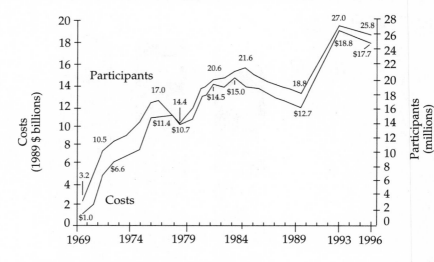

Source: House Committee on Ways and Means.

The food stamp participation rate among the poor was 68 percent, with 10.4 participants per 100 U.S. population in 1996 compared with 8.1 participants per 100 in 1978.

All public assistance recipients are eligible to participate in the food stamp program except SSI recipients in states that provide food stamp benefits in the form of increased SSI payments. Other households with net incomes at or below the poverty level after certain allowable deductions are subtracted are also eligible, but striking workers and most postsecondary students are not. An estimated 91 percent of all food stamp recipients have gross incomes below the poverty level. Forty-eight percent of them also receive public assistance, and 25 percent also receive SSI (1992 statistics).

Households receive monthly allotments of food stamps based on their income and household size. Although recipients would undoubtedly find cash easier and sometimes less demeaning to use, most retail stores accept food stamps in lieu of cash for any food except alcoholic beverages, tobacco, or hot, ready-to-eat foods. In 1996 the maximum monthly food stamp allotment for a family of four was $397, based on the Department of Agriculture's thrifty food plan of roughly $1 per meal for each person. This amount is reduced by 30 percent of a household's net income (after specified allowable deductions) based on the assumption, similar to that used in calculating the poverty threshold, that a family spends 30 percent of its income on food. In 1996 monthly benefits averaged $73 per person. Benefit levels are adjusted annually to reflect changes in food prices. The food stamp allotment is supposed to enable a family to maintain what the USDA calls a "nutritionally adequate" diet, but this regimen requires knowledge of nutrition, planning skills, storage space, equipment, and low-cost markets—resources infrequently available to the poor.

The food stamp program is jointly operated by the federal and state governments and is available in all states. The federal government finances the direct cost of food stamps and a share of state administrative costs. Program administration and distribution of food stamps are the responsibility of the state.

After a slow start in the 1960s, the program grew rapidly during the 1970s. While the expansion of food stamps in the 1970s paralleled the growth of cash welfare in the late 1960s, it also provided a subsidy to the working poor. The two most important factors contributing to the growth of the program were (1) more generous benefits and removal of obstacles to participation and (2) increased use as a result of extensive media publicity and the outreach efforts of public and private groups. Not surprisingly, participation in the program is also responsive to economic conditions, rising during recessions and declining during recovery. The USDA estimated that each 1 percent rise in the unemployment rate might add about 800,000 participants.

By the late 1970s record food stamp expenditures prompted diverse attempts to contain burgeoning program costs. To ensure that aid is not channeled to the nonneedy, Congress instituted numerous safeguards against fraud and waste. Regulatory requirements and financial incentives were employed to improve state administration of the food stamp program, including reporting requirements to verify eligibility and bonus payments to states maintaining low rates of error. The federal government took an increasingly aggressive role in investigating allegations of food stamp fraud and abuse. Charges of widespread fraud have never been substantiated, and although past administrative errors in determining eligibility and computing benefits have been a source of political frustration and embarrassment, they have not added greatly to program costs or to the overall number of food stamp recipients.

The concern that food stamps be restricted only to those who cannot support themselves also led Congress to establish a work requirement for recipients. Except for persons with child care responsibilities and persons already working or in school, all able-bodied persons between the ages of 18 and 60 years in households receiving food stamps must register for employment and accept suitable work paying the prevailing rate for the job in the locality. In addition, most states have established their own employment and training programs for employable food stamp recipients as mandated by the Food Security Act of 1985. The most common feature of these programs is the provision of job search assistance.

Since 1977 Congress has imposed a spending cap on the food stamp program in a vain attempt to hold down costs without slashing benefit levels. In each year that food stamp expenditures have threatened to exceed the authorized aggregate ceiling Congress has been faced with the choice of suspending benefits completely upon exhaustion of appropriated funds or approving supplemental expenditures sufficient to support benefits through the end of the fiscal year. Predictably, Congress has repeatedly opted for such last-minute extensions. Despite its ineffectiveness as a mechanism for restraining food stamp costs, the spending cap remains in federal law.

The program has been successful in targeting benefits on the basis of need and offering assistance to the working poor. Food stamp revisions enacted in 1977 focused on lowering income ceilings for eligibility and eliminated the "cash purchase" requirement, which previously prevented some very poor households from participating in the program. During the latter part of the 1980s Congress liberalized benefits and eligibility rules and authorized 50 percent federal cost sharing for optional state outlays aimed at informing low-income households and homeless persons about the food stamp program.

According to the USDA, two out of every three food stamp households are headed by women, one-fifth include members aged 60 or over, and three-fifths include children. In 1993 the average size of a household receiving food stamps was 2.6 persons. Some families not considered poor by official poverty standards are beneficiaries of the program because various costs may be deducted from a family's gross income to compute eligibility and benefit amount. In addition to a $131 standard disregard per month (in 1994), 20 percent of monthly earned income is deducted to make up for work-related expenses, payroll deductions, and income taxes. Work-related dependent care expenses up to $175 per month per dependent or $200 per month for dependents under the age of 2 and up to $231 monthly shelter expenses exceeding half of counted income may also be deducted. As of 1995, households were also able to deduct amounts paid for legally obligated child support. In 1994 a household of three (with children above age 2) with a gross monthly income of $1,263 could have been eligible to receive $233 in monthly food stamps by deducting as much as $790 a month, leaving a net monthly income of $473 to qualify for receipt of food stamps, as follows:

Gross monthly income	$1,263
less standard deductions	−131
dependent care	−175
shelter	−231
20% of earnings	−253
Equals net monthly income	473
Maximum monthly allotment	375
minus 30% of net monthly income (574 × .30)	−142
Monthly food stamp allotment	233

The importance of the food stamp program as a significant component of federal antipoverty efforts is beyond dispute. Although the program fails to meet the complete nutritional needs of recipients, it has improved access of the poor to essential food supplies. Perhaps more important, the food stamp program remains one of the few federal initiatives that extends aid to the working poor. By so doing, it preserves some sense of equity for that segment of the population neglected by the welfare system. Nevertheless, the food stamp program has not been exempted from the welfare reform axe. The 1996 welfare reform bill was advertised as saving $55 billion over six years, $27.7 billion—more than half—coming from food stamp cuts. Involved are across-the-board benefit cuts, special cuts affecting households with high shelter costs, cuts affecting unemployed but childless workers, denial of food stamps to legal aliens, and miscellaneous cuts for other groups eligible for food stamps. The Center on Budget and Policy Priorities calculates that about two-thirds of the benefit reductions will be borne by families with children, about half by families with incomes below 50 percent of the poverty line.[3] Most legal aliens will be totally denied food stamps. The low-income elderly will lose about 20 percent of their food stamp benefits. The unemployed between the ages of 18 and 50 who are not raising minor children will receive food stamps during only three months out of each three years. The thirty-year expansion of the food stamp program is clearly at an end.

Nutrition Programs

Federal food assistance focusing on child nutrition complements the broader food program as a vehicle for aid to the American poor. A variety of programs provide breakfast, lunch, and milk to more than 30 million children in private and public schools and day care centers, at a federal cost in 1996 of $6.1 billion. Federal aid is provided through state agencies in the form of cash or commodities that subsidize meals for children, with special aid targeted at children from low-income families.

By far the largest of the child nutrition programs is the school lunch program, with a federal cost of $4.0 billion in 1996. About 25 million children—more than half of the elementary and secondary student population—receive subsidized lunches. Federal reimbursement is based on all meals served regardless of children's family income, and additional assistance is provided for meals served free or at reduced cost to children from poor or near-poor families. In 1995 about 11.8 million children from poor homes received free lunches at an average federal subsidy of more than $1.50 per meal, 1.7 million children from near-poor homes received reduced-price lunches, and 11.3 million children from more affluent homes received subsidies averaging a few cents per meal.

The school breakfast and special milk programs are smaller in scope, yet they too have a significant impact on child nutrition. In 1996 appropriations for these programs amounted to $816.5 million and $21.9 million, respectively. Some 4.7 million received free or reduced-priced breakfasts (mostly in schools in low-income areas), and another 700,000 received full-price meals. Similarly, the special milk program provided 228 million half-pints of milk to 60,000 children monthly in participating schools, institutions, and summer camps. In order to eliminate program overlap, only schools that do not participate in other child nutrition programs are eligible for the special milk program.

Child nutrition programs reach outside the traditional school setting in summer camps, day care centers, and local health clinics. The summer food program benefits about 1.9 million children, and 1.2 million children receive meals at child care centers. The summer food program will take a modest cut from the 1996 welfare reform, shaving reimbursement rates by about 20¢ per meal, but the child and adult care food program, which primarily supports meals provided to children in child care centers and family day care homes, will take a nearly $2.5 billion hit.

Two additional programs—the special supplemental nutrition

program for women, infants, and children (WIC) and the commodity supplemental food program—channel aid to low-income, pregnant, and postpartum women and to infants and children up to age 5 whose inadequate diets may endanger their health. Participants receive food or vouchers to buy food that meets USDA nutritional requirements appropriate to the age and health status of the child or mother. Within federal guidelines, state and local agencies set income eligibility levels within 185 percent of the poverty level. In 1996 almost 6.5 million persons (1.5 million women, 1.7 million infants, and 3.2 million children) participated in WIC at a cost of $2.8 billion. Other programs provide cash and food commodities to Native Americans living on reservations, to soup kitchens, and to nutritional programs for the elderly. The federal government spent approximately $900 million on these initiatives in 1996.

The school lunch and breakfast programs have yielded gains, but some serious flaws remain in serving the poor. Millions of eligible children do not receive free or reduced-price lunches. The process of establishing eligibility can be complicated for the applicant and can create a great deal of paperwork for the schools. In some schools children who qualify for free or reduced-price lunches are required to stand in separate lines, eat at designated tables, or use distinctive lunch tokens. The involved certification procedures and stigmatization of children may discourage many needy children from applying for free meals. While the advances resulting from child nutrition programs since the mid-1960s are significant, their shortcomings underscore the special barriers that can accompany programs of indirect, in-kind assistance to the poor.

Social Services

As federal programs for the poor expanded, Congress increasingly acknowledged the importance of social services in helping the poor cope and in preserving some stability for future generations. The scope of social services is so broad as to defy definition and may include adoption and foster care, counseling, day care, services to the disabled and elderly, health-related services, information and referral, and legal aid. Merely identifying a problem, even if nothing can be done to relieve it, is regarded as a social service.

The social services block grant consolidated the funding of several categorical programs and is the largest (constituting over 50%) of eight federal program sources supporting social services. The 1981 provisions of the block grant eliminated a number of regulations imposed upon federally funded social services under Title XX of the Social Security Act. The changes reflected the Reagan administration's desire to channel greater decision-making power to the states. For example, states were no longer required to provide a minimum level of services to public assistance recipients or to adhere to federal income eligibility limits. However, the majority of states impose income eligibility as they did prior to the 1981 law because of cuts in Title XX funding. In addition, states can now design their own mix of services, establish their own eligibility requirements, and allocate federal funds without providing matching funds from state treasuries.

Title XX funding has declined in the past decades. In order to counteract rising federal expenditures for Title XX, which had reached $4 billion by 1972 ($10.7 billion in 1988 dollars), in 1990 Congress established a ceiling for annual program outlays of $2.8 billion. The ceiling has held social service costs well below growth rates in other federal in-kind assistance programs and has led to real reductions in spending. Adjusted for inflation and population growth, the federal contribution for social services dropped 58 percent between 1977 and 1994.

Changing Institutions

Virtually all federal in-kind assistance programs—medical services, shelter, food, and social services—displayed a strikingly uniform pattern of development throughout the 1960s and into the 1990s. In funding these programs the federal government responded to the immediate needs of the poor, demonstrating a consistent preference for in-kind rather than cash aid, and ultimately searched for ways to control costs as federal outlays ballooned. Compared with the above programs, community action has been a unique federal initiative manifesting markedly different goals and philosophy. The community action approach carved a history all its own as it struggled to assume a distinctive role in federal antipoverty efforts.

A component of President Johnson's antipoverty initiatives in the mid-1960s, the community action experiment tested a bold, unprecedented approach to the problems of the poor. Rather than responding to the immediate needs of Americans in poverty or even to the long-range personal barriers to individual advancement (e.g., lack of education and training or the need for family planning), community action embraced the ambitious goal of structural and institutional change in an attempt to alter some of the fundamental social, political, and economic forces that trapped the poor in poverty. Unlike other federal programs in aid of the poor, community action had as its goal not just to raise the effective income of the poor but to change the very conditions and institutions that have prevented millions of Americans from escaping poverty.

The structure of community action efforts represented a departure from the traditional antipoverty programs. The architects of the Great Society recognized that the administrators of federal programs were normally far removed from the populations they served and that the tradition of grudging and paternalistic assistance contributed little to individual self-esteem or to the collective abilities and potentials of the poor. The Great Society sought an alternative strategy for fighting poverty that included participation of the poor in the design and operation of the programs that served them. The effort to involve the poor in the decision-making process, including the choice of services and delivery systems, was intended to promote as much discretion and innovation as possible at the local level. Ultimately, three primary vehicles for this new approach emerged: the community action program (CAP), legal services, and community development corporations.

The CAP was a product of the Great Society's Economic Opportunity Act of 1964. It funded the establishment of almost 1,000 community-based agencies in urban neighborhoods, rural areas, and on Indian reservations. The poor were represented on CAP planning boards and in many cases were hired to help operate the programs. The community agencies quickly became catchalls for projects aiding the poor, acting as sponsors for a variety of social programs funded by federal, state, local, and private agencies. Yet their primary goal continued to be the development of mechanisms through which the poor could make their needs known to local government officials, civic organizations, employers, and labor interests who were in a position to offer direct local assistance.

In bypassing state and local elected officials and directly funding private organizations to operate programs, CAPs generated tensions and eventually prompted congressional action to restore political control over antipoverty efforts to local elected officials. This shift was completed in 1981, when Congress dissolved the Community Services Administration (which administered the funding of the local agencies) and incorporated its budget in a community services block grant (CSBG). The majority of the money from CSBG, $429 million in 1996, is allocated to community agencies formerly supported under community action and tribal organizations to provide a range of services to assist low-income individuals. A small amount of discretionary funds is devoted to such programs as community economic development, rural housing, migrant farmworker services, and youth projects.

In 1985 and 1987 Congress added two related community action efforts—the community food and nutrition program and community services to the homeless. Despite reduced funding and pressure from the executive branch to eliminate CSBG entirely, the community agencies persevered. Yet it would be a mistake to view the activities of these agencies as fulfilling the promise of the community action philosophy of 1964, for in most communities they have neither the power, the resources, nor, in some cases, the will to mobilize and represent the poor. Nevertheless, the surviving community agencies have continued to convey the needs of the poor to less sensitive institutions while offering a broad range of services more consistent with traditional approaches to federal antipoverty programs.

Closely related to the community agencies is Volunteers in Service to America (VISTA), also established by the 1964 antipoverty law. The agency enlists volunteers for the antipoverty effort. VISTA volunteers undertake a variety of projects in low-income communities, ranging from legal aid to community development to disaster relief. In 1971 VISTA and other volunteer programs were placed under ACTION, a new independent agency. The Reagan administration, despite its exhortations on behalf of voluntarism, repeatedly attempted to eliminate VISTA.

The late 1980s and the 1990s saw a revival of federal commitment to voluntarism. President Bush and influential members of Congress advanced vague blueprints for new volunteer efforts in metaphors of thousands of points of light. In 1993 the National Service Trust Act combined ACTION with the National Commission on National and Community Service and the White House Office of National Service to form the Corporation for National Service. The Corporation oversees President Clinton's AmeriCorps, which comprises three components: AmeriCorps*VISTA, AmeriCorps*USA, and AmeriCorps*National Civilian Community Corps (NCCC). The three entities engaged approximately 25,000 volunteers in community service in 1996.

AmeriCorps*VISTA was funded at $41.4 million in 1996. Its approximately 4,000 volunteers typically work individually in nonprofit organizations aimed at helping the disadvantaged. AmeriCorps*NCCC is a full time service program for men and women 18 to 24 years of age. The volunteers work in teams and live in housing complexes on NCCC campuses. Their assignments typically focus on maintaining and improving the environment. AmeriCorps*USA is the largest of the three, funded at $402.5 million in 1996. Its members work in a number of settings—tutoring teens, teaching elementary school students, starting neighborhood crime watches, building urban parks, providing assistance to the homebound, and the like. AmeriCorps volunteers receive a modest living allowance and health benefits. For a year of service they also receive a $4,725 education award to be used to pay off student loans or finance schooling or vocational education.

A companion entity, the National Senior Service Corporation, provides service opportunities to people 55 years of age and older as "foster grandparents" to children with special needs ($66.1 million in federal funds in 1994 and 24,000 seniors strong), as senior companions to assist elderly in independent living ($29.8 million in funding and 12,000 volunteers in 1994), and as senior volunteers in local services ($34.4 million annually and more than 450,000 volunteers). In each case the states provide matching funding.

A second primary vehicle of the community action initiative, the antipoverty legal services program, became one of the most controversial antipoverty experiments. As the interface between the poor and the institutions that community action sought to change, the legal system was a natural target of those attempting to intervene on behalf of the poor. Whether in landlord-tenant disputes, disputes concerning wage garnishments for unpaid debts, excessive interest charges and shoddy workmanship by ghetto merchants, or conflicts with police and juvenile authorities, the poor are the most likely to confront the legal system and the least prepared to cope with it. Although traditional legal aid societies have long provided some services to the poor, the antipoverty program was the first federal effort to expand access to legal services to help the disadvantaged in coping with the legal system.

Most of the cases undertaken by legal services projects involve fairly routine matters. In a typical year about 30 percent of a caseload of 1 million cases deals with family disputes such as divorce, child support, and custody of children; 21 percent with housing problems; 18 percent with income maintenance cases; 12 percent with consumer cases; and the remainder with education, juvenile, and health cases.

In its brief but stormy history the legal services program in the Office of Economic Opportunity (OEO) made friends among the poor and disenfranchised but also made many enemies within established power bases. As the effort to dismantle OEO reached its peak in 1973, several years of harsh criticism focusing on the legal services program culminated in the transfer of legal aid efforts to an independent Legal Services Corporation (LSC). The 1974 legislation creating the corporation included a wide range of restrictions on the agency and its attorneys, including bans on representation in cases concerning school desegregation, nontherapeutic abortions, and certain criminal cases. Later amendments to the Legal Services Corporation Act lifted a variety of other restrictions originally passed in 1974, including representation of juveniles and the use of corporation funds for research, training, and technical assistance related to the delivery of legal services.

During the 1980s, assaults on federal funding of legal services continued and the controversy over the mission of the LSC intensified. Both Congress and the LSC restricted legal services lawyers from handling cases relating to congressional redistricting, lobbying, strikes, and boycotts and most suits against government agencies. The Reagan administration attempted to do away with the corporation by appointing board members favoring its demise. Congress managed to keep the LSC alive through annual appropriations bills but at reduced funding in real terms. Adjusted for inflation, the $350 million appropriation for 1992 was about one-third below the funding a decade earlier. The 1996 federal budget funded LSC at $526 million.

In addition to the federal legal services program, state or local government programs, such as a public defender program, provide legal assistance to the poor. The Supreme Court has ruled that states and local governments must provide legal representation for impoverished persons accused of criminal offenses. In 1986 about $1 billion was spent by state and local governments to handle approximately 4.4 million cases, at an average cost per case of $223. Given the attacks on the LSC and the meager assistance provided by states and local governments, legal representation for the poor remains in a precarious position, with resources declining into the mid-1990s.

The third vehicle for community action adopted by the Great Society policymakers experimented with a radical approach to solving some of the fundamental chronic problems that contributed to poverty. The vision of the community development corporations (CDCs) was to support a variety of community-based enterprises. The CDC traces its history to Robert Kennedy's 1966 tour of Bedford-Stuyvesant, the passage of the Special Impact Amendment to the Economic Opportunity Act, and the formation of the initial set of CDCs, including the Bedford-Stuyvesant Restoration Corporation.[4] Available information indicates that fewer than one hundred first-generation CDCs were formed during the 1970s, but their focus shifted from economic development to housing development. In the 1980s the number of CDCs expanded significantly.[5]

Contrary to popular impressions, some CAPs have survived severe attacks and are active, albeit in modified form compared with the form envisioned for them by the Great Society antipoverty warriors. For example, the Local Initiatives Support Corporation (LISC), a private, nonprofit community development group, provides financial and technical assistance to CDCs. Founded in 1980, it raises funds from corporations, foundations, and government for CDCs in low-income neighborhoods that are unable to secure funds from banks. LISC claims that it has helped raise more than $1 billion of investment in over 525 CDCs. Made up of representatives from civic groups, social welfare agencies, businesses, and churches, CDCs are grass-roots organizations put together to bring needed services and development to impoverished neighborhoods. Between 1,500 and 2,000 CDCs existed in the early 1990s, supported by funds from private corporations, foundations, and the federal government appropriate to the community development block grant, HUD neighborhood development demonstration programs, and Office of Community Services discretionary funds.

The most aggressive elements of the community action concept are gone, frequently co-opted by the very institutions and power structures they were designed to challenge on behalf of the poor. CDCs are criticized for providing a pseudo impression of local community control because their resource base is typically controlled by entities outside the neighborhood, for providing a convenient rationale for blaming redevelopment failure on the neighborhood rather than on external conditions, and for radicalizing community self-help efforts. Yet some of the surviving indigenous local organizations display sensitivity to the needs of the poor. Community agencies and similar organizations created at the state or local level continue attempts to organize the poor and to provide a wide range of essential services on their behalf.

The Overlap of Cash and In-Kind Aid

The overlap of cash and in-kind assistance is inevitable and in many cases desirable. For example, virtually all public assistance recipients are eligible to receive Medicaid, and 96 percent do; 86 percent get food stamps; and approximately 30 percent live in subsidized housing, though this percentage is dropping rapidly. Some families on public assistance receive none of this in-kind assistance, while others may benefit from several programs. Virtually all elderly social security recipients in need of health care qualify for Medicare or Medicaid.

The most obvious—and intended—result of this overlap is an increase in the well-being of recipients. Some proponents of in-kind assistance hope that the eligible needy will benefit from as many programs as possible. But there are serious problems not only in coordinating eligibility for these benefits but in adjusting the level of these benefits as outside earnings or other income sources change. Administering most of these programs separately exacerbates the problem.

Program-induced disincentives to work can have a devastating effect on recipients who might be able to supplement their assistance with earnings but are also most likely to benefit from one or more in-kind programs. As an AFDC family's earnings rise, its members are confronted with a decrease in benefits for each dollar earned and failure to qualify for much-needed in-kind assistance. To the extent that earnings raise the household's counted income, food stamp benefits are reduced or eliminated. Housing subsidies and school lunches may also be affected. Considering the low earnings opportunities open to most AFDC recipients to begin with, income and payroll taxes as well as outlays for transportation, work clothes, and child care frequently make dependence on welfare economically more attractive than work. Providing financial and in-kind assistance at levels that simultaneously allow a reasonable minimum standard of living and encourage work force activity is one of the thorniest problems in welfare reform.

In view of the multiplicity of income support and in-kind programs and the diversity of eligibility rules and certification procedures, there is room for persons to exploit the system. No doubt some have, but the inequities resulting from duplication have often been exaggerated. For example, a GAO study found that participation in multiple programs was largely a function of family size—large families face multiple needs and therefore tend to participate in more programs. A single affordable cash assistance program could not provide for many needs. A system coordinating earnings with cash and in-kind assistance is needed and has been supplied, albeit with gaps in its coverage and meager funding relative to the obvious need.

Notes

1. Barbara Wolfe, "A Medicaid Primer," *Focus* (University of Wisconsin—Madison, Institute for Research on Poverty), spring 1996, 1.

2. Martha R. Burt, "Critical Factors in Counting the Homeless: An Invited Commentary," *American Journal of Orthopsychiatry,* July 1995.

3. David A. Super et al., *The New Welfare Law* (Washington, D.C.: Center on Budget and Policy Priorities, 14 August 1996), 17–21.

4. Randy Stoecker, "The Community Development Corporation Model of Urban Development: A Political Economy and an Alternative," occasional paper, Department of Sociology, Anthropology and Social Work, University of Toledo, March 1996.

5. Avis C. Vidal, "Rebuilding Communities: A National Study of Urban Community Development Corporations," occasional paper, Community Development Research Center, Graduate School of Management and Urban Policy, New School for Social Research, New York, 1992.

4. Programs for the Next Generation

Train up a child in the way he should go and when he is old, he will not depart from it.

Proverbs 22:6

The child was diseased at birth, stricken with hereditary ill that only the most vital men are able to shake off. I mean poverty—the most deadly and prevalent of all diseases.

Eugene O'Neill

The architects of the Great Society of the 1960s envisioned that federal efforts in aid of the poor would eradicate poverty. Not only has poverty remained, and in greater numbers, but cutbacks in funding during the 1980s and fundamental changes in programmatic approach in the 1990s, not yet completed at the end of 1996, have shown the nation's growing reluctance to provide the level of support necessary to meet even the most basic needs of Americans below the poverty level.

The immediate needs of the poor—income, food, shelter, and health care—continue to place pressing demands on government funds. Yet the costs of these efforts should provide a constant reminder that preventive strategies aimed at reducing the ranks of the poor in the future should complement the provision of assistance that alleviates the immediate deprivation of the poor. Funds for the prevention of poverty may not show definite, positive results for many years, but they are still the cornerstone of help in an affluent society.

The obvious focus of prevention efforts is the next generation, the children of the poor. The federal role in attempting to shield the next generation from poverty has centered on three major areas: birth control, child care, and education. Assisting couples in keeping family size within the limits of their desires and means will aid the next generation to begin at a lesser disadvantage. Providing care to preschool children can not only compensate for the neglect of physical and social development that is the lot of many poor children during their crucial formative years but also allow their parents to work. Investing in the education of the next generation can better equip the children of the poor to compete and free them from dependency.

The heavy reliance on the direct provision of services to the next generation—as opposed to additional cash assistance to the poor for these purposes—is hardly accidental. In some cases the in-kind approach is the only way to ensure effective aid; for example, cash assistance to defray the costs of birth control information or devices would probably not increase the availability or use of contraception by the poor. Direct provision of other services, such as education, is warranted because of economies of scale and abiding interest in a universal system of education.

Birth Control

The close relationship between large families, unwanted births, and poverty is well documented. As the number of youngsters in a household increases, so does the probability that the family will be destitute. Unfortunately, data support the adage that "the rich get richer and the poor get children." Inadequate contraceptive practices may be more responsible than parental desires for larger families among the poor. Government surveys provide conflicting evidence on desired family size. The Census Bureau found virtually no difference in the number of lifetime births expected by women in families with less than $10,000 annual income and those in upper-income families (2.2 and 2.1 children, respectively). In contrast, the National Center for Health Statistics found that women in families with incomes less than 1.5 times the poverty level expected to have 2.7 children on average, compared with 2.2 children for women in families with incomes three times the poverty level. The expectations of higher fertility rates by low-income women may reflect their experience. Low-income women are clearly more likely to have unwanted births. A National Center for Health Statistics survey in the 1980s indicated that 16 percent of women in households with incomes less than 1.5 times the poverty level had had at least one unwanted birth in the five previous years, compared with 7 percent for the upper-income group. Lack of universal access to birth control information, devices, and services may prevent low-income women from exercising the same degree of choice as more affluent women, or it may be simply that their relations with and influence on the men in their lives are that different.

Over the years, family planning has become increasingly prevalent and the quality of birth control methods has improved. In addition to scientific advances in bedroom technology, these gains reflect changing laws and societal values associated with birth control. A highly controversial issue just a quarter-century ago, making birth control information and devices available is approved by the vast majority of the American public today.

Controversy persists, however, about the right to abortion. In *Roe v. Wade* (1973) the Supreme Court struck down restrictive state laws regarding abortion, particularly during the first three months of pregnancy, but sixteen years later the Court ruled that states may restrict the right to abortion. In 1968 about seven of eight adults opposed abortion when its sole justification was the desire not to have another child. On the eve of the 1989 Supreme Court decision fewer than five of eight Americans held this view.

According to the Office of Population Affairs of the Department of Health and Human Services (DHHS), the birth rate for adolescents aged 15 to 19, which declined from 68.3 to 50.6 births per 1,000 between 1970 and 1986, increased by 23 percent between 1986 and 1991. Sexual activity among adolescents increased over the entire time period from 29 percent of females aged 15 to 19 having ever experienced sexual intercourse in 1970 to 42 percent in 1980, 52 percent in 1988, and then leveling off between 1988 and 1995. The likelihood of pregnancy decreased over the time period due primarily to increases in contraceptive use. Adolescent legal abortion rates rose during the 1970s to 42.7 per 1,000 in 1980, remained stable throughout most of the decade, and then declined in the early 1990s.

The continued importance of family planning efforts is illustrated by the rising proportion of births out of wedlock, which have increased fivefold since 1960. As a result, more than one of every four births in the United States is without the blessing of church or state license. Out-of-wedlock births are rapidly catching up with divorce as the principal cause of single-parent families. More than three-fifths of all black births and about one of every six white births happen out of wedlock. More than 70 percent of births among teenagers are out of wedlock, and among black teens the number is an alarming nine of ten (figure 4.1). Out-of-wedlock births have also increased among women above high school age, who in the early 1990s accounted for more than three-fourths of out-of-wedlock births, compared with half in 1975. More than 50 percent of the approximately 5 million children receiving AFDC in 1993 were born out of wedlock. It is notable, however, that the number of births per 1,000 unmarried women has declined in recent years among blacks, while it has continued to rise among whites. Also, between 1982 and 1992 the percentage of never-married mothers fell markedly among high school dropouts and slightly among high school graduates but rose sharply for those with at least some college educa-

Figure 4.1. Births to unmarried teens as a percentage of all births to teens, 1973–1993

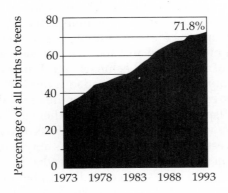

Source: Children's Defense Fund, *The State of America's Children, Yearbook 1996* (Washington, D.C., 1996), 47.

tion. Also, contrary to some suppositions, 70 percent of out-of-wedlock births are to women over 20 years of age, 17 percent to those aged 18 and 19, and 13 percent to girls under 18.[1]

Charles Murray, author of the book *Losing Ground* during the 1980s, continued to make headlines during the 1990s with the argument that the combined availability of AFDC, food stamps, and housing assistance is the primary cause of births to unmarried women.[2] The influence of his arguments on the 1996 welfare legislation was obvious. Nevertheless, most antipoverty scholars reject that explanation, noting that:

The rise in out-of-wedlock childbearing is a societywide trend

Lack of self-esteem and other factors aside from welfare can be demonstrated among the explanations for such childbearing

The purchasing power of welfare benefits has been falling, while births outside of marriage have been increasing

States with higher welfare benefits do not have higher rates of out-of-wedlock births

The teen birth rate is much higher in the United States than in countries with more generous welfare benefits[3]

Nevertheless, out-of-wedlock births pose one of the most troubling and challenging problems for public policies in aid of the poor. While unwanted births stem in part from the poor's limited access to family planning services, complex social and psychological forces have also contributed to the rise in out-of-wedlock births and subsequent increases in single-parent households. The lack of meaningful life options for many impoverished young women appears to render motherhood an attractive alternative, perhaps providing a sense of purpose and achievement. Whatever the causes, an increasing number of female-headed households clearly portends greater poverty and dependency in the years ahead.

In rearing offspring, teenage single mothers especially face diverse difficulties with potentially lasting effects on both mother and child. A child restricts the teenage mother's ability to acquire a basic education and secure a job. Families headed by young mothers are seven times as likely as other families to be poor and are extremely likely to end up on welfare. Whereas about 300,000 families on AFDC are headed by unwed teenage mothers, nearly 40 percent of mothers receiving assistance in 1993 gave birth before age 19. Such families accounted for approximately half of AFDC expenditures in an average year in the early 1990s. Even if teenage parents marry and support their offspring, their education is likely to be interrupted, and their job opportunities may be limited for life. There is also considerable evidence that early parenthood leads to larger families, placing continuing economic burdens on the household and society.

Recognizing the relationship between family size, out-of-wedlock birth, and poverty, the federal government actively promoted family planning services during the 1960s, 1970s, and 1980s. In more recent years the government has devoted special attention to the prevention of adolescent pregnancy, but with little success. Prior to the 1960s, family planning services were generally available only through private physicians and clinics. As part of the social security amendments of 1967, however, the Child Health Act required that family planning services be made available to AFDC recipients. A 1970 law established a population affairs office, now in the DHHS, and authorized funds for family planning services, training, information, and educational programs through Title X of the Public Health Service Act. The program helps fund more than 4,800 family planning clinics and serves some 5 million individuals each year through its nationwide network.

Family planning clinics in the United States are concentrated in low-income areas. A third of the clientele are under 20 years of age. Total funding for family planning services rose during the 1960s and 1970s; it has since declined somewhat. In 1996 federal and state governments spent roughly $500 million on family planning services, 87 percent of it contributed by the federal government. The federal support is channeled through Medicaid, Title X of the Public Health Service Act, the social services block grant, and the maternal and child health block grant. Title X of the Public Health Service Act provides the single largest source of family planning agencies' income: a third of the total in 1996, funded at $193 million. State public health departments administer more than half (57%) of the clinics and receive two-thirds of Title X monies. Planned Parenthood is the next most common provider of clinic services. Clinics receiving Title X funding must accord priority to low-income individuals and teenagers, and poor patients must be served without charge. Other individuals are generally charged minimal fees.

The welfare reform law passed by Congress in 1996 offers incentives for states to seek policy answers to the out-of-wedlock birth issue. It offers a $20 million bonus to each of five states that produce the most dramatic drop in out-of-wedlock births over a two-year period without raising the abortion rate. To date, states seem to be pursuing a strategy that work requirements for welfare recipients, requiring paternity information as a prerequisite for public assistance, pursuit of delinquent child support, and cutting any incremental benefits to childbirth subsequent to entering AFDC will address the problem. This approach seems at odds with substantial earlier research that a combination of family planning, birth control, and promotion of self-esteem as a key to abstinence is the most effective approach to the problem.

As a result of increasing expenditures in support of family planning, the number of women served by federally funded programs rose from nearly 1 million in 1968 to some 4 million two decades later. Roughly five of six clients had incomes below 150 percent of the poverty threshold. An additional unknown number of low-income women received family planning services from private physicians. In view of the fact that nearly 8 million poor and near-poor women were in need of organized family planning services in 1987, millions of eligible low-income women of childbearing age did not receive subsidized family planning services. There is little reason to believe that access has improved in the 1990s.

The 1980s brought controversial changes in federal policies regarding family planning. Despite increasing public acceptance of birth control and a stated goal of reducing future welfare costs, the Reagan administration sought to reduce federal family planning expenditures and to shift program responsibility to the states. Funding dwindled as conservatives emphasized chastity at the expense of contraception. No one argued with the premise, but few options seemed available for changing teenage conduct. The DHHS issued regulations barring funds for family planning organizations that advocated abortion or provided abortion counseling or services. These regulations were challenged in court, and no organization was denied funds because of them.

The Supreme Court's 1989 *Webster v. Reproductive Health Services* decision approved a restrictive Missouri abortion law. A number of states have enacted laws requiring mandatory waiting periods for abortions and information in the aftermath of the 1992 Supreme Court case *Planned Parenthood of Southeastern Pennsylvania v. Casey,* in which the Court upheld the state's right to encourage the choice of childbirth over abortion. While the Court rulings may portend a reversal of the 1973 *Roe v. Wade* decision, the courts have thus far upheld the right of choice. Still, those who abhor abortion the most are often the strongest opponents of both sex education and contraception, believing that knowledge is more likely to bring indulgence than restraint. Without judging the morals of the various viewpoints, it seems reasonably clear that unless effective contraceptive use increases, poor and near-poor women will be differentially affected by any ban on abortions.

In a given year, three out of one hundred women aged 15 to 44 have an abortion, approximately 91 percent of these occurring during the first trimester. Teenagers, minorities, and the poor are more likely than others to have an abortion. Poor women are three times more likely than non-poor women to have an abortion. Three of five pregnancies (excluding miscarriages) by unmarried women are aborted, and these women account for four of five total abortions. Seventy-five percent of women having abortions report interference of a child with work or school as the reason for the abortion, two-thirds say they cannot afford a baby, and 50 percent say they do not want to be a single parent or report difficulties with their husband or partner.[4] The obvious questions are, Why the pregnancy then? and Whose decisions were involved?

Federal funding of abortions through Medicaid has been limited since 1991 (under the Hyde Amendment to DHHS funding) to cases in which abortions are necessary to save the life of the mother and, since 1993, in which the pregnancy is due to rape or incest. A number of states have refused to comply with the limitations, and litigation continues in a number of jurisdictions. Fifteen states and the District of Columbia use their own funds to pay for abortions, financing approximately 177,000, or 11 percent, of 1.6 million total abortions annually in the United States. As a result of the Hyde Amendment, the number of federally funded abortions declined from 295,000 in 1977 to 165 in 1990. But that does not necessarily mean a diminution of the number of abortions occurring.

Lower welfare costs are only a part of the total savings that accrue from family planning programs. The driving reason for providing assistance to prevent the birth of unplanned children is not dollar savings but rather the reduction of human deprivation. Family planning services can substantially improve health among the poor. Having more children than desired and too close together contributes significantly to infant mortality, mental retardation, physical defects, and premature births. Frequent pregnancy is recognized as a health hazard to the mother as well, draining her energy and contributing to high maternal death rates.

Studies by the DHHS indicate that fertility control is the most effective means of reducing infant death rates and improving maternal and infant health, particularly among teenagers, who are more likely than older women to suffer from maternal and infant morbidity. Ancillary health benefits are associated with family planning efforts as well; for example, physical examinations help to detect cervical cancer and other diseases. Finally, the long-term payoff of fertility control lies in the fact that children in smaller families tend to receive better care and are less likely candidates for a life of poverty than children in larger families. While wiser decision making and a more widely shared ethos of abstinence is obviously to be preferred, government birth control programs have unquestionably helped reduce poverty by minimizing the number of unwanted children. Most Americans appear to defend the right of a woman to make her own choice regarding childbirth. The challenge is to get that decision made before rather than after the occurrence of pregnancy. No more significant victory could be achieved in the battle against poverty. But all of the relevant experience demonstrates that that can best be accomplished by (1) convincing young women from poverty backgrounds that they can truly take control of their own lives and (2) imposing responsibility for birth upon the fathers when it occurs.

Child Care

Marital dissolution, out-of-wedlock births, maternal employment, and geographic mobility all have increased the demand for nonmaternal child care. For poor families especially, access to safe and affordable care may prove one of the most important determinants of self-sufficiency. The federal government plays a vital role as a sponsor and funder of child care services, although in recent years its support for low-income families has lagged far behind its child care activities on behalf of middle- and upper-income families.

Widespread federal support of child care for the poor began during the Great Society era, when the federal government took on an expanded role in meeting the needs of the youngest generation. Increased work force participation by women of all classes and increased incomes led to programs that would provide care to low-income children while their mothers worked or attended school. In 1993 the labor force participation rate of mothers with children under age 18 was 67 percent, five times higher than in 1947. The full-time employment rate was 46 percent, part-time employment was 16 percent, women unemployed but actively seeking employment made up 5 percent. The 1993 labor force participation rates of mothers ranged from 75 percent for those with children 6 to 17 years of age to 54 percent for those with children under the age of 2.

The social services block grant, authorized under Title XX of the Social Security Act and administered by the DHHS, is the principal source of direct federal support for child care services. The program began during the 1970s as a structured system of grants to the states for a variety of social services, but in 1981 total funding was cut by 20 percent and the various grants were consolidated into a single block grant to each state. The 1996 appropriation for the social services block grant amounted to $2.8 billion, only half its real value in the peak year of 1977.

The block grant formula allows states wide latitude over the allocation of funds among a variety of social services. Forty-five states and territories use at least a portion of the funds for child care, and these programs account for approximately one-quarter of total social services block grant outlays. Social services block grant funds may be the sole source of funding for a child care program, but more often they supplement state dollars. States offer a variety of programs, most of them targeted to children in low-income families who are at risk of abuse or whose mothers work or participate in training programs.

In addition to the social services block grant, other programs assist low-income families indirectly with their child care needs. For example, two programs administered by the Department of Agriculture address the nutritional needs of low-income children in day care. The child care food program, authorized by the National School Lunch Act, is the largest source of direct federal assistance for child care. These programs provide funding and commodities to the states, which then make free or reduced-cost meals available to eligible children in day care. The rules governing means-tested social programs also have child care implications. AFDC, federal housing assistance, and the food stamp program disregard a portion of child care expenditures from a beneficiary's income when determining financial eligibility for benefits. AFDC disregards up to $175 of income spent on child care per month for each child aged 2 or older and up to $200 per month for each child under age 2. The food stamp program allows deductions of expenditures up to $175 per month, and public housing programs do not place a specific limit on income that low-income households may deduct in order to qualify for public housing.

Numerous other federal programs and regulations help poor families meet their child care needs. Four child care programs have been created by Congress since 1988. The Family Support Act of 1988 required states to guarantee child care assistance to parents enrolled in the JOBS program. In 1992 more than 102,000 JOBS participants received paid child care benefits for more than 162,000 children. Funding in 1996 was $850 million. A second program, Transitional Child Care, funds child care for families for twelve months after they leave AFDC for employment. It was funded at $268 million in 1996, having served 265,000 recipients in 1992. The Omnibus Budget Reconciliation Act of 1990 included two state child care grant programs. The At-Risk Child Care program, funded at $300 million in 1996, serves low-income families with children under 13 years of age that, while not currently receiving AFDC, are judged to be at risk of soon appearing on the roles in the absence of child care assistance to support work or training activity. Finally, the child care and development block grant provides support to low-income families with incomes up to 75 percent of the state's median income. It provided $935 million in 1996 and is expected to grow to help meet the demands of the work requirements in the new welfare reform law. For example, the budget it requested for FY 1997 seeks to serve 70,000 more children from low-income families than were served by the FY 1996 budget.

Federal payments to states for these federal child care programs totaled nearly $2.5 billion in 1995.[5] Despite this investment, JOBS child care assistance served 13 percent of adult welfare recipients. Although many confront exemptions based on the age of their children, limited state funding under the federal matching requirement results in long lines awaiting assistance and encourages liberal use of the exemption option in some states. In addition, shortages of some types of child care, such as that for children with special needs, limits child care possibilities. The Personal Responsibility and Work Opportunity Reconciliation Act of 1996 provided some $14 billion in child care funding over a six-year period, a 30 percent increase over prior planned allocations. The enriched funding is expected to support the movement of more mothers into jobs since the new law requires public assistance recipients to work after a maximum of two years of support and denies them further benefits anytime during their lifetimes after five years.

As to other programs, the Department of Education considers child care expenditures a cost of attendance in calculating Pell educational grants; the Job Training Partnership Act and other educational and employment programs set aside funds for child care; some areas use community development block grant funds for child care facilities or services; and programs for American Indians include a child care component. Yet provision of child care in aid of the poor is a small and shrinking portion of the total federal child care commitment. In 1988, for example, tax expenditures and direct federal outlays devoted to child care totaled $5.7 billion, but only $1.6 billion was targeted to low-income families. The 1996 commitment should redress that balance somewhat but will not tilt the system sufficiently to favor the poor.

The child and dependent care tax credit is the federal government's largest child care assistance program. Any taxpaying family with work-related child care expenses may take a credit against federal income tax liability for a portion of actual child care expenditures up to established limits. The credit is moderately progressive, sliding down from 30 percent of actual child care costs for families with adjusted gross incomes of $10,000 to 20 percent for those with adjusted gross incomes above $28,000. The child and dependent care tax credit is not refundable; it can only be used to lower the amount of income tax owed. Thus, families with incomes too low to pay taxes are unable to receive the value of the credit. Because the credit is claimed only upon filing the tax return, after the taxpayer actually pays out of pocket for child care, it is of limited value to families that cannot afford the up-front costs of child care. Estimated federal tax expenditures for the credit were $2.7 billion in 1994, virtually all of which benefited nonpoor families.

The favorable tax treatment of employer-provided day care benefits is another form of indirect child care aid. In 1988 such aid cost the treasury $65 million; no more recent data appear to be available. Child care assistance plans, like other fringe benefits, are more frequently available to workers with higher incomes. Even when employers offer child care assistance to low-wage earners, their lower marginal tax bracket makes an income exclusion less valuable to them than it would be to better-paid employees.

Demographic realities have made child care a central policy issue. More than two-thirds of women with children under age 18 are in the labor force, including half of all mothers with infants. Balancing work and child rearing proves very difficult for many of today's families, particularly those headed by a single parent. Adequately supporting that essential need remains an unmet challenge. Welfare reform promises to force the issue.

Child Support

In 1994 one out of every five children lived in poverty, compared with one out of seven two decades earlier. The single-parent family and the related financial abandonment of children by absent fathers are the major factors contributing to the rise in the number of poor children. The declining real value of the minimum wage and AFDC benefits, reduced funding for employment and training initiatives, and a decline in the earnings of unskilled and deficiently educated young adults are additional factors.

More than one-quarter of all children now live with only one parent. In 1992, 17.6 million children under the age of 18 lived with only one parent, a 114 percent increase from 1970. In 1992 the overwhelming majority of these children—88 percent, or 15.5 million—lived with their mothers; however, the number living with single fathers has been growing and was 2.2 million, or 3.3 percent of all children, in 1992. In 1992, 37 percent of children in single-parent families had a divorced parent, 24 percent had a separated parent, and 34 percent had a parent that had never been married. Disproportionately high poverty rates characterize single-parent families with children, particularly female-headed families. Eighteen percent of families headed by a single father and 46 percent of those headed by a single mother are poor, compared with only 8 percent of two-parent families. Almost 11 percent of the mothers of poor children worked full-time year-round.

Few Americans would question that parents have the responsibility to support their children, but defaulting on a consumer loan often draws tougher treatment than does failure to support one's children. Only one out of three divorced, separated, never-married, or remarried mothers with children receives child support payments, and those payments tend to be meager. In 1991, the most recent year for which data appear to be available, child support received by custodial mothers averaged $3,011 and child support received by custodial fathers averaged $2,292. This represented about 17 percent of the average total income of the custodial mother and 7 percent of the income of the custodial father.

Child support awards traditionally have been determined by courtroom judges on a case-by-case basis. However, the Family Support Act of 1988 required states to establish support guidelines as rebuttable presumptions of the appropriate support levels to be applied in child custody cases. In 1992, 54 percent of custodial parents were awarded payments as part of judgments—56 percent of custodial mothers and 41 percent of custodial fathers. Only 37 percent of those awarded payments received payments, and only 26 percent received full payments. Of a total of $17.7 billion owed for child support in 1991, 33 percent, or $5.8 billion, was not paid. The percentages are significantly lower in the case of women below the poverty level. Receiving payments due does surprising little to change the poverty status of these women, however. In 1989, 1.2 million, or 37 percent, of the 3.2 million women raising children alone and with incomes below the poverty line were supposed to receive child support. If payments due had been made, only 140,000 would have received enough to escape the poverty level. This reflects the reality of the poor income generation capability of the fathers once attached to these women.

Despite child support guidelines, awards vary greatly among parents who bring their cases before a judge, and parents who do not rely on the legal system generally receive no guarantee of support.

Mother's current marital status	Percentage awarded support	Average amount received, 1989
Remarried	79	$2,931
Divorced	77	3,322
Separated	48	3,060
Never married	24	1,888

When it comes to children, absence apparently does not make the heart grow fonder—fathers become less likely to pay support as time passes.

The status of child support as a "family issue" has colored government reaction to it. All states recognize supporting children as a legal responsibility whether the offspring is born out of wedlock or into a legally established family, but sanctions often have been mild or rarely invoked. The reluctance of Congress to intervene in family matters and the structure of a welfare system designed for impoverished widows kept the federal government from enacting child support legislation until midcentury. In 1950 Congress took the initial step of requiring welfare officials to report to state law enforcement officials the desertion or abandonment of AFDC children.

As increasing numbers of divorced, separated, and never-married mothers joined the AFDC rolls during the 1960s and early 1970s, new legislation expanded the federal role, culminating in the child support enforcement program in 1975. The law required states to designate an agency to administer the program and provided for the establishment of a child support enforcement office in the DHHS to coordinate the national effort. Primary responsibility for collections remained with the states, but the federal government assumed a role in funding, monitoring, and evaluating state programs.

In 1984 Congress required more stringent state enforcement mechanisms and augmented federal financial assistance available to states to enforce child support obligations. The law mandated that states take measures when a noncustodial parent fails to provide timely support by garnishing wages, imposing liens on property, withholding tax refunds, requiring the delinquent parent to post bond to guarantee payment, or providing credit bureaus with information on delinquent parents. It also extended the deadline for paternity determination to a child's eighteenth birthday and ordered states to establish nonbinding guidelines for child support awards. The federal government in turn accepted greater responsibility for improving interstate child support enforcement and established a federal parent locater service to aid in tracking down parents found delinquent in support of their offspring.

Several states, most notably Wisconsin, improved on the 1984 federal child support reforms. These initiatives inspired several broader measures included in the Family Support Act of 1988. Among the most important child support provisions of the law were that:

Judges must adhere to state child support guidelines or justify in writing departures from the guidelines.

Judges must revise awards every three years if a parent requests revisions.

States must require genetic testing in all contested paternity cases and must meet federal standards for determining paternity. The federal government absorbs 90 percent of laboratory testing costs.

All child support orders must provide for immediate wage withholding.

States must obtain both parents' social security numbers as a prerequisite for issuing a birth certificate and must establish automated systems for tracking absent parents.

A commission was authorized to study the issue of interstate child support enforcement, a vital concern of both custodial parents and state governments, for making a move out of state had been one of the surest ways of evading child support payments.

The Child Support Recovery Act of 1992 made it a federal crime to willfully fail to pay a past-due child support obligation for a child living in another state. In 1996, $2.1 billion was spent in child support enforcement programming, with estimates of $12.5 billion in collections—almost $6 collected for every $1 spent in administration. This represented a 38 percent improvement over 1982 by some estimates. In addition to collections, more than .5 million paternities were determined, 4.4 million absent parents were located, and more than 1 million support obligations were determined. Most of the collected funds are used to offset the assistance the families receive from public assistance programs. AFDC families receive up to $50 of any child support collected each month plus any current support over and beyond assistance given them. The 1996 welfare reform law included several provisions related to child support. The law established a federal case registry to track delinquent parents across state lines and a national directory of new hires to permit state agencies to facilitate procedures for direct withholding of child support from wages. In addition, the law sought uniformity in rules and procedures governing interstate cases, establishment of central registries of child support orders and collections, and expanded ability for states to seize assets, revoke drivers' licenses, and require community service of parents delinquent on child support.

Ensuring that absent parents support their children financially has emerged as a critical social policy issue. Widespread divorce, separation, and out-of-wedlock birth ensure that most Americans will be touched in some way by single parenthood. Improving the awarding and retrieval of child support will not end child poverty; the low earnings of some parents preclude contributions large enough to raise their children out of poverty. But holding absent mothers and fathers to their financial obligations will improve the living standards of children, however marginally. Enforcement of the law may also discourage some parents from shirking responsibility for supporting their children, and it may even reduce the number of unwanted children.

Education

A teacher's job extends far beyond the three Rs as changes in family structure, maternal employment, and work force requirements place increasing demands on American educational institutions. Children and adolescents from impoverished families, in particular, often require special attention in order to overcome social and educational shortfalls. Inadequate diet and mothers' drug or alcohol abuse during pregnancy can impair learning abilities; inadequate verbal and sensory stimulation in the early years leaves some youngsters poorly prepared for schooling; and child abuse or other family crises distract attention from learning. Children from poor families need extra support from the very start in order to improve their opportunities to achieve academic success.

The community organizations and schools that serve low-income areas often are unable to meet educational needs without outside support. Although education is perceived as a local responsibility, many low-income communities experience a shortage of financial and other resources and a surplus of deteriorating school facilities and children who require special attention. States began to address this problem during the 1970s, often after a court order, by investing more state education funds in school districts with a concentration of low-income neighborhoods. Since 1970 the average state contribution has increased from 41 percent of total public primary and secondary school revenues to 50 percent. Pending and anticipated legal challenges suggest that educational funding formulas will be an issue throughout the remainder of the decade.

The nation spends more than $500 billion a year on elementary through postsecondary education. The lion's share (85–90%) are state, local, and private expenditures. Federal dollars assist more than 50 percent of students by paying for some portion of their postsecondary education. Estimates of the proportion of federal funds targeted to poor children attending elementary and secondary schools vary widely (table 4.1).

Head Start

With many mothers working outside the home and a rising interest in early education, a growing number of families depend upon preschool programs to help socialize their children. Only a minority of public school systems offer prekindergarten classes, howev-

Table 4.1. Estimated Federal Investment in Education for Low-Income Individuals, FY 1997

	Appropriations (millions)	Beneficiaries with Low Incomes (%)
Elementary and secondary		
Head Start	4,000	90
Title I	7,194	
Education of the handicapped/disabled	4,036	55
Vocational education	1,026	
Native American education	350	
Bilingual/immigrant education	262	
Total	$16,868	
Postsecondary		
Pell grants	6,413	60
Guaranteed student loans	2,652	
College work-study	830	36
Supplemental educational opportunity grants	345	40
TRIO programs	500	
Perkins loans	158	33
Veterans' education	850	
Total	$11,748	

Sources: U.S. Congressional Research Service; Budget of the United States.

er, and low-income families cannot afford to pay the tuition charged by for-profit preschools.

A major initiative of the Great Society antipoverty efforts was the establishment in 1965 of Head Start, a program designed to address the developmental needs of children from poor families. The program now serves more than 796,000 children and has an annual budget of $4.0 billion in FY 1997. The Early Head Start program began in 1995 in response to research indicating that the earliest years are key to child growth and development. Early Head Start serves pregnant women and children under the age of 3. In FY 1997 it accounted for 4 percent of the total Head Start budget and served 25,600 children. Head Start offers a unique and important source of educational support for poor children. The program has a lower than usual student-teacher ratio. Like other antipoverty efforts, it has emphasized the employment of subprofessionals and volunteers to relieve teacher work loads and to provide additional attention to children. Parental involvement is a major goal of the Head Start effort, and many Head Start employees are mothers of children participating in the program. Bringing parents into the day-to-day operation of Head Start centers has proven an effective way to advise parents about child-rearing practices and to help them become more active participants in their children's education.

Longitudinal evaluations of Head Start and similar programs indicate that they have a lasting effect by improving school performance and employability in later life and that they are cost effective. Compared with children in similar circumstances who do not receive early education, Head Start enrollees are more likely to graduate from high school and to find work. A testimony to the program's demonstrated effectiveness is that it has continued to escape the budget cutters' axe during the parsimonious 1980s and 1990s. Yet funds are adequate to enroll only one in five impoverished children.

Elementary and Secondary Education

A national commitment to equal educational opportunity for children from all economic backgrounds has provided the fundamental rationale for federal involvement in public elementary and secondary education. Federal dollars have focused on the needs of children residing in neighborhoods with a high concentration of poverty, where schools often lack adequate facilities and resources and where students may require supplemental educational services.

The Title I program, reauthorized by Congress in 1994 and known as Chapter 1 when first authorized in 1965, is the primary vehicle for federal aid to the disadvantaged within the nation's public schools. The bulk of these funds are distributed to local educational agencies to supplement programs for students in low-income areas, with particular emphasis on providing supplemental support of reading and math instruction. Funds are also available for state-operated programs serving handicapped, migrant, neglected, and delinquent children.

The Department of Education estimates that 75 percent of Title I funds support basic educational services, such as reading and math instruction. The remaining 25 percent are allocated for support services, including health care, transportation, and guidance counseling. Children in secondary schools are eligible for Title I assistance, but spending is concentrated on kindergarten and elementary school students. Evaluations indicate that Title I–funded education improves students' reading and mathematics performance, but because of the dearth of funding in the upper grades, assisted children tend to lose ground as they get older.[6] In FY 1997 the Title I appropriation was almost $7.2 billion. Title I typically assists approximately 6 million students nationwide. Title I funds are distributed in block grants to state educational authorities, who in turn allocate funds to schools in areas that serve large numbers of disadvantaged children. Prior to the 1994 reauthorization Title I funds were spread to nearly 70 percent of public elementary schools, including a high percentage of schools with a low percentage of low-income children. The 1994 reauthorization sought to focus Title I funds to high-poverty schools and increased requirements for showing performance improvements by students. Despite reform, the need is so extensive and the resources are so constrained that only one-third to one-half of children needing assistance receive it, and many receive only a limited range of the full services needed.

Federal funds also address the educational needs of specific population groups, including disabled, immigrant, and Native American children, regardless of family income. During the past two decades Congress has expanded aid to handicapped children, including youngsters with emotional or psychological problems and learning disabilities such as dyslexia. The goal of the federal government has been to ensure that all disabled young people receive a tuition-free education in the least restrictive environment. States may receive up to 40 percent of the national average expenditure for each disabled child enrolled.

Federal government support for the education of Native American children dates back to the end of the nineteenth century. Today more than 300,000 Native American children receive federal assistance. Support of bilingual education is a more recent and controversial federal investment. It is estimated that nearly 3 million limited English proficient (LEP) students were enrolled in public elementary and secondary schools in 1994. Approximately 6,400 of 15,000 school districts enrolled LEP students, 6 percent of them serving a student population of at least 40 percent LEP. Most of the students receiving bilingual education aid are the offspring of poor Hispanic immigrants, although assistance exists for those who speak Chinese, Portuguese, or other languages. The bilingual program is structured as a capacity-building competitive grant program. For FY 1997 bilingual and immigrant education aid aimed at helping children learn English was funded at approximately $262 million to serve approximately 441,000 students.

Federal support for vocational education dates back to 1917. Current federal appropriations account for about one-tenth of the estimated \$10 billion devoted to vocational education in public schools. Vocational education programs serve primarily high school students who are not college bound, with a portion of funding earmarked for disadvantaged and disabled students. Current vocational education initiatives nationwide include the tech-prep model, focused on linking secondary and postsecondary programs through the joint teaching of academic and occupational skills, and the career academy model, which organizes curriculum around a specific occupation or industry cluster in a "school within a school" environment.

The School-to-Work Initiative

Two colliding forces in the 1980s were parents to a school-to-work initiative in the 1990s. Though not designed as an antipoverty program, one of those parenting forces was intimately related to declining earning power, and a successful program could do much for preventing or remedying poverty. On the one hand, the earning power of those without a college education began a long-term decline; on the other hand, a slowed rate of productivity growth was perceived as a prime cause of the strained ability of U.S. industry to compete in international trade. The first force sparked a concern for the "forgotten half," and the latter saw work force development as the key to restoring productivity growth and international competitiveness.

A proposal much discussed between the Departments of Education and Labor during the Bush administration became the Goals 2000 Educate America Act early in the Clinton administration. The funding was minor, designed to spark state interest in fulfilling the program's six goals without being provided with federal funding to do so:

Every child enters school ready to learn

A 90 percent high school graduation rate

Students leave grades 4, 8, and 12 having demonstrated competency in challenging subject matter and prepared for productive employment

American students lead the world in science and mathematics by the year 2000

Universal adult literacy

Drug- and violence-free schools

A National Education Goals Panel was to develop national education standards for key academic subjects and tests to assess shortcomings and progress. Though the goals were to be voluntary, it was hoped that a periodic state-by-state assessment would keep the states alert and give local schools a guide for testing their achievements. A National Skill Standards Board was to be created to develop and implement a nationwide system of voluntary occupational skill standards that schools could use to guide their skill training programs, students could attain as credentials for use in job searches, and employers could rely on as certificates of competence. Political opposition has prevented the successful implementation of either approach. The Goals 2000 budget was $350 million for FY 1996 and $491 million for FY 1997. There is as yet no measure of its contribution.

German youth apprenticeship practices were the primary motivator for the School-to-Work Opportunities Act of 1994, although the U.S. initiative was structured quite differently from its model. States were to be inspired by small grants to involve schools, employers, and other stakeholders in a combination of school-based and work-based learning. No model was prescribed; there was only a concept. The classroom experience was to be restructured so that students could learn how their academic subjects related to the world of work. Teachers were to work with employers to develop broad-based curriculums to help students understand the skills needed in the workplace. Teachers and students were to work in interdisciplinary teams to design projects capable of teaching both the academic subjects and their workplace relevance. Employers were to provide workplace learning opportunities in which the real-life relevance of academic subject matter could be tested, broad transferable skills could be learned, problem solving experience could be gained, and workplace discipline could be experienced. Connecting activities and organizations were to be developed to tie the school, the workplace, and the home together in a learning partnership.

In FY 1994, $100 million was taken for the purpose from the Job Training Partnership Act and the Carl Perkins Vocational and Applied Technology Act, followed by appropriations of $245 million for FY 1995, $350 million for FY 1996, and $400 million for FY 1997. Every state was given an initial planning grant; then one-time five-year implementation grants were awarded to eight states in 1994, nineteen in 1995, with most of the remainder expected to be involved by the end of 1996. It is far too early to assess results, but the progress to date appears promising. By the end of the second year, federal funds had gone to 818 local partnerships through state implementation grants or direct federal grants. Eleven states reported on 210 partnerships involving 135,000 employers and a half-million students in 1800 schools. The employers provided 39,000 work-based learning sites and nearly 53,000 slots for students. Though not required to do so, the reporting states were spending $1 of their own funds for every $2 of federal funds.[7] Annual performance measures have been developed to assess progress and outcomes. A national evaluation is due in September 1998, and the initiative is designed to "sunset" at the close of 2001, the expectation being that the states will continue with their own funds thereafter.

Heartening as the anecdotal evidence is at the end of 1996, the most obvious problem is the program's limited focus on in-school youths. Nothing in the legislation imposes that limitation, but it is obviously easier to involve those already in school than it is to entice back and enroll those who need it most.

Postsecondary Education

Despite the increase in the number of college graduates, the sheepskin's value in the marketplace has not diminished. It is still one of the surest avenues out of poverty, although poverty itself is a formidable barrier to college education. In 1993 a typical family with an income at the 25th percentile of all American families would pay 23 percent of its income to meet average tuition and room and board costs at the average public university, compared with 19 percent in 1975. Only one in eight young adults with a family income of less than $10,000 was enrolled in college in 1988, compared with more than half of those with family incomes of $50,000 or more (figure 4.2).

Because educational and motivational barriers to a college education often emerge before a student reaches college age, several programs assist disadvantaged high school students. These initiatives, commonly known as the TRIO programs, provide a variety of services through grants to colleges and other agencies. Recipient institutions use the funds to support basic skill instruction and remedial education, help in obtaining financial aid, personal and academic counseling, and stipends for low-income students, who are mostly first-generation college students. Although these programs reach only about 700,000 poor youths, those who participate are significantly more likely than their peers to enroll in and graduate from college. TRIO programs were funded at $500 million for FY 1997.

The federal government makes its commitment to postsecondary students in the form of grants, loans, and work opportunities. In

Figure 4.2. Percentage of high-school graduates aged 16 to 24 enrolled in college the October following graduation, by family income, 1994

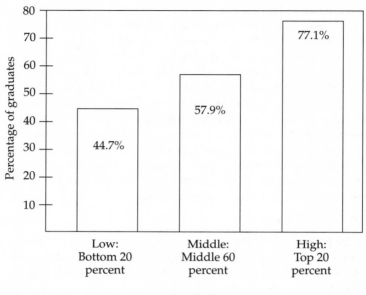

Source: U.S. Bureau of the Census.

1996 an estimated $33.7 billion in federal, state, local, and school funds were available through these programs. Federal assistance during the 1980s shifted from grants to loans, and two-thirds of the funds are now devoted to various loan programs.

Despite shifting priorities, the Pell grant program still allocates the largest pot of federal postsecondary assistance dollars, $6.4 billion in FY 1997. Pell grants aid students from families who cannot afford to attend a postsecondary educational institution. In the 1995–96 school year nearly 4 million students at 6,000 educational institutions received Pell grants. A student eligible for the maximum award may receive 60 percent of education costs or $2,700 annually, whichever is less. In 1996 an estimated 3.6 million students—70 percent of them with family incomes below $20,000—received Pell grants. Educational opportunity grants, which provide supplementary aid to students who would not otherwise be able to attend a postsecondary institution, provide assistance to smaller numbers of students.

The guaranteed student loan program enables postsecondary students and their families to obtain low-interest loans through banks and other lenders. The two primary student loan programs are the William D. Ford Direct Loan Program and the Federal Family Education (Stafford) Loan Program. The federal government encourages lenders to offer loans at interest payments ranging from 8 percent to 12 percent by providing them reinsurance against default and interest payment subsidies. Students obtaining Stafford loans, the most common variety, may borrow up to $23,000 during their undergraduate years. While applicants must meet family financial requirements to qualify, the program allows middle-income as well as poor students to obtain loans. The two programs provided more than $26 billion in educational loans in 1996. It is not known how many of the 6.5 million loan recipients in 1995 were students from low-income families.

The college work-study program makes federally subsidized employment available to low- and moderate-income students. Federal grants are awarded to qualifying institutions, which develop and provide jobs for students with demonstrated need. Most colleges participate in the program, providing students up to twenty hours of work a week during the academic year and up to forty hours a week during the summer. The federal government pays 70–80 percent of wages, which cannot be set lower than the federal minimum wage. During 1996 an estimated 713,000 students participated in the program, earning an average of $1,000 each. For FY 1997, $830 million in funding was appropriated to support an estimated 960,000 jobs for eligible college students.

Men and women who have served in the American armed forces may receive educational assistance administered by the Department of Veterans Affairs. Measured by either cumulative outlays or numbers of students served, the GI Bill has been one of the most massive federal commitments to student financial assistance and has served as a key vehicle for the advancement of young people from low-income families. Congress has revised the GI Bill four times since its first enactment in 1944. Under the current Montgomery GI Bill, recruits who complete three years of active duty with an honorable discharge may qualify for $417 per month in basic educational benefits for up to thirty-six months while in an educational program, up to a maximum of $14,400. Men and women who complete two years of active duty plus four years of service in the military reserves may receive approximately $300 per month in benefits up to a maximum of $10,800. In 1996 more than 285,000 veterans and 86,000 reservists participated in the All-Volunteer Force Educational Assistance Program, at an expenditure of $742 million. The Department of Veterans Affairs also expended $108 million to assist 725,000 eligible dependents of veterans whose deaths or permanent or total disabilities were connected to their service. Additional veteran education support in 1996 came in the form of work-study payments ($22 million), other loan guarantees ($169 million), and the Post-Vietnam Education Act ($72 million). The Office of Public Affairs of the Department of Veterans Affairs estimates that veteran education benefit costs have totaled $71 billion over the life of the agency.

Investing in the Future Labor Force

Basic educational competency—mastery of the three Rs and communication—is becoming increasingly essential to gain even an entry-level job; more education is necessary for those who wish to advance their careers. Because of the increase in the number of students who fail to acquire a basic education, all levels of government, business enterprises, and other private groups are placing emphasis on preschool, elementary, and secondary education.

The future of postsecondary education may prove more problematic. The cost of higher education has been rising far more rapidly than inflation during recent years, placing college beyond the financial grasp of a growing number of young people. Part-time attendance has increased because fewer students can afford to attend college on a full-time basis, and the proportion of students aged 25 and over is growing rapidly. These developments will require changes in the nature of government assistance to postsecondary education.

Child Welfare Services

Children's aid programs were the first social welfare services provided by the federal government; they date back to the Taft administration. While child and maternal services are not aimed exclusively at children of poor families, most beneficiaries are from low-income families. Problems of child neglect, abuse, and emotional disturbance are not found exclusively in indigent homes, but it is hardly surprising that poor children face more than their share of such problems. Consequently, children from impoverished

Figure 4.3. Reports of child abuse or neglect, 1976–1993

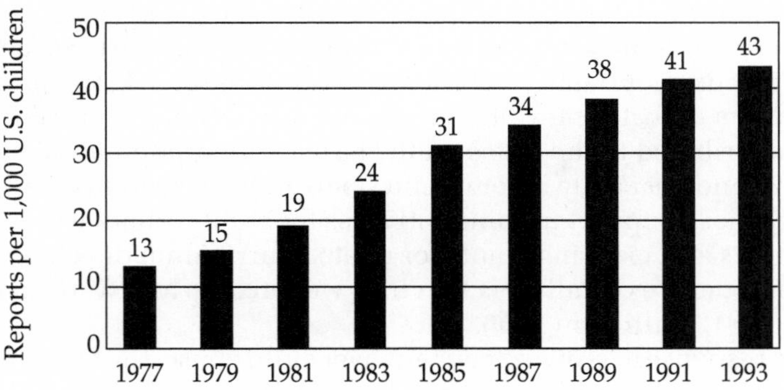

Source: Children's Defense Fund, *The State of America's Children, Yearbook 1996* (Washington, D.C., 1996), 69.

homes are likely candidates for assistance offered by child welfare programs.

According to reports to child protective service agencies, in 1993 more than 3.0 million children were alleged victims of child abuse and neglect, four times as many as in 1976 and 25 percent more than in 1988 (figure 4.3). Increased numbers of at-risk children, inadequate child welfare services, and reduced funding have resulted in an overburdened child welfare system. Consequently, only the most severely abused children are served and many children are left without care.

Federal programs to promote child welfare address a broad range of problems, including child abuse, foster care, adoption, runaway youths, and research related to these problems. By far the largest federal child welfare expenditures are allocated to support poor children in foster care. This assistance, formerly provided as part of the AFDC program, is now channeled through the states as an entitlement for all foster care children meeting AFDC eligibility criteria; the individual states determine the level of payments to foster parents or institutions. In addition to income support, foster care children receiving this federal assistance also become automatically eligible for Medicaid benefits. Federal outlays for monthly benefits to 267,000 children in foster care totaled $3.4 billion in 1996.

The states also receive federal grants for the provision of child protection, foster care, adoption, and other welfare services to children and their families without regard to income. These discretionary funds are intended to encourage state-administered activities that promote family stability, assist children at risk, and provide adoption or foster care alternatives when necessary. Federal funds are distributed to the states on the basis of their population below age 21 and per capita income, and small additional grants are made available to support training activities for child welfare workers or students and teaching grants for related curriculum development. Total federal expenditures for child welfare services were an estimated $1.3 billion in 1996.

In response to growing concern over child abuse, the federal government provides grants to states in support of prevention and treatment efforts and child abuse and neglect services. It also sponsors projects to facilitate and encourage the adoption of children with special needs. A separate federal program supports shelters and counseling or referral services for youths who run away from home. Finally, the federal government provides modest support for ongoing research and demonstration projects in the field of child welfare, including studies of the special needs of abused, disadvantaged, and foster care children and training grants for child welfare providers.

Compared with the size and scope of federal expenditures for child care and education, the federal investment in child welfare services hardly looms large, though it has grown significantly in recent years. In part, limited outlays reflect a historical view of child protection and welfare as predominantly state, local, or private responsibilities. Yet as public awareness of child abuse, neglect, or inadequate supervision and protection has increased, the impetus for federal involvement in and encouragement of state activities has grown. For a small minority of children at risk, these federal programs ensure continued state efforts and research activities to address their pressing needs.

No coherent program of federal aid to assure the future of low-income children exists. Nevertheless, the investment in scattered programs is substantial, and these children would undoubtedly be worse off without the assistance. The challenge is to assess the effectiveness of what now exists, compare it with the need, fit the pieces into a coherent program, fill the gaps, and assure adequacy. There can be no better investment in the nation's future.

Notes

1. Sharon Parrott and Robert Greenstein, *Welfare, Out-of-Wedlock Childbearing, and Poverty: What is the Connection?* (Washington, D.C.: Center on Budget and Policy Priorities, January 1995), 6–8.

2. See the following by Charles Murray: "The Coming White Underclass," *Wall Street Journal,* 29 October 1993; "Welfare and the Family: The U.S. Experience," *Journal of Labor Economics* 11, no. 1 (1993); and "Does Welfare Bring More Babies?" *Public Interest,* spring 1994.

3. Parrott and Greenstein, *Welfare, Out-of-Wedlock Childbearing, and Poverty,* ix–xi.

4. Planned Parenthood web page, www.pp.fa.org.

5. U.S. General Accounting Office, *Welfare to Work: Child Care Assistance Limited: Welfare Reform May Expand Need,* GAO/HEHS-95–220 (Washington, D.C., September 1995).

6. D. W. Grissmer et al., *Student Achievement and the Changing American Family* (Santa Monica: RAND, Institute for Education and Training, 1994).

7. National School-to-Work Learning and Information Center, *Report to Congress, 1996,* www.stw.ed.gov.

5. Opportunities for the Working Poor

Anticipate charity by preventing poverty; assist the reduced fellow man . . . so that he may earn an honest livelihood, and not be forced to the dreadful alternative of holding out his hand for charity. This is the highest step and the summit of charity's golden ladder.

Moses ben Maimon

The goal of the Economic Opportunity Act of 1964 was "to eliminate the paradox of poverty in the midst of plenty in this nation by opening to everyone the opportunity to live in decency and dignity." To accomplish this goal more is needed than the provision of cash or goods and services, which might lessen poverty but fail to attack its causes. Dignity in this society depends upon self-reliance for all of those capable of meeting its rigors. Programs that encourage self-support through employment are crucial to the elimination of poverty in the long run. As an old proverb moralizes, "Give a man a fish and you feed him for a day. Teach him to catch a fish and you feed him for life."

Those in need of self-help programs face a variety of impediments. Among the unemployed are those who lack the skills to compete effectively in the labor market and qualified workers who are unable to locate a demand for their skill. There are also some, not counted among the unemployed, who are too discouraged by their failure to find work to continue to look. Many are precluded from effective labor market participation by ill health, disability, or age. Others are blocked by aspects of their personal conduct that impede their search for work, repel employers when they apply for work, or prevent successful job performance once they find work. Many individuals work yet remain poor. They are part-time workers who need full-time jobs and persons employed at wages so low that even full-time work does not raise them above the poverty standard. These underemployed and low earners, when added to the unemployed and discouraged, constitute the subemployed, a measure of which would provide a more realistic indication of the universe of need for employment and training services.

Aid in overcoming these obstacles includes preparation for work, the creation of job opportunities, finding access to jobs, and improving on-the-job performance to retain and advance in employment, once obtained. The range of self-help programs for the jobless but employable poor is wide, but its resource base is shallow; assistance to the employed poor is limited in both range and resources. Some programs focus on the supply side of the labor market, preparing the poor for gainful employment. These include both the educational programs discussed in chapter 4 and the employment and training programs launched in the 1960s. Other programs have sought to stimulate the demand for labor through equal opportunity laws or job creation, directly via the creation of public-sector jobs (widely used in the 1970s) or indirectly through subsidization of private-sector wages. A third group of programs seeks to improve the functioning of the labor market for the poor, matching supply and demand more effectively and setting minimum-wage standards. Finally, several programs incorporate all three approaches, targeting a specific geographical area or population group.

Both the number of programs designed to promote self-reliance and their budgets increased rapidly during the 1970s; their budgets suffered during the 1980s, then stabilized in the 1990s. Meanwhile, without adding to the total resources, Congress expanded the number of programs until demands for consolidation became a major political issue in the early 1990s. The General Accounting Office became particularly vociferous on the issue during 1994 and 1995, charging that there were as many as 163 overlapping "employment training programs," adding to costs and impeding efficiency.[1] However, to reach that number, the GAO had included some programs that did not involve training, some that provided for training incidental to accomplishing unrelated objectives of unrelated programs, and some that provided training for nondisadvantaged populations and had even counted subtitles of antipoverty programs as independent entities. Not that the issue of program multiplication was invalid, but for overlap among antipoverty training programs a more appropriate number might have been 11 or 12. Although efficiency could have been enhanced by some consolidation, the issue became submerged in the congressional devolution arguments of 1995 and 1996, the preferred solution apparently being to combine the budgets of designated programs into block grants to the states, leaving it to them to resolve the multiplicity. There emerged S. 143, the Workforce Development Act, and H.R. 1617, the Consolidated and Reformed Education, Employment, and Rehabilitation Systems Act (CAREERS). However, in the tensions of the 1996 election campaign the two houses of Congress were never able to resolve the differences between the two approaches, which remain in limbo at this writing.

Work Force Development Programs

The first major employment programs were instituted during the Great Depression in the 1930s and provided at least part-time work to a large proportion of the unemployed. Since their primary purpose was employment rather than training, the programs were dismantled when full employment was achieved during World War II. In contrast, what were called manpower development and training programs in the 1960s, employment and training programs in the 1970s and 1980s, and work force development programs in the 1990s began in response to widespread concern about continued poverty despite economic growth. They have emphasized education and training to prepare the jobless poor for available jobs.

Federal job training programs for the disadvantaged began with $10 million appropriated as part of the 1961 Area Redevelopment Act and rose more than a thousandfold within two decades before declining sharply and then more slowly to a level where the ability to serve no more than 5 percent of those declared eligible is often cited (figure 5.1). The second major step was the 1962 Manpower Development and Training Act (MDTA), originally targeted at workers displaced by automation but quickly redirected toward the needs of the impoverished. President Johnson's antipoverty initiatives experimented with a wide variety of training programs, most of which Congress consolidated—along with MDTA programs—under the Comprehensive Employment and Training Act (CETA) in 1973, which was replaced in 1982 by the current Job Training Partnership Act (JTPA). The term *work force development* has been attached to proposed legislation but has yet to become law. It is intended to encompass programs for the mainstream as well as the disadvantaged, as shown in table 5.1.

Employment and training programs have provided a wide variety of services at various times, although each individual enrollee receives only a limited number of forms of assistance:

Assessment to evaluate skills and needs

Career counseling

Job search assistance

Figure 5.1. Federal support of employment and training programs, 1975–1996 (1989 dollars)

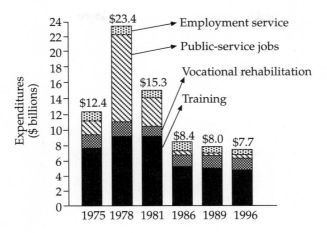

Sources: U.S. Office of Management and Budget, Budget of the U.S. Government, various years; U.S. Congressional Research Service, Department of Labor, Employment and Training Administration.

Basic education needed for employment

Classroom occupational training

On-the-job training

Public-sector employment

Stipends or other support services, including child care and transportation assistance

Placement services

The poor often lack adequate knowledge of the labor market and the contacts needed to secure jobs related to their skills. Job development, information on available opportunities, instruction in job search techniques, and referrals to employers increase the likelihood of finding employment. Basic education, vocational training, counseling, and work experience make the poor more attractive to potential employers. The programs primarily assist targeted populations, including youths, the handicapped, welfare recipients,

Table 5.1. Federal Work-Force Development Program Budgets, Program Years 1993–1997 ($ millions)

Program	Program Year					
	1993	1994	1995	1995 recision	1996	1997
JTPA state formula grants	2,947.1	3,367.8	4,428.9	(1,495.5)	2,4187.7	2,927.1
Title II-A adult training	1,015.0	988.0	1,054.8	(98.0)	850.0	895.0
Title II-B summer youth	840.7	876.7	1,738.6	(871.5)	625.0	871.0
Title II-C year-round youth	676.7	608.7	598.7	(472.0)	126.7	126.7
Title III dislocated workers	414.7	894.4	1,036.8	(15.6)	880.0	1,034.4
JTPA federal programs	1,381.1	1,519.0	1,613.1	(85.0)	1,489.8	1,588.0
Title III discretionary grants	152.9	223.6	259.2	(13.5)	220.0	258.6
Native American programs	61.9	64.2	64.1	(4.3)	52.5	52.5
Migrant farmworkers' program	78.3	85.6	85.7	(5.7)	69.3	69.3
Job Corps	996.1	1,040.5	1,099.5	(10.0)	1,093.9	1,153.5
Other national activities	135.4	105.6	104.6	(51.5)	54.1	54.1
Community jobs, older Americans	396.1	410.5	410.5	(14.4)	373.0	463.0
State programs	87.2	90.3	90.3	(3.1)	82.1	101.9
National programs	308.9	320.2	320.2	(11.3)	290.9	361.1
Unemployment compensation	2,265.8	2,485.3	2,374.0	(60.7)	2,306.8	2,345.8
State operations		2,072.8	2,132.8	(9.0)	2,080.5	2,119.5
Contingency		387.1	224.6	(51.7)	216.3	216.3
National and other		25.4	16.6	(0)	10.0	10.0
Employment service	894.6	968.3	922.3	(7.0)	820.7	824.4
Allotment to states	811.0	832.8	845.9	(7.0)	761.7	761.7
National activities	83.6	85.5	76.4	(0)	59.0	62.7

TAA aid	211.3	220.4			346.1	324.5
TAA training and benefits		206.9			279.6	276.1
NAFTA training and benefits		13.5			66.5	62.7
Vocational education	1,169.5	1,176.3	(67.3)	1,178.1	1,080.7	1,132.0
Basic state grants	972.8	972.8	(0)	972.5	956.1	1,007.1
Tech-Prep education	104.1	104.4	(67.3)	205.3	100.0	100.1
National and other		99.4	(0)		24.6	24.9
Adult education and literacy	304.7	304.9	(23.3)	302.2	259.6	354.5
State programs	254.6	254.6	(15.5)	293.4	250.0	345.3
National and other	41.3	8.8	(7.8)	8.8	9.6	9.2
Key work force investment		255.0	(676.5)	803.8	6,754.4	6,754.4
School to work	0.0	100.0	(25.0)	250.0	350.0	400.0
One-stop career centers		50.0	(20.0)	120.0	110.0	150.0
Pell grants					4,914.0	5,919.0
State student incentive grants					31.4	50.0
Goals 2000 education reform	0.0	105.0	(91.5)	393.3	340.0	476.0
JOBS for welfare recipients	1,000.0	1,100.0	(330.0)	1,300.0	1,000.0	1,000.0
Other						433.8
Totals					$15,903.8	$17,954.3

Source: National Governors Association, *Current Development in Employment and Training* (Washington, D.C., various years).

workers displaced by large-scale layoffs, the elderly, farmworkers, Native Americans, and veterans.

Training Disadvantaged Adults

JTPA, the largest government training program for the poor and deficiently educated, provides a variety of assistance involving all three levels of government and the private sector. Within limited federal rules, local boards comprising private and public officials plan and supervise program activities that are then carried out by public and private education and training institutions. By the mid-1990s these private industry councils and state job training coordinating councils, largely limited to JTPA oversight, were beginning to give way through state government reorganization to work force development departments and councils of various kinds having a wider range of multiprogram oversight and jurisdiction.

JTPA's predecessors, MDTA and CETA, provided stipends to support enrollees while they were engaged in work experience and classroom training, along with minimal on-the-job training (OJT). However, the concern grew that some enrollees were attempting to extend their training periods in order to continue receiving the stipends, which under CETA had been set at the minimum-wage level. Stipends were eliminated under JTPA, which during the 1980s stressed OJT and short-term job search assistance, in order to shorten the duration of enrollments and maximize the number served within limited budgets. However, few employers were interested in getting involved in OJT in order to receive a subsidy that generally reimbursed only about half of an enrollee's wage for the first five hundred hours of employment; most employers who did participate treated the funds as a subsidy for having hired less attractive workers and provided little or no training. Job search training, while low-cost, proved to be able at best only to assist inadequately skilled workers to obtain jobs just like the low-paid ones they had previously held. By the early 1990s, JTPA's Title II-A training for some 175,000 disadvantaged adults each year had swung back to a training mix more comparable to that which had existed under MDTA and CETA, though the absence of stipends still limited the numbers who could afford to continue in classroom training until substantial skills were attained, and the abolition of public service employment limited work experience opportunities:

	1982 (%)	1987 (%)	1991 (%)	1994 (%)
Classroom training	48	34	44	59
Work experience	29	8	6	5
On-the-job training	12	24	15	14
Job search and other minor assistance	11	34	35	22

A combination of the limited funding available and the limited backgrounds of those to be trained has kept both classroom and OJT throughout the history of MDTA, CETA, and JTPA concentrated on preparation for relatively low-skilled jobs. Throughout, ten occupational categories have accounted for half of all occupation-specific training: clerk/typist, secretary or word processor; electronic assembler; machinist; custodian; nurse's aide; salesperson; licensed practical nurse; accounting clerk or bookkeeper; food service worker; and computer operator. JTPA was criticized during the 1980s for "creaming," that is, for serving the most qualified of the eligible population and neglecting the most needy.[2] The JTPA system responded in the late 1980s and early 1990s by making more explicit the importance of serving the hard-to-serve by making that a key element of the system's performance standards and by providing extra incentive monies for quality service to people in these categories.

Despite changing emphases, the outcomes have been remarkably consistent over the entire thirty-five-year history of training for disadvantaged adults. Most of the skill training is performed by postsecondary public vocational and technical training institutions and community colleges, though a substantial amount occurs at private proprietary schools. Since stipends are no longer available (though subsistence allowances, transportation costs, etc., are sometimes provided), the major provision to the recipient is free tuition. About three-quarters of those who complete their training courses obtain jobs, mostly in training-related positions. Women's wages generally reflect greater proportionate advancements over their pretraining earnings than do men's, but the gains of both are sufficient to provide a positive cost-benefit ratio. Improved employment stability is generally a greater contributor than enhanced wages to those positive outcomes. However, as noted, the combination of scarce funding and limited education and work experience backgrounds leads to training in relatively low-paid occupations. Hence, though the pay is above what would have been available without the training, it is rarely enough to bring a single-earner family of any substantial size above the poverty line.

A study of classroom training under CETA in the 1970s demonstrated that those whose training lasted fewer than twenty weeks experienced only one-sixth the gains of those few who trained for more than forty weeks.[3] It was not surprising, therefore, that during the late 1980s, when the average training duration had shrunk to fewer than twenty-four weeks, a comparison between the subsequent earnings of adult JTPA participants and a control group who had not been enrolled showed only modest gains for adults and negative returns for youths, whose enrollment was even briefer.[4] The treatment group of that study had an average enrollment duration of 3.3 months, with those in classroom training averaging 5.0 months and those in OJT or job search training averaging only 2.0 months.[5]

The men in the trainee group experienced a 57 percent earnings increase between their last preprogram year and their first postprogram year, but five years later, despite a 26 percent increase in earnings, their earnings advantage over their control group was only $300 to $500 per year, which was not statistically significant. However, the adult women trainees experienced a 75 percent earnings increase the first year and another 40 percent increase by the end of the fifth year, when the control group was $400 behind, which was statistically significant at their earnings level.[6] The provision of an access route into previously inaccessible jobs may have been as much a factor in the women's success as the actual training. The addition of an emphasis on displaced homemakers—those forced into the labor market by divorce or widowhood or simply freed up for it by the maturing of their children—as a new target group probably added to the success. For them, mentoring approaches in which employers assigned experienced employees to guide the new hires proved to be particularly effective. However, a scarcity of funding for child care was an obstacle for those displaced homemakers with children still at home. The impact on both outcomes and child care requirements of the rising proportion of welfare recipients among JTPA II-A enrollees from 32 percent in 1990 to 42 percent in 1994 has not been measured.

Even though the average duration of JTPA training increased from twenty-four weeks in the 1980s to thirty-two weeks into the 1990s, the program suffered from the same forces that increased the earnings advantages of college graduates over all persons having less education and training and dictated that, on average, only those with postgraduate training were able to keep their real incomes from declining. Those completing JTPA classroom training during 1993 and 1994 found a positive relationship between training du-

Table 5.2. JTPA Title II-A Placement and Retention Wages by Classroom Training Duration, 1993–1994

Training Hours	Percentage of Total Enrollments	Hourly Wage at Training Termination	Weekly Wage at 13-Week Follow-Up
Up to 480	64.9	$7.13	$273.45
481–639	10.2	7.47	281.65
640–799	6.1	7.50	287.46
800–959	4.3	7.38	274.57
960–1,199	4.3	7.63	288.08
1,200–1,439	3.0	7.88	306.46
1,440–1,599	2.0	8.01	301.92
1,600–1,919	2.0	8.14	323.90
1,920–2,079	0.8	8.22	314.61
2,080 and over	2.6	8.47	329.45
Mean		7.38	284.20

Source: Office of Policy and Research, Employment and Training Administration, Department of Labor.

ration and placement and retention wage, but the margin was by no means as great as it had been under CETA (table 5.2).

Nevertheless, the average program completer, if employed full-time year-round, would have earned $14,760, and the short-term trainee would have earned $14,260, both approximately the poverty wage for a family of four, while those few in training for a full year or more would have earned $16,940, almost supporting an additional family member at the poverty level. That differential would have to prevail for at least seven years for the longer-term trainee to have been paid for the extra time spent in training at the wage rate that would have been available after the shorter training period, a disturbing fact since the controlled comparison showed the earnings advantage of the male trainees narrowing over the first five years while that of the women was widening. Interestingly, that consistent increase in wages with enrollment duration does not prevail for either OJT or basic education, supporting the view that subsidizing OJT under JTPA buys a job, not training.

In addition to JTPA, the vocational education program provides limited funding to assist adults. At least 15 percent of the federal funds involved must be used for postsecondary vocational education programs provided by community colleges, technical schools, and adult education programs. However, no data are available to separately assess its returns for vocational education for youths in the same settings.

Youth Programs

Vocational education, the JTPA in-school and summer youth employment program, the Job Corps, and the targeted jobs tax credit either exclusively or primarily assist youths or young adults. Vocational education represents the oldest federal direct investment in training, dating back to the 1917 Smith-Hughes Act. Current federal appropriations (under the Perkins Act) amount to just over $1 billion (table 5.1). The program serves primarily non-college-bound youths or young adults, with some funds set aside for the disadvantaged and the handicapped.

Federal vocational education legislation in 1968, 1976, and 1984 intensified set-asides, seeking to persuade the states to emphasize the training of various disadvantaged groups; in 1984, for instance, the emphasis was on the economically disadvantaged, the handicapped, single parents, women preparing for nontraditional occupations, and the incarcerated. A 1986–87 assessment was discouraging, however. The federal funds, which were outweighed ten to one by state expenditures, were inadequate to provide substantial leverage. The disadvantaged and handicapped were more likely to show up in training for low-level service occupations, leaving high-quality vocational education for their opposites. In general, the higher the poverty rates and the lower the academic achievement, the fewer the vocational courses offered and the less the access to area vocational schools providing more extensive course offerings. Particularly instructive was the finding that the more occupationally specific the training, the less it was utilized in enrollment, completion, and subsequent job placement.[7] On the basis of these findings, evaluators recommended integration of academic and vocational curriculums, augmented assistance to at-risk students to enable them to succeed in more demanding courses, an emphasis on placement efforts, improved linkages between secondary and postsecondary training, and a general improvement in the quality of the vocational offering in those schools with high concentrations of poor and low-achieving students.

The congressional response was the Carl D. Perkins Vocational and Applied Technology Act of 1990 (better known as Perkins II). The integration of academic and vocational education would use vocational training more as a tool for career exploration than as a method of occupational preparation and more as an approach to learning than as specific skill instruction. Articulation between secondary and postsecondary work force preparation recognized that few worthwhile occupations could now be adequately prepared for in high school alone. Vocational education's responsibility for the transition from school to work recognized the floundering that inevitably occurs if the school merely provides classroom instruction and leaves it to the school leaver to discover opportunities for application.

But public education is a ponderous machine that changes slowly. A GAO review of the first two years under the 1990 amendments found only limited change.[8] Team teaching by vocational and academic teachers was in place in only 14 percent of schools for 4 percent of vocational/technical students, but plans were being formulated for expansion. The fact that approximately one-half of the students in the high schools surveyed participated in vocational/technical education programs indicated that enrollments in such programs were not limited to a student body that could be labeled "vocational." Tech-prep programs in which two high school years and two post-high years were spent in integrated preparation for an advanced occupation, and for which approximately 10 percent of the federal funding was earmarked, were found in 18 percent of schools, involving 11 percent of vocational/technical programs and 8 percent of students in 1990–91. Plans were declared for substantial expansion of those programs in subsequent years.

Nevertheless, Congress chose to delete from the specified allowable activities under the act the cooperative education programs enrolling 430,000 high school students in 1989–90 and accounting for 8 percent of total high school enrollment. These integrated, not vocational and academic learning, but vocational training and part-time employment and on-the-job experience. Such programs are not prohibited, however, and will undoubtedly survive. Eliminating the set-asides, it was hoped, would bring into the mainstream of higher-quality employment preparation those who might have been segregated into low-quality programs. The results remain to be seen. A distribution formula that provides small states two or three times the federal funds per student as the large states would seem to carry a bias against school systems with concentrations of disadvantaged and handicapped students, The 1992–93 GAO review found no net increase or decrease in the enrollment of the economically and academically disadvantaged, the disabled, or students with limited proficiency in English, though half of reporting districts claimed addition and expansion of services for such students.

Looking at vocational education from the postsecondary end produced similar findings. Of the 93 percent of two-year colleges offering vocational/technical programs to 43 percent of their enrollment, only 21 percent offered tech-prep programs in 1990–91, but that figure rose to 36 percent the following year, with 58 percent either having been engaged or engaged then in developing such programs. Few had postcompletion data adequate to determine outcomes and differentiate between advantaged and disadvantaged placement rates.

All in all, there appeared to be little reason to question earlier conclusions that secondary-level vocational education was playing a significant career exploration role but was experiencing relatively few training-related placements, primarily because few students of high school age had made a lasting career choice. On the other hand, postsecondary enrollees (recipients of about 40% of the total federal funding but making up less than 40% of enrollment) had more work and life experience, knew what they wanted to do, had favorable training-related placement rates, and increased their earning power thereby. However, the gains are concentrated among those enrolled in longer-term community college and technical courses rather than in short-term training for rudimentary skills. Assessment of the 1990 new departures will have to go on for several years before a definitive answer can be provided, but they represent promising directions, and progress appears to be under way.

The outcomes and outlook for the youth titles of JTPA, II-B and II-C, are less propitious. The post-1986 National JTPA Study found both male and female youths among JTPA enrollees to actually be falling behind their counterpart control groups in the race for higher incomes. The treatment group raised their earnings from $2,900 during the year before training to $4,600 in the first year following training and $7,600 in the fifth year. However, the control group began at $4,800 for the year following the training of their counterparts and actually experienced higher earning growth during the first three years than the former trainees before falling behind in the fourth and fifth year to finish at $6,800 earned in the fifth year. The earnings patterns of the young female enrollees were similar, rising from $2,000 in the year before enrollment to $3,300 in the year after and $5,400 after five years. However, the experience of women in the control group was parallel, despite the lack of training, rising from $3,400 to $5,200 over the same five years, outearning the treatment group slightly during the first two years and then falling behind equally during the final two years.[9]

Although the law allows local administrators to offer participants a wide variety of services, the summer youth employment program funds primarily work experience programs. Most enrollees work thirty-two hours a week at government agencies, schools, or community organizations for seven weeks at the federal hourly minimum wage. The law requires localities to assess the reading and math skills of participants and to allocate at least some funding to teaching the three Rs. Both the summer and year-round programs are designed to offer work experience and earnings as an incentive to stay in or return to school as well as a source of needed income. Both programs have been substantially enriched since the devastating late 1980s study. About half of the summer youth enrollees receive academic enrichment as well as work experience. Half of the year-round enrollees receive basic skill training, and 25 percent receive skill training, raising the total employability enhancement rate from 39 percent in 1990 to 54 percent in 1994. Nevertheless, the limited time spent in either remedial education or work experience could hardly be expected to accelerate substantially the learning and earning experience of youths confronting major barriers. The only mystery is why those enrolled actually fell behind their nonenrolled controls during some years.

The widely touted 1993 study has been a major factor in creating a negative image for remedial programs for out-of-school youths and spreading the message that "nothing works" for them. It was used by the new Republican congressional majority in 1995 to impose a dramatic recision from the already appropriated budget of that year and to perpetuate that budget cut in subsequent appropriations (table 5.1). As part of the effort to soften the image of hardheartedness as the 1996 election approached, the summer youth JTPA budget was restored to its 1993–94 level but not to its prerecision 1995 level, but the year-round program has yet to recover. The enrollment figures of 158,000 for the year-round program and 555,000 for the summer program during program year 1994 appear to have become the norm.

Perhaps the 1995 youth budget crash should have been expected. The 1992 JTPA amendments, responding to charges of creaming, had stipulated that at least 50 percent of youths served by the youth titles must be out of school and no less than 65 percent must be facing serious barriers to employment. Under these circumstances, only major rehabilitation efforts could have been expected to have substantial payoff—but not in the available time frame. There are successful programs for out-of-school and at-risk youths, but they require more commitment and investment than is generally found in run-of-the-mill JTPA youth programs. Even though the behavioral characteristics of many low-income youths had been deteriorating, training duration had been falling. One week of rehabilitation for each year of accumulated disadvantages could hardly be expected to work miracles. Employers had shown no eagerness to employ youths of suspect backgrounds when they had a ready supply of adult women, older workers, and immigrants to draw from. The few programs that had demonstrated success with the disadvantaged youth population had been characterized by at least a year's enrollment duration, integrated combinations of basic education, skill training, and on-the-job experience, visible connection to jobs of promise, mentoring by respected adults, opportunities for high-profile community service, and the possibilities of further educational advancement upon demonstrated success. These youths have shared decision-making responsibilities within their programs and gained a greater sense of empowerment than that available through antisocial activities. There is no reason to expect success with lesser commitment.

That willingness to invest substantially and at length in the rehabilitation of severely disadvantaged youths has been the source of over three decades of plaudits for the Job Corps, despite its continued high cost the least changed survivor of President Johnson's Great Society antipoverty efforts. Despite being costly ($15,300 per trainee in 1993 compared with $3,700 for each JTPA youth enrollee), observers across the political spectrum have acknowledged its achievements. A 1982 study of the Job Corps found a $1.46 return to society for every $1.00 invested in this residential training program.[10] In the sixth edition of this book Sar Levitan claimed a $4.46 net return on every public dollar expended and noted that Congress had rejected the Reagan administration's attempts to abolish or scale back the program in the early 1980s.

However, in the harsher atmosphere of the 1990s this program too was subjected to more critical analysis, though it had not yet suffered budget cuts. The program's high costs throughout its history have been primarily attributable to the use of residential facilities to remove severely disadvantaged youths from their presumably debilitating environments. Though there was some use of Job Corps facilities by nonresidents by the mid-1990s, it amounted to less than 10 percent. The typical Job Corps participant is an 18-year-old, minority, high school dropout who has never had a full-time job and who reads at the seventh-grade level. The GAO found that of 63,000 students who left the Job Corps in the year ending 30 June 1994, 68 percent had two or more barriers to successful employment, such as not having a high school diploma, lacking basic skills, receiving public assistance, and having limited English proficiency.[11] That was true of 39 percent of enrollees in JTPA nonresidential youth programs.

As of 1995 there were 111 Job Corps centers in 46 states providing a total of 43,000 training slots and ranging in capacity from 120 to 2,234 trainees. Thirty centers were classified as conservation centers and were operated by the Departments of Agriculture and Interior. The skills they taught were related to construction and conservation activities, which could be learned in an out-of-doors, rural setting, and labor unions were often involved in the instruction. The other 81 centers were operated by private corporations and nonprofit organizations and emphasized classroom training. In program year 1993, three-quarters of the entire Job Corps budget was allocated to center operating costs; the remainder was spent on contracts for outreach, recruitment, screening and placement services, facilities acquisition and construction, student allowances, and other such costs. At the center level, it is difficult to separate the residential costs from the instructional costs because of the amount of effort invested in teaching the values of personal conduct and social interaction. The GAO in its 1995 intensive study of 6 centers concluded that 23 percent of the center budgets were spent on residential living expenses, 22 percent on social skills instruction, 22 percent on basic education and job skill training, 21 percent on administration, with the remaining 12 percent covering all other.

Job Corps instructional techniques have been praised as models in instructing youths and adults who have failed in or have been failed by the school system. Its enrollees are 16- to 24-year-old socially disadvantaged volunteers who apply through various outreach and screening contractors. Training programs are open-entry and self-paced, allowing students to enter at any time and progress at their own pace. Each Job Corps center offers basic education, vocational skill training, personal and vocational counseling, health care and recreational activities, as well as room and board. Students can stay as long as two years, but the average stay is eight months. Each receives a base allowance of about $50 a month at the beginning, rising to $80 after six months. Incentive bonuses of $25–80 are awarded for exceptional ratings on performance evaluations. A bonus of $250 can be earned for graduating from high school, achieving a general education development (GED) certificate, completing vocational training, or getting a job. An additional $100 bonus is paid if the job is training-related.

The latter responds to one of the rising crescendo of complaints about the Job Corps. The GAO study noted that although 59 percent of Job Corps enrollees obtained jobs and another 11 percent continued on to further education, one-half the jobs were low-skill, low-pay jobs unrelated to the training provided. In the six centers studied, 22 percent had dropped out before obtaining any significant training, 40 percent had been engaged in vocational training they had not completed, and 36 percent had completed their vocational programs; 2 percent were classified as "other." Forty percent of center funds, it was lamented, were being spent on those who did not complete their assigned vocational training. However, the GAO also found that those who completed their vocational training were five times more likely to obtain a training-related job than those who did not, and training-related jobs paid 25 percent more than the others. A survey of employers found them well-pleased with their Job Corps hirees, but they reported that those hirees, like most youths, tended not to stay long, 30 percent working less than one month and only 20 percent staying for six months or longer, 45 percent quitting, 22 percent being fired, and 13 percent being laid off.[12] Another questioned aspect was the long tenure of many center contractors and sole sourcing to nine labor unions without competitive bidding.

None of these complaints is new to those familiar with the history or evaluations of the Job Corps. The dropout rate has always been high, a consequence of the combination of the backgrounds of the youths, their distance from home, and the training discipline involved. In fact in recent years the concern has been expressed that the discipline has not been tight enough, leading to some unfortunate incidents in the centers and their surrounding communities. The Job Corps gains have always been attributable to those who stayed long enough to make a difference in their lives. In the midst of the block grant devolution discussions in the Congress during 1995 and 1996, there were some proposals that the administration of Job Corps centers be turned over to the states in which they were located, but few governors appeared to be standing in line for the responsibility. The findings of a new assessment of the Job Corps, currently under way, are scheduled for release in 1997, but no sharply different findings are expected. Meanwhile, since these difficult years passed without any budget cuts, one could reasonably assume that the Job Corps has reached a level of stability to be envied by other programs.

The targeted jobs tax credit (TJTC), enacted in 1978 and in effect during almost all of the period from 1979 to 1994, provided subsidies to employers who hired 16- to 22-year-olds living in low-income households, welfare recipients, and handicapped individuals undergoing vocational rehabilitation, among other groups. Sixty percent of those certified for the credit were youths. The TJTC appears to have been heavily used by large retail and fast food service firms. An estimated 9 percent of economically disadvantaged youths who were eligible and employed during the 1980s were hired under the tax credit.[13] It has been difficult to assess the worth of the tax credit. A recent summary of the evidence suggests modest positive employment effects for economically disadvantaged young adults under the TJTC. It is estimated that 75,000 to 100,000 jobs were subsidized by the tax credit at any point in time at a cost of $1,500 (1991 dollars) per net job created. The accompanying net employment estimate is that 40–50 percent of the jobs subsidized were net employment additions.[14] Conversely, a significant proportion of employees hired under the program would have been employed without it; the program therefore provided windfall profits to these employers. The tax credit was idled after 1994 and was not mentioned among the tax credits advocated during the 1996 election debates. Whether attention will return to it remains to be seen.

Handicapped

In 1996 the working-age severely disabled constituted about 10 percent of the total working-age population. Some 49 million Americans had a limitation in a functional activity or a social role. The Census Bureau estimated that 33.4 percent of those individuals with a work disability had less than a high school education. Fewer than a third of the disabled 24 to 64 years of age were in the work force in March 1996, including one in nine who were unemployed. Federal support of vocational rehabilitation dates back to 1921. Current federal vocational rehabilitation assistance, authorized by the 1973 Vocational Rehabilitation Act, provides services to handicapped persons regardless of their income, but many of the disabled are poor. A 1996 GAO report identifies 130 federal programs, administered by 19 different agencies, that provide services to people with disabilities. Sixty-nine of these programs are targeted exclusively to people with disabilities. Of these, 26 provide direct employment services, such as skill training and job search assistance. These employment-focused programs provided an estimated $2.5 billion to $6.1 billion in services to the disabled in 1994.[15]

The law requires administrators to give priority to the potentially employable handicapped who most need assistance. Between 1980 and 1986 federal funding for vocational rehabilitation declined by 7.5 percent. However, Congress in 1986 required that appropriations be adjusted annually for inflation. Vocational rehabilitation was funded in FY 1997 at approximately $2 billion to serve 1.2 million eligible individuals in the rehabilitation system. Vocational rehabilitation and other services enable the handicapped to work, but income support dominates government disability policy. Vocational rehabilitation represents less than 5 percent of total government expenditures for the handicapped. Most cash assistance programs require applicants to prove that they are incapable of work, which discourages them from pursuing rehabilitation. The 1996 GAO appraisal of employment-related programs targeted at the disabled concluded that such programs generally lacked interagency coordination, yielding duplicate services and service gaps simultaneously. The report also concluded that these programs were only infrequently evaluated in terms of their effectiveness.[16]

Welfare Recipients

Federal extension of AFDC to two-parent families in 1962 was soon followed by the introduction of voluntary work programs for welfare recipients. A decade later Congress mandated enrollment by welfare parents whose youngest child was at least 6 years old. However, because of limited funding and numerous exemptions only a minority of welfare recipients actually participated in work programs.

Limited support for employing and training adult AFDC recipients came from the work incentive program (WIN), initiated in 1967. WIN underwent few changes until 1981, when the Reagan administration severely reduced its funding and allowed the states to operate a number of alternative work-welfare programs, including a "workfare" program that required recipients to "work off" their welfare grant. Few states used their own funds to replenish federal budget cuts, and most continued to operate rudimentary job search programs that emphasized immediate employment instead of training. By the end of the 1980s, federal WIN funding was less than a fifth of what expenditures had been at the decade's beginning, after adjusting for inflation.

In the work-related provisions of the 1988 Family Support Act (FSA) Congress used a carrot-and-stick approach to bolster education and training assistance for AFDC recipients. The FSA required states to establish JOBS programs making education, training, and support services needed for employment available to AFDC recipients. States could choose whether to provide services directly or through local service providers. Congress specified minimum acceptable participation and targeting requirements that had to be achieved in order for a state to receive its full share of federal funding. The minimum participation requirement rose from 7 percent of AFDC recipients in 1991 to 20 percent in 1995, with a requirement that 55 percent of funds be spent on designated target groups. The federal government supplied matching funds to the states up to a maximum of $600 million in fiscal 1989, which had risen to $1.3 billion by 1995.

In requiring the states to progressively increase participation of recipients in JOBS, the law set a goal of reaching an average of 40 percent of single-parent families by 1995 and 75 percent of two-parent families by 1997. Exemptions were significantly tightened, requiring participation by parents whose youngest child was at least 3 years old, though states could require parents with 1- and 2-year-olds to enroll. Parents who refused to enroll risked losing their personal welfare payment, although payment for the children would continue. Despite these initiatives, approximately 50 percent of adults receiving AFDC were exempted from JOBS, usually because they had a young child to care for. Because of its budget, capacity, and capability constraints JOBS served about 25 percent of the remaining nonexempt population.[17]

Studies predating JOBS showed that training programs for welfare recipients generally could have a positive but modest impact on earnings but that, on average, low-cost services such as short-term job search assistance did not generate access to better jobs than would have been attainable without assistance. JOBS allowed states flexibility in offering a variety of education, training, and work programs to encourage more comprehensive service. However, JOBS funds were rarely used for skill training. Instead, welfare agencies typically used JOBS budgets to provide basic education, GED preparation, job search training, or work experience, relying upon JTPA funds for skill training. As noted earlier, the proportion of welfare recipients among JTPA enrollees rose from 32 percent to 42 percent between 1990 and 1994, and their weekly placement wages were $267 in the latter year, compared with $234 for the total II-A enrollment.

JOBS permitted use of temporary subsidies to employers to encourage hiring and training of AFDC recipients in public- and nonprofit-sector organizations as a last resort in gaining work experience. To remove obstacles to successful participation and completion of a training program, Congress expanded federal child care assistance, allowing families attaining self-support through work to retain entitlement for child and health care services for up to one year, although states could require payment for health coverage during the second half of the year. Program administrators were to give priority to long-term welfare recipients and to young parents with little education or work experience.

Evaluation of the success of JOBS in reducing welfare dependency was difficult because the JOBS management information system tended to overemphasize accountability for process measures such as the number and type of participants and to underemphasize outcome measures. Despite this, in evaluating JOBS performance the GAO noted that the states had generally done a reasonably good job of tracking participant outcomes in their local programs. All but one state monitored the number of JOBS participants entering employment, 42 states monitored the hourly wage at placement, and 26 states monitored job retention rates.[18] But that was not enough to save either the JOBS program or its AFDC parent from the rigors of the 1995–96 attack on antipoverty programs.

At the end of 1996 the Department of Health and Human Services was undertaking development of JOBS outcome measures, but, though the findings might be instructive, it was too late to save the program, which had already been abolished by the Personal Responsibility and Work Opportunity Act passed by the Congress and signed by the president two months before. Among the fundamental issues of the assessment will be the relative weights of at least two potential goals—obtaining employment quickly and obtaining the education and training needed to acquire better-paying jobs. A GAO survey of twenty-seven state JOBS directors determined that 21 percent of JOBS participants entered employment in 1993. The GAO found that few JOBS programs across the nation had a strong employment focus. However, those programs that did stress employment with the individual participant and aggressively forged links to employers showed promising results in promoting work among welfare recipients. In 1994 approximately 600,000 welfare recipients were JOBS participants in an average month. Fewer than 65,000 of these were in work experience programs or on-the job training. In contrast, the greatest concentrations of participants were in other interventions: 120,000 in postsecondary education; more than 85,000 in GED programs; 80,000 in job skill training; and 145,000 in short-term job search and job readiness activities. But these numbers were small given the more than 5 million adults on AFDC.

President Clinton promised in his 1992 campaign to "end welfare as we know it," but once in office he was reluctant to do so. Not so the House of Representatives, which in 1995, soon after the accession of a Republican majority, passed a stringent bill that the Senate resisted for a year before passing with substantial softening compromises, only to have it vetoed by President Clinton. It was more the coming election than further compromises that led to the passage of the Personal Responsibility and Work Opportunity Act in August of 1996. As noted earlier, the new act ended AFDC as an entitlement and substituted the Temporary Assistance to Needy Families (TANF) block grant program. In ending AFDC it also ended JOBS, replacing its long-term and even plodding employability development approach with imminent requirements for work activities in exchange for time-limited assistance. TANF recipients must work after two years of assistance. Twenty-five percent of all families in each state are to be engaged in work activities or to have left the public assistance rolls in FY 1997, and 50 percent by FY 2002. Work activities include unsubsidized or subsidized employment, OJT, work experience, community service, or up to twelve months of vocational training. Providing child care services to others participating in community service or engaging in up to six weeks of job search can count toward the work requirement, with limitation on the proportion of a state's caseload that can be so engaged. Families receiving assistance for five years, or less if the state chooses, will be ineligible for further cash assistance under TANF, except for a 20 percent exemption for those found to be nonemployable. Some non-cash assistance options will remain for the states through other funding sources. The new law also mandates mutual assessment of recipient skills and aptitudes and encourages development of personal employability plans guiding needed education, training, and job placement and intervention. TANF implies a faith that job opportunities for those on public assistance rolls can be identified for which recipients are or can be job-ready. There is no past experience to support that supposition, which will be put to the test soon in states with prescribed shorter grace periods and by the end of the century in the nation as a whole.

Dislocated Workers

Dislocated or displaced workers are individuals with significant previous job tenure who have lost a job due to slack work, job abolition, or plant closure. The Congressional Budget Office has estimated that, on average, some 2 million American workers were displaced annually during the 1980s. Displacement has continued at a similar rate into the 1990s. Although not necessarily poor, dislocated workers face the prospect of impoverishment if they remain unemployed for long periods. In 1982, in the midst of severe budget cuts for employment and training programs, concern for the rising numbers of workers displaced because of foreign competition and automation led Congress to incorporate a new training component into JTPA for these workers, Title III. Initially the program was relatively small, but funding grew over time as policy focused on economic dislocation, in part to justify relaxation of international trade barriers. In 1988 Congress authorized a tripling of funding, to the $1 billion level; appropriations for FY 1997 reached $1.3 billion. The expansion of funding in programs for dislocated workers in the late 1980s and 1990s is in sharp contrast to funding of programs for disadvantaged adults and youths, which can best be described as stagnant over this time period.

JTPA Title III programming built on the foundation of the Trade Adjustment Act (TAA), which offers benefit payments and reemployment services to workers who lose their job or have their hours of work or wages reduced as a result of an increase in imports. However, Title III services are available to victims of any large-scale dislocations. Services include training, job search and relocation allowances, as well as weekly trade adjustment allowances following exhaustion of unemployment benefits as long as the individual is enrolled in a certified training program. A variant of TAA, the NAFTA Transitional Adjustment Assistance program took effect with the North American Free Trade Agreement in 1994. To access benefits or services, workers must provide evidence that their job loss or reduction in wages or hours is due to increased imports from, or movement of jobs to, Canada or Mexico.

Data on dislocated worker programs reflect a population that has been well and steadily employed and needs primarily to be restored to that status. Fewer than a third of program participants are poor or near poor. For those with substantial skills local project operators have emphasized short-term, low-cost assistance designed to get them back to work without additional training. Two-thirds of enrollees receive job search assistance, which often lasts no more than a few days. Nevertheless, the proportion receiving retraining fluctuated from 56 percent to 64 percent between program years 1990 and 1994. And the training paid off. In program year 1994, when 188,000 were enrolled, those trained had a placement rate at termination of 76 percent and a wage recovery rate of 93.6 percent, compared with 63 percent and 86.2 percent, respectively, for those Title III participants who were not retrained. Unlike in the case of JTPA Title II-A disadvantaged adults, Title III placement rates and placement wages have not been correlated with their length of training, being more dependent upon their current skills. Although a fifth of enrollees did not complete high school, a factor related more to their age than to their predilections, they have made little use of remedial help—only one in twenty participants receive basic education instruction. Yet 71 percent of all JTPA Title III participants in 1994 and 1995 were placed, and 73.4 percent remained employed at a thirteen-week follow-up. Training gains were indicated by the fact that 76 percent of those who undertook skill training were employed at completion and at follow-up. However, the superior position of those who did not appear to need retraining was indicated by the fact that their prelayoff wage had averaged $12.52, their placement wage averaged $10.52, and their follow-up wage averaged $10.76, compared with $11.45, $9.75, and $9.82, respectively, for the skill trainees. That the placement wages were less than the predisplacement wages is an indication of the losses from displacement and the difficulty of catching up with the gains of longevity despite additional training. According to one estimate, the average displaced worker loses $80,000 of earnings. The authors concluded that retraining of at least two years' duration—equivalent to the time it takes to obtain an associate's degree—would be necessary to restore their earning power.[19]

In separate 1988 legislation, the Worker Adjustment and Retraining Notification (WARN) Act, Congress required establishments employing more than one hundred full-time workers to provide two months' notice to employees who lose their jobs because of plant shutdowns or major layoffs. The advance notice was to cushion job loss by allowing workers to initiate their job search sooner than they otherwise would have, reducing unemployment duration and resulting in better job matches. Evidence suggests that WARN decreases joblessness by only small amounts on average but that it has been associated with somewhat higher postdisplacement earnings.[20] Nearly one-half of employers who gave WARN notices reported that their displaced employees found new jobs more quickly than otherwise would have been the case. Sixty-one percent of employers experienced little or no costs as a result of the notices. But the alternatives available, even with warning, are limited by local labor market conditions.

Elderly

The senior community service employment program, designed to alleviate joblessness among the poor aged 55 or older, is the only remaining adult public service jobs program. Individuals in households with incomes below 125 percent of the poverty line are eligible to participate in the program. Funded at $463 million in fiscal

1997, the program is one of few employment and training efforts that has not faced severe funding reductions. The funds provided about 150,000 part-time jobs.

An unusual provision of the senior employment program requires the Labor Department to allocate 78 percent of the funds to eight national contractors (the largest being Green Thumb, Inc., and the National Council of Senior Citizens) and the remaining 22 percent to the states. The majority of participants work in recreation centers and parks, social service agencies, schools, or nutrition agencies for the elderly. Apart from their experiences on the job, few enrollees receive any training. Participants are permitted to work twenty to twenty-five hours per week up to thirteen hundred hours per year. The median length of stay in the program is almost a year, but because some participants remain for much longer the mean is nearly two years.

Adult Education

Nearly 90 million American adults have deficient literacy skills. Congress passed the Adult Education Act (AEA) to help the states fund programs that enable adults to acquire the basic skills they need in order to benefit from job training, as well as to increase their life satisfaction. AEA's state grant program makes grants to the states on the basis of the number of people who are at least 16 years old, are not required to be in school, and lack a high school degree. In 1995 about 4 million adults were enrolled in classes funded by the program. Federal funding for that year was $252 million, and state and local sources provided an additional $890 million. Federal funds outweighed state and local contributions to the program from 1966 to 1980, but the opposite condition has prevailed since.

Programs funded under AEA play an important part in providing the basic skills needed by the clients of federal employment and training programs such as JTPA and vocational education. The National Literacy Act of 1991 amended the AEA and authorized several new programs. Major provisions included the creation of a National Institute for Literacy, the establishment of state and regional literacy resource centers, and the requirement for the Department of Education to develop model indicators of program quality to guide states in developing their own indicators for improved program evaluation.

It is easier to ascertain AEA's input than its output, with 59 percent of the funds going to local education agencies, 15 percent to community colleges, 14 percent to community-based organizations, and 12 percent to other entities.[21] The program lacks a specific goal, but its availability is an obvious boon to programs like JTPA and JOBS, which are struggling to improve the employability of those lacking basic education as well as job skills.

Native Americans

Of the various programs designed to serve Native Americans only the JTPA Section 401 Indian and Native American (INA) program will be mentioned here. There were 180 grantees, mostly Indian tribes, serving 24,425 participants in program year 1994, down from 28,106 in 1990. Though nearly three-fourths of the participants were high school graduates, 55 percent had low reading skills and 68 percent had low math skills; 53 percent had not worked during the previous year. Therefore, 14 percent received basic skill training, while 27 percent were given occupational skills and another 27 percent work experience; 7 percent were provided training while on the job. Because of the economic conditions on Indian reservations, only 50 percent of INA participants were placed in jobs, averaging $6.17 an hour. However, a total of 80 percent had some positive outcome; they either found a job, obtained a GED, returned to school full-time, advanced to further education or training, or attained a skill proficiency or a worksite training objective. All would have preferred job placement, but the other outcome provided some positive use of time.

The Effectiveness of Employment and Training

Evaluations indicate that employment and training programs enhance the earnings and employment of participants, although the effects vary by service population, are often modest because of brief training durations and the inherent difficulty of alleviating long-term deficiencies, and are not always cost effective within a benefit-cost framework. Employment and training programs for adult women have consistently been shown to produce modest earnings gains that persist over time. The gains have been associated with almost all types of interventions (e.g., OJT, classroom training, work experience, job search assistance, basic skill training), and earnings increases have been shown as resulting from increases in both hourly wage rates and the number of work hours. Earnings gains of adult men, though positive, have been more modest than those of adult women. Job search training has proved to be an effective strategy for facilitating employment, but since it does not increase job skills, it generally returns its disadvantaged users to their previous level of earnings. Displaced workers lose jobs in which they have invested longevity and have been rewarded for seniority. Therefore, retraining them cannot be expected to immediately return them to their previous level of earnings. The impact of employment and training programs for youths, especially males, has seldom been positive in terms of earnings gains. Job Corps training is an exception; it has consistently shown a significant positive earnings impact, as well as positive benefit-cost ratios, but at a high cost per enrollee because of the cost of providing residence.

Employment and training programs enhance participants' employability, but the gains are modest, perhaps in part because funds are inadequate to provide lengthier training. Congress has displayed a propensity for establishing new programs without substantially increasing appropriations. Current funding permits limited assistance to only about one in fifteen of those who are eligible for assistance. Classroom training is demonstrably more effective than many other possible services for many of the disadvantaged, but it requires lengthy participation and is consequently often expensive. It is a sobering thought that human resource investment on behalf of the nondisadvantaged generally returns about 10¢ for every dollar annually, really not a bad rate of interest.[22] For instance, with the cost per participant in JTPA II-A at $2,165 and per entered employment at $7,378 in 1994, the added annual earning capacity could not be expected to be more than $738 for a disadvantaged worker. In addition, strict limits on stipends and support services have precluded many eligible persons from enrolling in or completing the classroom training—the poor cannot eat training. Finally, the virtual eradication of the public service jobs program in 1981 removed a potent weapon from the antipoverty arsenal because even during economic recovery periods many of the poor may be unable to find work.

After nearly thirty-five years of experience the value of "second chance" training has been proven, but so has the old adage that "you get what you pay for." Funding has been available to enroll no more than a margin of those eligible. Training durations have always been limited by available funds, which have not kept up with inflation. Training of such short duration could prepare only the moderately disadvantaged for low-level jobs; this is better than nothing but far from what it could be.

Employment Service

Established in 1933, the federal-state employment service—the Job Service—attempts to match employers with job seekers, who are mostly unemployed or poor, through a nationwide network of more than eighteen hundred offices. Changing congressional mandates have pulled the service in a variety of directions since the 1960s. Severely deficient and declining funding and competing pressures to assist unemployment insurance recipients, employers, the poor, veterans, welfare clients, food stamp beneficiaries, and other groups have precluded local offices from offering comprehensive services to the millions who seek assistance. The employment service has responsibilities to many different programs, some unrelated to its original labor-exchange role. Reduced budgets have forced persistent staff cuts, eliminating personalized services such as counseling and leaving job seekers to rely on self-help access to information about job openings. Nevertheless, though the number served has tended to decline in recent years, the number placed has been maintained (table 5.3).

Of the nearly 19 million served in 1994, 2.9 were economically disadvantaged. The basic fact remains that the public employment service ends up with the jobs that are hardest to fill and the applicants that are hardest to place just because the other job matches occur informally. But that fact makes the service even more essential. Computerization is expanding the reach of the public employment service but reducing its control of the placement function. All Job Service listings are now on the Internet, accessible to all with the capability of using it. America's Job Bank, a computerized national labor exchange network, links the state employment service offices across the nation to help job seekers and employers find each other. In April 1996 there were 400,000 job listings and 5.3 million applicant inquiries. Also on the Internet, America's Talent Bank, operated nationwide through the public employment service system, provides a database of résumés that employers can search through electronically.

Declining federal funding and a greater permissiveness within the system were resulting in a greater diversity among the various state systems at the end of 1996. The national emphasis on one-stop career information services, not all of which were in the hands of the public employment service, was bringing about radical changes in the system. Many states were in the process of substantially reorganizing their work force development systems, with differential impacts on the roles of their public employment service agencies. One could posit that more change was under way in the system, for better and for worse, than at any time since the inauguration of antipoverty efforts in the 1960s.

Table 5.3. Employment Service Performance, Program Years 1992–1994

	Program Year		
	1992	*1993*	*1994*
Total applicants	21,346,336	20,195,029	18,809,907
Received some services	11,994,392	11,827,016	11,990,268
Referred to employment	7,971,650	8,094,603	8,217,656
Job placement by ES	2,697,298	2,734,265	2,681,839
Individuals placed as percentage of those referred	33.6%	33.8%	32.6%
Entered employment	3,266,120	3,308,217	3,358,152
Percentage of applicants entering employment	15.3%	16.4%	17.9%
UI claimant applicants	10,436,910	9,235,977	7,662,050
Referred to employment	2,439,458	2,336,603	2,223,657
Percentage referred to employment	23.4%	25.3%	29.0%
Cost per entered employment	$240	$249	$246
Job openings received	5,743,558	6,342,957	6,619,420
Job openings filled	3,372,369	3,557,852	3,525,136
Percentage of job openings filled	58.6%	56.1%	53.3%
Average wage at placement	$7.78	$7.89	$7.27
Total expenditure ($ millions)	$782.3	$824.1	$825.2

Source: National Governors Association, *Current Developments in Employment and Training*, 16 March 1995.

Equal Employment Opportunity

Job discrimination has been a major cause of poverty among blacks, Hispanics, other minority groups, families headed by females, and the aged. The federal government took halting steps in the 1940s to combat racial discrimination in the workplace, but not until the 1960s did all three branches broadly challenge many discriminatory employment practices. Major equal employment opportunity laws include:

The 1963 Equal Pay Act, requiring that men and women be provided equal pay for equal work.

Title VII of the 1964 Civil Rights Act, forbidding employment discrimination on the basis of race, sex, religion, or national origin. It specifies unlawful employment practices, including both disparate treatment and disparate impact. The 1972 State and Local Assistance Act allows the federal government to terminate aid to states and localities that violate Title VII.

Executive Order 11246, signed by President Johnson in 1965, requiring federal contractors with contracts in excess of $10,000 to abide by the provisions of the Civil Rights Act and to set and implement affirmative action plans.

The 1967 Age Discrimination in Employment Act, which currently bans discrimination against workers aged 40 or older.

The 1973 Vocational Rehabilitation Act, which enjoins contractors and programs receiving federal funds not to discriminate in the hiring and promotion of qualified disabled individuals.

The 1990 Americans With Disabilities Act, requiring that state and local governments and private employers of fifteen or more employees not discriminate against qualified individuals with a disability. The act requires employers to make reasonable accommodation for the disabled unless such would cause undue hardship to the employer.[23]

The Civil Rights Act of 1991, which overturned several Supreme Court decisions weakening antidiscrimination efforts and also substantially increased the penalties for violating equal employment opportunity laws.

In addition to congressional and presidential action, many states have enacted antidiscriminatory laws. Some of these laws are tougher than the federal regulations and apply to small firms that are often exempt from federal coverage.

Antidiscriminatory efforts in the 1960s focused on the hiring and promotion process, an approach that can reduce but not necessarily prohibit bias. For example, an employer may fulfill the letter of the law by soliciting and considering applications from minorities but never actually hiring any. For this reason the federal government, especially the Supreme Court, subsequently placed more emphasis on results instead of intent and process. In *Griggs v. Duke Power Co.* (1979) the court forbad superficially neutral employment practices that, while not job-related, had an adverse impact on protected classes. The occasion was recruitment and selection examinations and high school graduation requirements that could not be shown to be job-related yet adversely impacted African American applicants. In *Steelworkers v. Weber,* in the same year, the Court endorsed an employer's voluntary racial affirmative action plan as long as it was designed to overcome an existing imbalance in employment relative to the population of the relevant labor market; was only temporary, lasting only until the imbalance was eradicated; and did not "unnecessarily trammel" the rights of the majority workers. The Supreme Court also expanded the interpretation of two post–Civil War laws, the Civil Rights Acts of 1866 and 1871, to proscribe job discrimination.

Until the 1980s, the Equal Employment Opportunity Commission (EEOC), established by Congress to enforce Title VII of the Civil Rights Act, and the Office of Federal Contract Compliance Programs, which monitors the executive orders, aggressively pursued antidiscriminatory policies. The EEOC did not initially possess direct enforcement authority, but after 1972 Congress allowed the agency to sue violators of equal employment opportunity laws. The agency targeted large employers and used class action suits to maximize its effectiveness.

Federal equal employment policy changed significantly during the 1980s. The Reagan administration limited enforcement to the most flagrant violations by requiring that intent to discriminate be established before remedial action was taken and by rejecting numerical affirmative action goals. Budget cuts reduced EEOC staff size, and the agency filed fewer court cases and did not initiate the class action suits and broad impact cases it had pursued previously. The Supreme Court rejected the Reagan administration's interpretation of equal employment laws throughout most of the 1980s but abruptly reversed itself in several far-ranging 1989 decisions that overruled several previous decisions, including *Griggs* but not *Weber,* and substantially weakened enforcement powers. Congress, still in Democratic hands, reacted violently in its Civil Rights Act of 1991, not only restoring conditions close to those previously overruled but increasing penalties by providing for jury trials and allowing limited compensatory and punitive damages.

President Bush was as aggressive as the Democratic Congress in pushing for the Americans With Disabilities Act of 1990. However, by the mid-1990s the tide seemed to be turning against equal employment opportunity enforcement, with increasing criticism centering upon affirmative action; it was increasingly argued that affirmative action's time had passed, that women and minorities were no longer in need of special assistance.

Minimum Wages

Even if discrimination were completely eliminated, the persistence of poverty among the working poor testifies to the maldistribution of societal rewards for work and the need for improvement. Even full-time employment is not a sure escape from poverty. In 1995 a worker would have had to earn $4.95 an hour and worked at least 2,000 hours annually to lift a family of three out of poverty. At the then minimum hourly wage of $4.25 a family head with two dependents working full-time year-round earned only 73 percent of the poverty threshold (figure 5.2).

In 1989 more than 3.8 million adults were employed at or below the minimum wage, which stood at $3.35 an hour, the same rate it had been since 1981, while the cost of living had risen by 40 percent during that period. In 1989 Congress raised the statutory minimum hourly rate to $3.85 effective 1 April 1990 and to $4.25 effective a year later. It remained at $4.25 until 1 October 1996, when it was increased to $4.75, and an increase to $5.15 per hour was mandated for 1 September 1997. Some 2 million American workers were employed at $4.25 per hour, and another 2.2 million received between this wage and $4.74 at the time of the 1996 change. It has been estimated that some 300,000 people, including 100,000 children, living in poverty will have household incomes above the current poverty level as a result of the increase to $5.15 in the autumn of 1997.

Though most of the low-paying jobs are filled by part-time or secondary earners, a significant number of employed family heads are unable to escape poverty. In 1993 one-fifth of all of the employable

Figure 5.2. Minimum-wage earnings for a full-time, year-round worker, 1970–1995

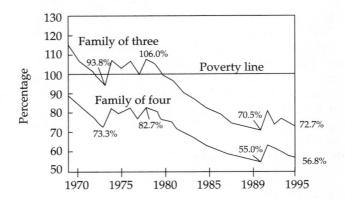

Source: U.S. Department of Labor.

poor aged 25–54—about 2.5 million people—worked full-time year-round without escaping poverty. Nearly one-half worked year-round but not full-time.[24]

The plight of the adult working poor receives little attention in the training and employment programs already described. These programs tend to be preoccupied with the unemployed, youths, and those outside the work force. The goal of most training programs is full-time employment; that this may be no real solution to poverty is often ignored, as are the needs of those who are already laboring at low-paying full-time jobs.

The minimum wage is perhaps the most direct and comprehensive measure to increase the earnings of the working poor. The objective of the Fair Labor Standards Act (FLSA), enacted in 1938, was to achieve, as rapidly as practicable, minimum-wage levels that would sustain the health, efficiency, and general well-being of all workers. Because an unduly high or rapidly rising minimum might price many low-productivity jobs out of existence, the gains from higher wages have to be balanced against the losses from job elimination.

On the assumption that a low-paying job is better than no job at all, Congress has acted incrementally and prudently in applying the law over the years. It has established minimum wages that directly affect only a limited number of employees at the bottom of the economic ladder. About four out of five nonsupervisory workers are covered by the minimum wage. Still not covered are about 10 million private-sector nonsupervisory employees, many of them in low-wage occupations, primarily in retail trade, service industries, and agriculture. A 1985 Supreme Court decision extended the federal minimum-wage protection to state and local workers.

The favorable impact of minimum-wage rates is reduced to the extent that employers find it unprofitable to retain or hire workers at the government-imposed wage levels, resulting in job loss or reduced work opportunities rather than higher earnings. True to the adage that there is no free lunch, the minimum wage does entail some costs. Because many factors are involved, it is difficult to determine the extent of job loss due to the federal minimum wage. The available evidence indicates that the minimum-wage legislation has raised the total income of the poor and that any losses it caused in employment and earnings were more than compensated by the increased earnings it brought to the majority. This is, of course, little comfort to individuals who lost their jobs as a result of such increases. Nor do studies of changes affecting those now employed tell the whole story. Future demand for labor might be dampened, closing off potential job growth for those who might otherwise have been hired.

Some advocates have argued for setting minimum-wage rates high enough to eliminate poverty among all full-time workers. Regrettably, such pronouncements are more rhetoric than serious policy alternatives. Reasonable people may differ on whether the minimum wage should be adjusted to a predetermined proportion—say, 50 percent—of average wages in American industry. There can be little doubt, however, that excessively rapid boosts in the minimum wage would cause serious economic dislocations and loss of jobs. It would be a case of killing the goose that lays the golden egg, even if the minimum wage would buy little gold. Eliminating jobs is not the way to fight poverty.

The earned income tax credit (EITC) is arguably less direct than the minimum wage in increasing the earnings of the working poor because of the delay between the act of work and the receipt of the tax credit. It does, however, have the advantage of not directly altering the wage bargain between employer and employee. The EITC and the minimum wage can be companion tools in fighting poverty. A family of four with one worker working full-time year-round at $5.15 (the post–September 1997 minimum wage) would earn $10,300. This worker would receive the maximum EITC of $3,560 and food stamps worth $2,876 and would pay $788 in payroll taxes. Earnings at the higher minimum wage plus the EITC and the value of the food stamps would exceed the applicable poverty line of $15,600.

The United States has experimented with differential minimum wages, differentiating on the basis of age and experience. In passing the 1989 minimum-wage amendments, Congress provided a subminimum wage equal to 85 percent of the minimum wage for teenagers with limited work experience during the initial three months of employment. The lower minimum wage could be extended for another three months if the teenagers were in certified training programs. The notion of a youth subminimum is based on the assertion that setting the minimum at some percentage of the statutory minimum during the initial six months of employment would encourage employers to hire young workers entering the work force. However, teenagers account for only a quarter of the low-wage earners, and employers willing to hire disadvantaged youths and AFDC recipients qualified for a generous subsidy under the TJTC, discussed above. Moreover, there is no guarantee that if more jobs became available for youths, the gains would not be at the expense of adult workers.

It is questionable whether a reduced minimum wage would have a significant impact on youth unemployment. The major causes of unemployment among black teenagers and other disadvantaged groups must be sought elsewhere. First, the liberalization and expansion of various income support measures, including AFDC, have offered a minimal measure of income maintenance to young women with children. Some may have preferred to subsist on relief rather than to work at very low wages. Second, some black unemployment reflects the fact that jobs once open to blacks in central cities disappeared with the exodus of middle-class white and black families. As jobs moved to suburbia, the demand for black labor declined. Many residents of slum areas become economically stranded because of inadequate public transportation. Third, an indeterminate but probably not insignificant number of individuals recorded as unemployed may be engaged in the subterranean economy, where their employment goes unrecorded. According to one estimate, one of every four black males residing in inner cities derives his income in the underground economy.[25]

Proponents concede that in order to minimize the dangers of unemployment and inflationary pressures, minimum wages should be raised no more rapidly than average wages in American industry. While little is known about productivity trends in low-wage industries, it is reasonable to assume that the rise in productivity in these industries is no greater than in the rest of the American economy. If this estimate is correct, a rule of thumb might be that boosts in the minimum wage should be no larger than average productivity increases plus increases in the cost of living.

Although coverage of the minimum wage has expanded over the years to include nearly nine of every ten nonsupervisory employees, Congress has failed on several occasions to maintain the purchasing power of the minimum wage. As noted above, in the 1980s the inflation-adjusted value of the minimum wage declined by nearly a third. One way both to adjust the minimum wage to increasing living costs and to avoid the discontinuities of infrequent but large jumps is to index the minimum to a cost of living in line with automatic adjustments applied to social security and other benefits. Congress has thus far rejected any proposal to index minimum wages.

While the past achievements of the minimum wage should not be downgraded, it would be unrealistic to rely too heavily upon it as a tool to combat poverty. The EITC is more important as an antipoverty weapon on behalf of parents, but it ignores the needs of the working poor who do not have responsibility for supporting children. The minimum wage provides help to all individuals. And a government check presumably is not as rewarding to wage earners as direct payment for their labors. Policymakers must consider the trade-off between boosting the minimum wage in order to reduce poverty and the possible elimination of jobs that might result. In the final analysis, conclusions regarding the impact of minimum-wage legislation upon aggregate employment and unemployment depend on value judgments, and whatever the conclusion, some relevant facts can be found to support it. If society is determined to reduce poverty at a more rapid rate than in the past, it will have to rely upon additional tools, including an expanded earned income tax credit.

Migrant and Seasonal Farmworkers

Many American farmworkers and their families live and work under conditions that are cruel and harsh by any standard. The conclusions of the 1978 presidential commission that examined the problems of migrant and seasonal farm laborers remain valid today: "They are ill-housed, undernourished, face enormous health hazards, are underpaid, underemployed, undereducated, socially isolated, politically powerless, excluded from much of the work-protective legislation that other American workers take for granted."

Migrant and seasonal farm work emerged as an occupation in the latter part of the nineteenth century, when farmers began specializing in a single crop. Large farms offered plentiful employment to immigrants from many countries, although the jobs were temporary and paid little. The first large-scale government program to import Mexicans began in 1917, coinciding with labor shortages and a temporary halt to immigration caused by World War I. Similar labor shortages during World War II led Congress in 1942 to authorize the importation of temporary Mexican farmworkers, called "braceros," whose ranks had swelled to 450,000 annually by the late 1950s.

Concern over the destitute plight of migrant and seasonal farmworkers led the federal government to end the bracero program in 1964. The decline of cheap immigrant labor and widespread consumer sympathy demonstrated through boycotts enabled laborers to gain some improvement in working conditions.

The migrant and seasonal farmworker population has decreased significantly due to mechanization and because large-scale operations have replaced family farms. The number of migrant workers, the poorest group, reached an estimated postwar high of 477,000 in 1959 before dropping by two-thirds during the next three decades. Illegal aliens probably add several hundred thousand to the official count of migrant and seasonal farmworkers.

Migrant and seasonal farmworkers, together with domestic workers and day laborers, are most likely to be excluded from the legal and social safety net protections afforded other workers. Most states exempt migrant and seasonal farmworkers from coverage under workers' compensation and unemployment insurance programs, and even if they are covered their meager earnings ensure that they receive little or no benefits. Children of migrant workers may have to interrupt schooling as their families move from job to job.

Workplace protection laws are more likely to exclude than to cover migrant and seasonal farmworkers. The federal minimum-wage law excluded farmworkers until 1966, and until 1978 it established a lower minimum for them. The minimum-wage, child labor, and overtime provisions of the current Fair Labor Standards Act remain riddled with exceptions excluding farmworkers. Even self-help opportunities are limited because farmworkers, unlike other workers, have no legal right to organize or join unions.

Federal social welfare programs have not completely neglected the pressing needs of migrant and seasonal farmworkers. Section 402 of JTPA Title IV provides a program for migrant and seasonal farmworkers. In program year 1994, 53 grantees served a total of 46,310 individuals. Because the program is designed to serve entire families, 65 percent received emergency services only, such as housing, meals, transportation, or medical assistance. The program has since increasingly focused on employability, with the percentage of participants attaining a skill enhancement up from 37 percent in 1990 to 51 percent in 1994. The program serves twice as many school dropouts and seven times as many participants with limited English proficiency as does JTPA Title II-A. To increase basic skills, one-half of trainees in JTPA Title IV received classroom training in 1994, up from 34 percent in 1990. Still, at a cost of $4,000 per completer, more than 60 percent are placed in jobs averaging $6.17 per hour. In addition, Head Start, Title I education funding, farmworker activities of the employment service, and the migrant health program all target migrant and seasonal farmworkers at an annual cost of $500 million.

Undocumented Immigrants

Between 1981 and 1990, 38 million individuals legally immigrated to the United States. Twelve million emigrated, yielding a net immigration of 26 million. There were more than 720,000 legal immigrants in 1995, 10 percent less than in 1994 and 20 percent less than in 1993. Although far from the major source of legal immigration to the United States, African immigration increased by 59 percent in 1995. This increase was largely due to the Immigration and Naturalization Service's new Diversity Program, which allows for up to 55,000 immigrants per year from countries that have provided relatively low levels of immigration in the past.

Federal law attempts to limit the number of immigrants but is often overwhelmed by foreigners seeking a better life and employers desiring cheap labor. Consequently, many undocumented aliens reside in the United States illegally, but their number is difficult to ascertain because, for obvious reasons, they avoid government enumerators. A large proportion of undocumented immigrants are undoubtedly poor; however, they may not be counted in the published statistics. Many were poor upon entering the United States, they may lack schooling or facility in English, and their illegal status often bars them from taking advantage of assistance that could help them escape poverty.

Estimates of the number of illegal immigrants vary widely, from 5 million to 15 million. To stem the inflow of illegal immigrants, the Immigration Reform and Control Act (IRCA) of 1986 instituted sanctions on employers who hired them. It was amended by the Immigration and Nationality Act of 1990. Employers face civil fines of up to $10,000 and a criminal penalty of up to $3,000 for each illegal alien hired, as well as a maximum six months' imprisonment. In the fifteen-month period after the sanctions were fully implemented on 1 June 1988 three thousand fines were levied; the average penalty was $4,600.

The 1986 immigration law also included a major humanitarian component in that it offered amnesty to large numbers of immigrants who had entered the country illegally. Almost 3.1 million illegal residents applied for amnesty under two separate provisions. Nearly 1.8 million applied under the program that granted amnesty to individuals who had lived in the United States continuously since 1982. Another 1.3 million applied for amnesty under a special agricultural worker program, which qualified farmworkers employed for at least ninety days between May 1985 and April 1986.

The vast majority of amnesty applicants were young single men from Mexico. Over half of the total lived in California. Contrary to popular stereotypes, only a minority of those applying under the post-1981 residency provision were farmworkers. Prior to immigration, 40 percent of them had been, but only 16 percent found their first U.S. job on a farm and only 6 percent were still employed in agriculture at the time of their application for amnesty. Instead, at the time of application most aliens performed unskilled work as operators, fabricators, or laborers (34%) or had service jobs (30%).

Refugees admitted to the United States under special provisions are another source of immigration, numbering about 100,000 annually. In recent years they have originated primarily from Southeast Asia and the former Soviet Union and have usually been poor. Almost half reside in California. The law requires the federal government to reimburse states for up to 100 percent of the costs of providing refugees with cash and medical assistance during their first two years in the United States, but Congress has not provided adequate funding for doing so.

Legal immigration since 1965 has given first priority in granting immigrant visas to spouses, children, parents, and, to a lesser degree, siblings of American citizens with the intent to unite families. Worker skills are given lower priority, and then only when there is a proven shortage of those skills within the country. Hence, whereas historically most immigrants were young men, many of whom were skilled workers, a rising portion of immigrants are outside of the active work force ages and lack either education or skills. As immigrants have competed for jobs more directly with women, poorly educated youths, and the aged, animosity has risen. An unprecedented proportion are recipients of various public programs.

California passed laws in 1995 and 1996 forbidding the provision of education and other services to the children of undocumented workers, their parents being already deprived and some of the children being automatically eligible by birth for American citizenship. The 1996 welfare reform legislation denied even legal immigrants access to Supplemental Security Income, food stamps, and other welfare provisions. From a historical position that immigration bettered the lot not only of the immigrant but of the domestic population at large, economists have begun to swing to the position that there are winners and losers, with the poor suffering from immigrant competition and the affluent profiting from lower labor costs and the balance between the positives and negatives still on the plus side, but by a narrow—and narrowing—margin.[26]

Economic Development Programs

For myriad reasons rooted in regional economic trends and often in unique local conditions, poverty tends to concentrate in specific geographic locations. Declining employment opportunities, high rates of out-migration, low per capita income, underdeveloped infrastructure, low educational attainment of the population, and a high percentage of minority components interact in some localities to produce labor surplus or "depressed areas." The areas themselves vary. Poverty pockets exist in otherwise prosperous metropolitan areas, in underdeveloped rural areas, and in isolated or stagnating regions cut off from the rest of the economy. Some are as small as an inner-city neighborhood or Indian reservation; others are as large as major sections of the rural South or Appalachia. The problems faced by rural and urban areas differ but are related. The out-migration plaguing many rural areas has resulted in an influx of unskilled migrants into the cities, whose affluent classes in turn have fled to the suburbs, creating poverty ghettos in the inner cities. Depressed urban and rural areas fail to attract new economic enterprise because they frequently lack adequate public facilities, and the work force tends to be deficiently educated and poorly trained.

While the history of federal efforts to promote business investment and create jobs can be traced to the New Deal programs of the 1930s, several federal economic development programs emerged in the 1960s and received increased emphasis under the Carter administration in the late 1970s. During the 1980s, funding for the major federal economic development programs—the community development block grant (CDBG) under the Department of Housing and Urban Development (HUD) and grant and loan programs under the Economic Development Administration, the Appalachian Regional Commission, and the Agriculture Department—declined substantially. Only a fraction of what the federal government spends for the above programs is allotted to specific economic development programs.

The Reagan administration sought to rely on free market operations and local or private-sector initiatives, including coordination of economic development activities with job training programs under the JTPA. In addition, it initiated "enterprise zones" as a vehicle for federal economic development assistance. The Bush administration favored similar policies, with then HUD Secretary Jack Kemp a strong proponent of enterprise zones.

Enterprise zones were economically distressed areas targeted for economic growth and job creation. During the 1980s thirty-seven states began more than five hundred enterprise zones and Congress established a federal enterprise zone program under the authority of the Housing and Community Development Act of 1987. The federal program mandated HUD to select 100 enterprise zones, one-third of them in rural areas, taking into account a number of criteria, including unemployment, poverty, income, and migration. Most states provide tax and regulatory relief to entice new businesses to locate within the zones. The initiative has continued during the Clinton years, with the typical label changes to denote political ownership, "enterprise zones" becoming "empowerment zones." The Omnibus Budget Reconciliation Act of 1993 authorized 9 empowerment zones and 95 enterprise communities. Urban empowerment zones receive $100 million, rural empowerment zones receive up to $40 million, and enterprise communities receive $3 million.

The viability of enterprise zones is still to be proven. Critics of the concept claim that enterprise zones often do not create new business but may attract existing business from other areas. In addition, tax incentives and relief from government regulations are rarely sufficient to lure new business into a distressed area. Other economic factors, such as the availability of a skilled work force, the state of the infrastructure, or general living amenities, are normally more important considerations. Finally, enterprise zones may be divisive to the community in that they may have adverse impacts on businesses and workers located within the zones or nearby areas.

The largest federal economic development program, the CDBG, with a $4.6 billion budget in 1995, supports various housing, public works, and economic development projects intended to benefit poor and moderate-income persons, remove urban blight, or meet community development needs. CDBG funding declined substantially during the 1980s, while the number of communities eligible for CDBG assistance increased, reducing the average community grant by a third.

The CDBG program has two components targeting urban areas with populations greater than 50,000 and a separate component for smaller communities, about 70 percent of available funds going to this purpose. The remaining 30 percent is allocated to participating states. Over a three-year period at least 70 percent of program funds are required to be used on activities that benefit low- and moderate-income people. Empowerment zones receive employer tax credits of 20 percent of the first $15,000 of wages or training expenses per enterprise, tax-free facility bonds of up to $3 million, and an additional $20,000 tax deduction for qualified business investments within the empowerment zone. About 13 percent of the urban funds are spent directly on economic development activities, including loans and grants to businesses for renovation and construction of commercial buildings, purchasing of equipment and land, and repair or construction of infrastructure, such as street repairs, and renovations of building facades. The small cities program spends about 11 percent of its funds on economic development activities.

The mandate of the Commerce Department's Economic Development Administration (EDA) is to encourage business investment and create jobs in areas where there is a labor surplus. Whatever the potential of the program, its very modest resources have been spread thinly. Although 90 percent of the U.S. population live in areas that are eligible for EDA assistance, the agency claims that it targets assistance to areas with high chronic rates of unemployment, high concentrations of low-income families, and high rates of business failures or farm foreclosures. EDA provides grants, loan guarantees, and technical assistance for public works and business development assistance projects, of which nearly 70 percent over the years has been awarded to communities for public works projects.

The Farmers Home Administration (FmHA) administers related programs focusing on rural economic development. Authorized by the Rural Development Act of 1972, FmHA programs provide grants, loans, loan guarantees, and technical assistance to develop business activity in rural communities. Priority for grants and loans is given to lower-income communities or communities that are unable to obtain credit from a private lender.

While federal aid to areas with a chronic labor surplus and high concentrations of poverty may offer significant boosts to local economies, it remains virtually impossible to separate the impact of federal policies from the impact of continual fluctuations in business cycles and regional growth trends. In itself, federal economic development assistance is rarely provided in the massive or concentrated doses necessary to reverse the economic decline of truly distressed areas.

The effectiveness of programs for distressed areas in fighting poverty is even less clear. The federal policies toward distressed areas rely on a "trickle down" approach, concentrating on aid to the business community and the development of infrastructure, assuming that such efforts will eventually generate new jobs that will help the unemployed in the future. While the attempt to provide incentives for businesses to locate or expand enterprises in areas where unemployment and poverty are high may be justifiable on other grounds, it is necessarily a long-range strategy with little immediate antipoverty impact. Economic development programs will seldom offer direct relief to the poor, but they may help to minimize disparities in regional growth, thereby lessening the high concentrations of low-income households that compound difficulties in alleviating poverty.

A substantial body of federal programming and funding seeks to enhance the earning ability and the potential for self-reliance of a variety of population groups experiencing more than their proportionate share of poverty. None of the programs is funded adequately to serve all or even a major portion of those eligible for it. None of the programs functions as effectively as it might, but that is the nature of reality. Society would be worse off in the absence of these programs, and its well-being could be enhanced by improving their performance and then enlarging their resource basis once that improvement is demonstrated.

Notes

1. See the following from the U.S. General Accounting Office: *Multiple Employment Training Programs: Overlapping Programs Can Add Unnecessary Administrative Costs,* Report to the Ranking Minority Member, Committee on Appropriations, U.S. Senate, GAO/HEHS-94–80 (Washington, D.C., January 1994); *Multiple Employment Training Programs: Overlap among Programs Raises Questions about Efficiency,* Report to the Chairman, Subcommittee on Labor, Health and Human Services and Education, Committee on Appropriations, U.S. Senate, GAO/HEHS-94–193 (Washington, D.C., July 1994); *Multiple Employment Training Programs: Major Overhaul Is Needed,* Statement of Clarence C. Crawford, Associate

Director, Education and Employment Issues, Health, Education and Human Services Division, GAO/T:HEHS-94–109 (Washington, D.C., 3 March 1994); *Multiple Employment Training Programs: Major Overhaul Needed to Reduce Costs, Streamline the Bureaucracy, and Improve Results,* Statement of Clarence C. Crawford, Associate Director, Education and Employment Issues, Health, Education and Human Services Division, GAO/T: HEHS-95–53 (Washington, D.C., 10 January 1995).

2. Sar A. Levitan and Frank Gallo, *A Second Chance: Training for Jobs* (Kalamazoo, Mich.: W. E. Upjohn Institute for Employment Research, 1988).

3. Robert Taggart, "A Review of CETA Training," in *The T in CETA,* ed. Sar Levitan and Garth Mangum (Kalamazoo, Mich.: W. E. Upjohn Institute for Employment Research, 1981), 103, 111.

4. Howard S. Bloom et al., *The National JTPA Study: Title II-A Impacts on Earnings and Employment at 18 Months* (Bethesda, Md.: Abt Associates, 1993).

5. James J. Kemple, Fred Doolittle, and John W. Wallace, *The National JTPA Study: Site Characteristics and Participation Patterns* (New York: Manpower Demonstration Research Corporation, March 1993), executive summary, 14.

6. U.S. General Accounting Office, *Job Training Partnership Act: Long-term Earnings and Employment Outcomes,* GAO/HEHS-96–40 (Washington, D.C., March 1996), 4–5.

7. Margaret J. McLaughlin, "Including Special Education in the School Community: National Information Center for Children and Youth with Disabilities," *News Digest,* 2 November 1993.

8. U.S. General Accounting Office, *Vocational Education: Status in School Year 1990–91 and Early Signs of Change,* GAO/HRD-93–89 (Washington, D.C., August 1993), 4–5.

9. General Accounting Office, *Job Training Partnership Act,* 6–7.

10. Mathematica Policy Research, Inc., *Evaluation of the Economic Impact of the Job Corps Program: Third Followup Report* (Washington, D.C., September 1982).

11. U.S. General Accounting Office, *Job Corps: High Costs and Mixed Results Raise Questions about Job Corps Effectiveness,* Report to the Chairman, Committee on Labor and Human Resources, U.S. Senate, GAO/ HEHS-95–180 (Washington, D.C., 1995), 2, 8.

12. Ibid., 10–16.

13. Lawrence Katz, "Wage Subsidies for the Disadvantaged" Working Paper 5679 (Washington, D.C.: National Bureau of Economic Research, July 1996), 16.

14. Ibid., 22–23.

15. U.S. General Accounting Office, *People With Disabilities: Federal Programs Could Work Together More Efficiently to Promote Employment,* GAO/HEHS-96–126 (Washington, D.C., September 1996), 5.

16. Ibid., 3.

17. U.S. General Accounting Office, *Welfare to Work: Most AFDC Train-*

ing Programs Not Emphasizing Job Placement, GAO/HEHS-95–113 (Washington, D.C., May 1995), 5.

18. U.S. General Accounting Office, *Welfare to Work: Measuring Outcomes for JOBS Participants,* GAO/HEHS-95–86 (Washington, D.C., April 1995).

19. Louis Jacobson, Robert LaLonde, and Daniel Sullivan, *The Cost of Worker Dislocation* (Kalamazoo, Mich.: W. E. Upjohn Institute for Employment Research, 1993), 137.

20. Bruce C. Fallick, "A Review of the Recent Empirical Literature on Displaced Workers," *Industrial and Labor Relations Review,* 50 (October 1996), 5–16.

21. U.S. General Accounting Office, *Adult Education: Measuring Program Results Has Been Challenging,* GAO-HEHS-95–153 (Washington, D.C., September 1995).

22. James J. Heckman, "What Should Be Our Human Capital Policy?" in *Of Heart and Mind: Social Policy Essays in Honor of Sar A. Levitan,* ed. Garth L. Mangum and Stephen L. Mangum (Kalamazoo, Mich.: W. E. Upjohn Institute for Employment Research, 1996), 326.

23. Herbert Heneman III, Robert Heneman, and Timothy Judge, *Staffing Organizations* (Middleton, Wis.: Mendota House-Irwin, 1997).

24. Lawrence Mishel and Jared Bernstein, *The State of Working America: 1994–95* (Washington, D.C.: Economic Policy Institute, 1994), 291.

25. James Heckman, "Murky Numbers on Black Economic Progress," *Wall Street Journal,* 22 August 1989, A14.

26. George J. Borjas, "The New Economics of Immigration," *Atlantic Monthly,* November 1996, 72–80.

6. Strategies to Combat Poverty

The needy shall not always be forgotten: the hope of the poor shall not perish for ever.

Psalms 9:18

America took great strides during the 1960s to combat poverty. The Great Society's antipoverty legislation launched a substantial effort to meet the needs of the poor. While the rhetoric of the war on poverty was muted in the 1970s, federal social welfare expenditures continued to increase. The titles of Great Society programs changed and their administrative structures altered, but most antipoverty initiatives persisted. The 1980s witnessed retrenchment of federal programs in aid of the poor, but few programs were completely eliminated. The 1990s were ushered in with calls to "end welfare as we know it," and in 1996 Congress took a significant step in that direction. Whether that signals a retreat in the battle against poverty depends upon the support given to the development of self-reliance among those pushed out of welfare entitlement.

The Evolving Welfare System

A three-pronged strategy undergirds the evolvement of efforts in aid of the poor. First, to satisfy basic needs, the welfare system assists the poor through the provision of cash support and in-kind services, including health care, shelter, and nutrition. Second, in an attempt to change the poor by bolstering their self-sufficiency, the welfare system extends education, training, and other services. Third, to allow the poor a greater voice in determining their own destiny, the welfare system has sought, to varying degrees at various times, to increase their access to American institutions and their participation in the planning and implementation of antipoverty programs.

This combination of programs and services was designed to provide a base of support for the current poverty population while at the same time building a ladder out of poverty for the next generation. The strategy is sound, but it has also proved to be expensive. Efforts to change the behavior of the poor frequently proved unsuccessful or met with political resistance. At the same time, the breakdown of two-parent families, drug abuse, and other social ills disproportionately affected low-income communities, placing new obstacles in the way of an escape from poverty.

The resources available to fight poverty have never matched the need, but federal outlays rose moderately under the Johnson administration. The entitlements incorporated in the Great Society legislation—those for the poor being a minor portion of the total—accelerated budget growth during the first Nixon administration. By 1973 total federal outlays (after adjusting for inflation) had more than doubled in the span of a single decade, leading to concerns that the "budget explosion" was fueling inflationary pressures. When the Nixon, Ford, and Carter administrations moved to restrain the growth of the federal budget in the 1970s, few doubted the need for such action. The fight centered primarily on whose ox was to be gored. Under the Reagan administration policy tilted in favor of the affluent and the military at the expense of programs targeted at the economically disadvantaged and those on the brink of impoverishment. During the Bush administration and the first Clinton administration retardant income growth prompted a political environment in which assistance to the poor was increasingly perceived as coming at the expense of the unassisted. With the economic pie growing less rapidly than in the sixties and seventies, a larger piece for one group was increasingly seen as attainable only by reducing the size of another group's piece. Concern for the plight of others proved less compelling than concern for self. "Ending welfare as we know it" by removing public assistance's entitlement status and placing time limits on assistance is a major step down that road.

Without judging the merits of this shift toward fiscal restraint, it is evident that the emphasis on opportunity and future advancement was sacrificed in attempts to halt the rapid expansion of federal outlays. The optimism of the Great Society was replaced by a resignation embodied in the prophecy, "The poor ye shall always have with you." Several factors may have contributed to the nation's unwillingness to sustain the struggle against poverty as a top priority. The most flagrant deprivation in America had been alleviated by the 1970s, and yet the Great Society's hope for a lasting victory over poverty had not been realized. Furthermore, the increasing reliance upon income transfers at the expense of programs designed to expand opportunity and self-sufficiency undermined political support for aid to the poor, reinforcing the image of government handouts without prospects for future advancement. Amidst the economic turmoil caused by deep recessions, slowed productivity growth, and stagnating real earnings, national policymakers failed to commit the resources necessary for a sustained drive to eliminate or at least reduce poverty.

The welfare system, as it has evolved over the past half-century, has fallen short of creating an orderly program for improving the prospects of the poor. Nor is it clear, considering the multiple and complex problems facing the poor, that a simple system could have been designed. While millions of Americans living in poverty have been given additional income through the expansion of public assistance and in-kind benefits, the nation has failed to develop a universal system to meet the basic needs of the poor and to blend income support with services that expand future opportunity and self-sufficiency. The challenge in the years ahead lies in the development of an integrated approach to reducing poverty, one that provides greater hope for advancement and self-support while focusing federal resources on those areas and groups with the greatest potential or need. Only through greater reliance upon programs that promise opportunity is the nation likely to reject policies of negativism and retrenchment for a more compassionate response to poverty in America.

The needs of the poor in the 1990s are no less pressing than they were three decades earlier. The poor continue to need both income and services, not one or the other. It is essential to provide direct income support that meets basic needs, but a lasting response to the problems of the poor must emphasize efforts that attack the causes of poverty rather than those that merely mitigate its symptoms.

It would be a grave mistake to overlook the advances made in the transfer system already in place. Although the several existing programs may seem disjointed and inefficient, in sum they form a fairly comprehensive, albeit not universal or uniform, system of income support. Each of the various programs has its own target group; some duplication is inevitable, but there are no longer major gaps in coverage. The food stamp program, unemployment compensation, and the EITC have extended some aid to the working poor, while the federation of adult public assistance categories has improved the lot of the disabled and the aged poor who cannot work. Welfare mothers have been caught in between. Should their priorities be child care or self-reliance?

Even assuming that a consensus can be reached on the amount of additional resources to be allocated for the attack on poverty, it is not obvious how these resources should be distributed and most effectively put to use. What share of any additional dollars should be allocated to raising the cash income of the poor, and what share to improving the quality and quantity of services that are offered to them? The poor are not a homogeneous mass. Additional income, perhaps combined with short-term medical insurance, may meet the needs of the many individuals and families who face a brief spell of economic misfortune, yet a cash grant alone, no matter how generous, would do little to improve the long-range prospects of poor people beset by multiple problems.

In providing basic income support to the disadvantaged, the public policy objective is to provide an adequate income floor at a reasonable program cost to provide the recipient with an opportunity for self-reliance without unduly compromising his or her work incentive. One dilemma created by this objective is classic. The higher the minimum guaranteed income, the better off the individual judged worthy of assistance but the higher the program cost. Work incentives are enhanced by minimizing the benefit reduction rate applied to the income guarantee in the presence of earned income. However, the lower the benefit reduction rate, the wider the range of preprogram income potentially affected by the assistance program, the greater the number of potential recipients, and the greater the program costs. Consequently, a grant adequate to fulfill basic needs and an effective benefit reduction rate low enough to preserve work incentives combine to create a very expensive antipoverty program. For this reason, the guaranteed income proposals advanced by the Nixon and Carter administrations failed to win congressional approval. For example, the Carter proposal would have established a minimum benefit level of 65 percent of the poverty level for AFDC recipients. Although considered a modest goal, it would have constituted a significant advance in building a base of federal support for the poor. Some critics believed that the proposals offered too little support to the destitute; others feared that the proposed guaranteed income was too generous, would push program costs to unacceptable heights, and would encourage indolence.

These fundamental trade-offs across program goals help explain why meaningful welfare reform is difficult to achieve. Agreement on program values and recipient behaviors consistent with those values is difficult enough. Agreement on the mix of program characteristics when pursuit of one value compromises progress toward another is particularly problematic. A viable assistance program seeks through incentives to increase the extent to which assistance is tied to behaviors consistent with the values reflected in desired outcomes.

A number of past and present program characteristics can be

viewed within an incentive context. The public assistance system historically has provided disincentives with respect to the formation of two-parent families, though the disincentives are far too small to explain trends in illegitimacy and family structure.[1] While decisions concerning family structure reflect only limited sensitivity to financial incentives, efforts to make cash benefits to unmarried teen mothers contingent on staying in school and to continuing to reside with their parents can be viewed as such an incentive. So too can "family cap" provisions that reduce or eliminate additional public assistance benefits for children born while the mother is on assistance or incentive payments to encourage welfare mothers to identify fathers and their locations to facilitate child support enforcement provisions. In each case the effort is to impose costs on undesirable behaviors or to directly reward positive behaviors. The risk is always the punishment of the innocent child.

Research evidence documents labor supply disincentive effects associated with public assistance programs. These are far stronger than family structure effects, perhaps explaining up to half of the labor supply differences between program participants and comparable nonparticipants.[2] Alteration of benefit reduction rates and eligibility rules have significant impacts. Extension of transitional Medicaid coverage to individuals leaving assistance for work and subsidization of child care for working recipients are recent examples of incentives in support of positive work behaviors.

The 1996 welfare reform law, The Personal Responsibility and Work Opportunity Reconciliation Act of 1996, can be viewed in this light. It is revolutionary in that it limits entitlement to the replacement program for AFDC, imposing a five-year limit on receipt of benefits and a two-year limit on assistance in the absence of work or satisfactory work preparation activity. The law's underlying philosophy is that exposure to public assistance programs can weaken individual resolve and that limitations therefore provide incentive for positive individual actions consistent with leaving the dole.

The 1996 welfare reform law underscores another reality: that incentives toward positive behavior are sensible only to the extent that access to responsible behaviors and associated outcomes is reasonably possible. Estimates are that up to 50 percent of adult recipients at the time of the change in law, as well as 30–40 percent of new adult recipients, may eventually be affected by the imposition of time limits on benefits. While conditioning receipt of benefits on meeting work requirements is a reasonable incentive, it must be recognized that many adult welfare recipients have very low earnings potential due to low-productivity characteristics, including but not limited to low educational attainment and limited work experience. As a consequence, few employers are standing in line to receive the services of these potential workers. Where employment is available and obtained, assistance needs are likely to continue due to low hourly rates of pay, again reflecting underlying productivity realities. A preview of this likelihood is found in the Michigan general assistance program, in which 20 percent of recipients found steady employment following imposition of restrictions on program eligibility. A related reality is that the cost of moving low-productivity welfare recipients to a significantly higher level of human capital and consequently to higher levels of earnings potentiality, is significantly higher than society heretofore has typically been willing to pay. In that regard, James Heckman's finding that human capital investment for the nonpoor pays off at a rate of about 10 percent is sobering. If the same rate of return could be posited for the poor, every $1,000 increase in annual earnings would require a $10,000 investment in skill development.[3]

There are also questions about the ability of today's labor market to absorb a potentially large number of additional low-skilled workers at wages sufficient to support family self-reliance, especially in times of high immigration, legal and undocumented. As a consequence, one may accept the need for a system of incentives reinforcing behaviors consistent with positive, underlying core values and yet question the wisdom of strict time limitations to public assistance entitlement. These fundamental problems in the low end of the labor market must be addressed if welfare policy is to facilitate or support a reasoned escape route from poverty. This is a perplexing challenge, one well summarized by Richard Freeman, a leading labor market expert. Freeman's comment was made in the context of less skilled young American men, but it is equally applicable to the challenge of less skilled welfare recipients, less skilled immigrants, or, particularly, all three combined: "How to improve the job market for less skilled . . . American[s] . . . and reverse the huge decline in their earnings and employment opportunities, is the problem of our times, with implications for crime and many other social ills."[4]

Components of a Comprehensive Program

Although the existing antipoverty safety net is substantial, it is not without tatters or inconsistencies. It suffers from lack of philosophical underpinnings and is far from comprehensive. The last half of the 1990s may be an inopportune time to press for comprehensiveness, but agreement on philosophy now may be an essential preliminary step in that direction.

Philosophical Underpinnings

It is our premise that the widespread withdrawal of support from antipoverty programs in recent years results from a zero-sum game perception that every public dollar expended comes directly from the pockets of the working nonpoor. If that assumption is correct, continuation and renewal of support depends upon changing the perception from dole to investment. But that shift is also essential in its own right. No survival can be truly satisfactory in these United States—even to the survivor—that is not based on self-reliance. That does not mean self-sufficiency. All of us rely on others for what we cannot do or do not care to do for ourselves. What makes life worthwhile is the assurance that we have done all that we reasonably could to support ourselves and those for whom we are responsible. A bonus is to make a significant contribution to others outside our personal responsibility. We justify support during childhood and youth as an investment in the future. We can accept idleness in old age as the reward of past productivity and contribution, but the aged are rarely really satisfied with their lot if they are not still making some useful contribution to those around them. The independently wealthy are never honored and probably never truly content unless they too can perceive a social contribution.

We also expect appropriate conduct from those we assist—and rightly so. We cannot for our own comfort let people starve and freeze on our streets, but we resent their accepting our largesse while indulging in counterproductive habits that we know would decrease our own productivity and well-being if we so indulged. Nevertheless, we must be certain that the incentive system works as we perceive it. Can we really expect right conduct from a young person if within a reasonable time horizon that right conduct cannot be relied upon to enhance his or her life's comforts and satisfactions?

Members of society have an obligation to act with rectitude. But society has an obligation to reward that conduct. If it does not, the continuance of that conduct cannot be predicted. For all of those reasons, the only acceptable antipoverty system contains programs that can be perceived as reasonably positive investments in the fostering of self-reliance. That system need not forgo temporary income support while the individual enhances future productivity that will repay that social investment. It need not deny continued support as long as the recipient is allowed and persuaded to make all the contribution toward self-support that he or she is capable of making and feels, in addition, that society has a reason to value his or her continued presence. A comprehensive program for addressing poverty must adopt a life cycle perspective.

Toward a Real Head Start

No greater contribution could be made to the alleviation of welfare dependency than the prevention of premature, out-of-wedlock pregnancy. Any education that promises to prepare youths for life should instruct them to effectively control their powers of procreation. The least prepared for parenthood are the least likely to avoid risking it, and their parents are the least likely to be effective in dissuading them. Too many families are ill equipped to socialize the young or even to teach them simple facts of life. While churches and other organizational entities can be effective in providing wise assistance, for too many children school is the only place where they might learn about the range of birth prevention technologies, from abstinence to contraception. Given the long-range cost consequences, federal funding of such instruction would be a forthright and potentially high-payoff investment. With those defenses in place, the abortion issue should rarely arise, should never be a response to irresponsible conduct, and should protect against only nonviability of the fetus or dire threats to the physical or mental health of the mother. The time to prevent unwanted children is before conception. Once a child is conceived, Medicaid—or a potential universally available health care alternative—should provide readily the full measure of prenatal and infant care needed for a reasonable shot at a healthy childhood and adulthood.

Training for effective parenting should be at least as ubiquitous as driver education, but at a minimum it can be required of those receiving various kinds of federal assistance. Such training should be an integral component of education for the appropriate age groups. Federal policy should mandate exposure to the needed training for all funded prenatal, infant, and child care, WIC, Head Start parents, and TANF recipients. One appropriate vehicle for that objective is Home Start or Early Head Start, a version of Head Start in which staff visit parents and children at home, providing an opportunity to teach parenting skills as well as to reach all preschool children of all ages at lower intervention costs than in daily center-based instruction.

Head Start funding has been commendably expanded but is still inadequate. Full funding should be a goal. As that goal is achieved, the objective of Head Start should shift from preventing the children of the poor from falling further behind to more fundamental objectives such as offering every child access to quality preschools. Federal funding should be the gap filler after parents and local and state policymakers, including school authorities, have been encouraged to meet the challenge to the best of their ability. Within the Head Start program, care will be necessary to assure that multiplication in quantity does not lead to subtraction in quality. The federal funding agent has the responsibility for close evaluative supervision to discover, prevent, or reverse any tendency to fall behind. Government may face a trap of surrogate parenting from birth to adolescence and beyond unless the cycle is somehow broken.

Quality will be best assured by stressing Head Start expansion within the school system. Community-based organizations have been important as champions of early childhood education among the poor and have been particularly effective in recruiting Head Start parents as aides. But those organizations have not been well instructed nor are they well positioned to monitor educational quality. An additional argument for elementary schools' conducting Head Start and other preschool programs is easier transition into kindergartens in the same familiar environment. Enlarging the role of the public schools in Head Start may speed the day when that responsibility can be assumed by local education systems.

Elementary and Secondary Education

The elementary and secondary education experience is the only universally available instrument for preparing young people for successful careers. There is wisdom in the long-term American preference for limiting the federal role to research, development, and assistance to overwhelmed schools. But widespread support and endorsement by the nation's governors and two successive presidential administrations of a set of national education goals invites an enlarged federal role. Unfounded criticisms by a few loud radical commentators should not be allowed to divert that consensus.

Of the goals currently set forth in Goals 2000, federal support for preparing the children of the socioeconomically disadvantaged to start school ready to learn is the objective of Head Start and other early childhood programs. Achievement of the goal of a 90 percent high school graduation rate is not far off. The challenge is to reduce the dropout rate of underclass youths, to remediate those that do drop out, and to assure the quality of the learning experience for all. Application of the school-to-work initiative to out-of-school and at-risk youths could be a major step toward that goal.

A third goal, that of making sure that American students leave grades 4, 8, and 12 having demonstrated competency in the assigned subject matter and prepared for productive employment in the modern economy, requires federal leadership in the establishment of national education standards, as well as increased educational support for those schools and students encumbered by overwhelming socioeconomic burdens. Following development of standards and tests to assess progress relative to standards, the next priority task is development of a system capable of assessing cognitive abilities rather than the ability of teachers to "teach to the test."

The goal of universal adult literacy is challenged by elusiveness in its definition. A concerted attack on adult literacy will be likely to find more success if it is pursued within the context of preparation for improved employment—an added burden for an already underfunded employment and training system.

The potential benefits of education goals for those still in school can best be provided through revitalization of the Elementary and Secondary Education Act. That will require abandonment of Title I as it has been administered in favor of concentration on the most poverty-impacted of schools, systematic reform within these schools, and a federal guarantee that stricter national standards will not be allowed to cause those schools and their students to fall further behind the rising norms.

School-to-Work Transition

Those who do well in school rarely have difficulty making the transition from school to work. But most who do well in high school choose to continue on to postsecondary education. Improving school performance should be the first priority. But there are many who learn more readily in a hands-on than in an academic environment and others so alienated from the schools that an alternative approach is essential. Those alternatives should be recognized for what they are. Few American teenagers are prepared to make a lasting occupational choice. The purpose of work-based learning in the teen years is fourfold: to motivate youths to learn what they should have learned in an academic setting, to offer career exploration opportunities in order to facilitate more realistic subsequent career choices, to offer the discipline of work experience, and, incidentally, to use earnings as a carrot to encourage continued learning.

Work-based learning opportunities will be limited at best. Nowhere have large numbers of employers proven willing to participate, and that scarce resource must be vigorously promoted and carefully husbanded. Experience in many communities has demonstrated that promotion by those in positions of prominence followed by demonstrations of substantial positive results can be effective in increasing employer involvement. Cooperative education is a proven approach, dependent for success primarily upon the effectiveness of the school staff in proselytizing employers and coaching the youths. Appropriately visioned, secondary-level vocational education is another potentially effective tool. Rather than preparation for specific, necessarily limited occupations, it can be transformed into a vehicle for hands-on learning of the practicalities of abstract concepts. That only one-half of school leavers ever make use in their employment of the occupation-specific courses taken in high school is often viewed as a mark of failure. If these courses are recognized as a career exploration experience and a motivation to stay in school longer, accumulating further academic preparation in the process, the roughly 10 percent federal matching expenditure for vocational education is more than justified.

The wage advantage of the postsecondarily educated has widened in the 1990s; therefore postsecondary career preparation must be emphasized. In that pursuit, Pell grants and educational loans have been essential and should be expanded though more vigorously monitored. But that set of priorities—secondary vocational education as career exploration and a vehicle for applied academic learning, postsecondary occupational preparation, and tech prep as a bridge between the two—will not happen unless the federal partner declares the priorities and exercises the modest leverage its minimal expenditures provide.

Second-Chance Programs

All federal employment and training programs confront the same obstacles. Barring serious mental or physical health limitations or dysfunctional lifestyles such as drug or alcohol addiction, employability can be enhanced through some combination of remedial education, skill training (whether classroom or on-the-job), and work experience. But the trainees must be motivated to succeed, and the providers need to commit resources to sustain the effort. The adult and youth components of the Job Training Partnership Act, dislo-

cated worker efforts, the welfare JOBS program, and vocational rehabilitation have all suffered from trying to do too much with too
little.

A realistic assessment must be made of the length and combination of remedial education and skill training required for each
client, and if no other source of income support is available,
stipends should be supplied to make training possible. The enrollees' progress needs to be continually assessed, and those not
performing adequately should be first warned and then dropped.

A sound program would select occupations substantial enough
to provide adequate incomes, fund training sufficient to prepare for
them, and require performance commensurate with success. Involved would be integrated recurrent and simultaneous combinations of basic education, skill training, and on-the-job application.
As already noted, whether the first time through or as a second
chance, anything short of the equivalent of a two-year postsecondary degree will be inadequate for earning wages above the
poverty level. The current expectation of too much from too little
might as well be abandoned. Whether the emphasis is on helping
the disadvantaged or the displaced or on the general upgrading of
the work force and enhancement of productivity, another priority
training challenge is to expand the role of private employers in that
effort. The 1992 Clinton notion of leveraging such employer involvement was too early abandoned.

Programs for Out-of-School Youth

Second-chance systems for out-of-school youths must recognize
the unique needs and dismal prospects of poorly educated youths,
particularly high school dropouts. While the conventional wisdom
is that "nothing works" for this population, recent conceptual development and systematic culling of the programmatic experience
of seasoned practitioners by Gary Walker and his colleagues have
yielded a set of core principles that appear to be critical to effective
programming for out-of-school, out-of-work youths.[5] Among the
principles are that each young person served must sense

> that at least one adult mentor associated with the program has a
> strong stake and interest in his or her success and consistently
> cares and acts on that interest;

> that the program has strong and effective connections to em-
> ployers, that placement into a paid position with one of those em-
> ployers is an immediate program priority, but that the initial
> placement is but one step in a continuing and long-term devel-

opmental relationship between the young person, the program, and the network of employers;

the need and opportunity to improve his or her educational skills and certification; and

that the program will provide support over a significant period of time, perhaps over several years.

That the involvement of caring, connected adults is critical to youth success is so obvious as to be easily overlooked. Most of us have only to reflect on own lives to recognize the impact that caring adults had in our own development. Most of us as parents count on the positive influence of other adults—coaches, counselors, religious leaders, scout leaders, teachers, neighbors—on our children as they grow and become increasingly attached to institutions other than their home. Providing these influences (many of which we take for granted) is critical for those youths for whom such influences have been absent. Walker and others argue that successful programs also exhibit effective connections to providers of basic support, such as housing, counseling, and medical assistance, and that they make strong use of performance incentives, positive peer group reinforcement, and leadership opportunities.

These principles must be applied within the context of a functional system that operates at a local level to extend opportunity. College-bound youths are guided by parents and school personnel through an information-rich support system to prepare and access a generally effective system of career preparation. The value of high school completion and the career paths beyond high school are not as clear or as smooth for the non-college-bound. The School-to-Work Opportunities Act of 1994 was designed to emulate for the non-college-bound high school graduate the essential features of the college-bound system. Youths and the schools that prepare them are to be supplied with information about workplace expectations. Employers are to be involved in designing curriculums and training teachers and guidance counselors about labor market requirements. Small, career-based learning communities are being developed as schools within schools to provide close personal involvement. Work-based learning connections allow youths to advance from field trips and job shadowing to work experience, internship, and apprenticeship and on to successful career placements.

But where is the out-of-school youth in this picture? Several entities could take the initiative, but local elected officials are probably in the best position to convene school administrators, employ-ers, community-based organizations, the correctional officers most likely to preside over the next step if the system fails, and others to combine their resources in building an equally effective system for those already out of school. Such a system must start within the communities where these youths are and involve reliable commu-nity-based organizations or create new ones that value youths and recruit and attract them. With that community base as the hub or anchor, adult "connectors" must supply the needed connections to alternative learning communities, peer support groups, social ser-vices, skill building, creative work experiences, and jobs—all of the resources that seem to work well for in-school youths but in a com-munity-specific mode. Funding based on average daily atten-dance—the key to public school finance—plus the dollars saved by keeping at-risk youths out of the correctional system, would go a long way toward meeting the four essentials of youth program suc-cess in an out-of-school setting.

Access to Jobs

Economically disadvantaged families with multiple problems need case-managed access to the full array of food, health, housing, in-come maintenance, and other social services, as well as employ-ment and training. Access must be seamless and available at what-ever point they confront the system. For employment and training services there is already the JTPA system, governed by State Job Training Coordinating Councils and Private Industry Councils, whose members usually include representatives from all the rele-vant organizations in the state and the community, respectively. For almost universal access there are the nearly two thousand offices of the oft-maligned but still essential sixty-year-old Job Service. De-spite decreasing resources, the Job Service continues its tasks of providing labor market information, matching the workers who are hardest to place with the jobs that are hardest to fill, and adminis-tering unemployment insurance.

At least a dozen states are now in various levels of reorganiza-tion, combining these entities and other relevant agencies in some form of work force services department, providing service through one-stop career and employment assistance centers, and guiding the whole through some sort of human resource investment coun-cil. They perceive their customer base as comprising employers re-cruiting help, job-ready job seekers needing primarily labor market information, and those facing multiple employment barriers and re-quiring case-managed access to a variety of remedial and support services. The trick is to serve all and neglect none in an era of declining resources. Encouraging models should be monitored, and knowledge of proven elements should be disseminated throughout the states so that they can design their own improved systems to fit their own realities.

Enforcement of equal employment opportunity laws gained new impetus under the enhanced powers of the 1991 Civil Rights Act. The Clinton administration restored aggressive enforcement, including mediation efforts, hoping to assure equal consideration for jobs for which applicants are qualified. But here too a sense of foreclosing opportunities for the majority is generating animosity toward affirmative action on behalf of the less favorably situated. Equal employment opportunity enforcement must continue with vigor, but the climate of opportunity for all must be extended to reduce divisiveness. As that is accomplished, access to skill enhancement must be provided to those previously denied opportunities because of their lack of qualification—another indicator of the need for second-chance programs.

Income Maintenance

With assisted self-reliance as the watchword, income maintenance separated from a past, present, or future work connection should be justified only by rare circumstances.

Three significant changes are needed in the unemployment insurance system. First, the adequacy of state trust funds should be assured by reasonable projection of outflows over time and by reforming the payroll tax to fit. Second, the federal extensions now voted by Congress in each recession should be automatically tied to the national unemployment rate, phasing in and out without further legislation. Third, those unlikely to become reemployed without remedial efforts and requiring such involvement as a condition of continuance should be identified early on. Meeting their needs would require ready availability of retraining, relocation, or other adjustment services and an ongoing public service employment program as a last resort for those who cannot obtain employment. A boost in the federal payroll tax supporting unemployment insurance is a potential vehicle for obtaining the necessary outlays to implement these reforms.

The social security old age pension reform requirement is straightforward. The retirement age of 65, chosen nearly sixty years ago, when the average age at death was five years short of that, cannot be justified today, when the average age at death is 75 and rising. In addition, the waste of human resources is unconscionable.

After forty years of employment, many elderly persons may prefer a change of pace. But that does not mean they crave idleness or that society is obligated to support them if they do. The social security retirement age should be raised commensurate with the longevity of the population, while thought and planning should be devoted to creating flexible forms of employment for those kept in the work force longer. Raising the retirement age would also be a major factor in restoring the economic viability of Medicare.

The support of widows and orphans is the oldest form of income maintenance. Yet it is also the most egregious example of unfinished business. A sixty-one-year-old entitlement program for which support of dependent children was the raison d'être has been destroyed because of antagonism toward their mothers with little thought of the consequences for this target population. The 20 percent exemption window is already overfull with those who have received benefits for more than five years, who will have to be expelled when the time limit takes effect unless drastic steps are undertaken. Substituting employment for the mothers in place of the dole to the family makes eminent sense if, and only if, appropriate supportive steps are taken. It is those former AFDC recipients who will clog the arteries of the new one-stop centers and require the attention of effective case managers. Child care assistance, Medicaid persistence, remedial education and skill training, reasonable access to available employment, guaranteed employment opportunities when the competitive labor market does not provide them, and an earned income tax credit or other form of wage supplement when earnings remain inadequate despite full-time employment must be available. Without those continued supports welfare reform is a farce.

Of course, every reasonable effort should be made to find acceptable private-sector jobs. For many welfare recipients the possibility of unsubsidized employment depends on the availability and amount of resources allocated to impacting their productivity. For some the costs necessary to prepare for unsubsidized employment may be prohibitively high in terms of the ratio of benefits to costs. This plus natural constraints on the rate of growth of private-sector employment suggests that any welfare reform that does not include an undergirding of public-sector employment is doomed to failure.

Experience has shown that the U.S. economy does not always generate an adequate number of jobs to employ the poorly educated and unskilled. Creation of jobs for them should be second only to the establishment of adequate training facilities for those who are sufficiently motivated to acquire new skills. The continued high level of unemployment among the unskilled, particularly among blacks and other minorities, indicates the need to generate government-supported employment—not make-work jobs—for those who cannot qualify for gainful employment in private industry.

Despite the gloomy foreboding of the present-day advocates of the ancient lump of labor fallacy, much of society's work is not being done and the needs are going to increase rather than disappear. Many jobs can be performed by relatively unskilled workers, whether in rural areas or urban centers. Stream clearance, reforestation, park maintenance, and housing rehabilitation are some of the traditional work-relief jobs. Many new jobs can be added in fields such as child care, health care, education, maintenance of public facilities, and renovation of slum areas. These jobs should be in addition to countercyclical job creation programs designed to help the victims of economic recession.

This is an expensive proposition, but without it the only way to build and maintain a work-based welfare system is to provide opportunities to engage in useful community service activities in return for benefits. Even that imposes additional supervisory and administrative costs. With opportunities for employment or useful community service, adequate child care, and health services in place, nearly all welfare recipients could fill an employment requirement and entitlement limitations would be unnecessary. However, if public service employment is not to become a new form of dole, it must be viewed as transitional work experience on the way to competitive public or private employment. Clear in all of this must be the fact that, particularly in the short run, the cost of any serious employment requirement is greater—though more desirable—than the budgetary costs of the dole.

Making Work Pay

Minimum-wage legislation in tandem with the EITC can play a significant role in reducing poverty. Major boosts in minimum wages tend to reduce overall employment. Nonetheless, there is a persuasive body of evidence showing that the wages of millions of workers tend to cluster around the statutory minimum wage. Prudent increases in the wage floor, therefore, can assist the working poor and reduce the inherent conflicts between transfer programs and work incentives. Protective legislation cannot be used to transform the nature of the general economy, but it can minimize its worst redistributive effects and have a major impact on promoting equal opportunity in the free market.

The minimum-wage reform needed is straightforward but not

easy to accomplish politically. The current practice of allowing the real value of minimum-wage rates to deteriorate between intermittent and delayed congressional actions prevents employers from planning their labor costs and reduces the meager incomes of minimum-wage earners. The 1996–97 increases do not significantly change this picture. The desired relationship between the minimum wage and the average hourly wage in private industry should be determined once and for all and a formula adopted for annual increments.

The plight of the working poor looms as one of the greatest barriers to the elimination of poverty. In the present transfer system any attempt to raise the nonworking poor out of poverty only creates unacceptable work disincentives for the millions of Americans working and yet still living in poverty or just above the poverty threshold. The importance of channeling aid to the working poor in order to preserve work incentives received increasing recognition during the 1970s. The EITC offers significant relief to the working poor through the tax structure; it serves as a wage supplement that builds upon the modest security of minimum-wage laws. As such, the EITC has been moving steadily in the appropriate direction—increasing the returns to employment for the working poor. It is necessary to continue to increase its value, to extend its benefits to the childless and single poor who are currently ineligible, and to base it upon family size.

In sum, a constructive and compassionate response to the working poor, as well as the nonworking poor who are employable, is to broaden opportunities for advancement and self-reliance through training and work. In the short term, work incentives should ensure that the rewards of work exceed the stipends of dependency. For the longer term, however, federal social welfare initiatives should focus on investments that enhance the ability of the poor to secure gainful employment and support their families with a decent wage.

But What Would It Cost?

Not as much as one might think. New moneys are less essential than reorganization. Where additional funds are needed, it is in the context of human capital investment that in a more sensible fiscal system would be part of an investment budget defended by its potential revenue return.[6] There are many examples:

While it is tempting to measure antipoverty efforts solely in terms of direct expenditures, the case for a federal role in family planning is a reminder that cost and contribution are not always synonymous. Particularly among the working poor, the size of households rather than the level of family income can be viewed as the key factor in forcing households below the poverty threshold, and programs to help the poor control the size of their families can bring major results in minimizing this trend. If a primary emphasis were placed on family planning efforts that helped the poor fulfill their own desires in reducing the number of unwanted children, at a negligible cost to the public, the next generation would have a far better chance of escaping the grasp of poverty.

Moreover, a great deal more could be accomplished through better allocation of existing dollars. The current social welfare system is a jumble of poorly integrated, and often conflicting income and in-kind programs. Income maintenance programs focus on families for the most part, but other interventions typically are aimed at individuals without regard to the family problems that often underlie social problems. Policymakers remain bound by the structures and strictures of existing efforts, and program administrators rarely venture beyond their narrow jurisdictions. As a result, dependent care, child and spouse abuse, crime, education, training, and health concerns, and many other challenges are too often addressed in a piecemeal fashion rather than as parts of a coherent whole.

Impoverished individuals who are elderly or disabled and families who become poor for short periods may receive adequate assistance through existing social programs. To meet their multiple needs, persistently poor families and young adults who grow up in such families require a system that integrates the various programs. Demonstration projects that attempt to implement such an approach to the needs of low-income families are under way in several communities. With leadership by the federal executive and legislative branches, such recasting of the family support system could become far more widespread.

More than thirty years ago this nation declared, in the words of its president, an "unconditional war on poverty." Now the question is whether to withdraw from the fray, justifying the withdrawal either by declaring victory or by blaming the victims. Current programs have in aggregate reduced the incidence of poverty. A coherent effort based on the philosophy of assisted self-reliance could in fact further reduce poverty as currently defined by assisting all those who are capable of working to prepare for work, by providing them with access to work, by supplementing their earnings when they are inadequate, and by providing them with income maintenance before and after work is realistically possible.

The cost would be substantial; in the short run it would be more than the cost of current piecemeal efforts. The current social security and Medicare crises can be avoided by more rapidly accelerating the retirement age while augmenting the gross domestic product, and consequently tax revenues, from the productive activities of experienced workers. A truly effective education, training, and employment system in the long run pays back far more than it costs. The current federal deficit controversy needs to be laid to rest by dividing the federal budget between consumption and investment, always balancing the consumption budget over the business cycle and balancing the investment budget against its projected returns—including investment in the nation's human capital and its productive employment. For now the primarily state and local education system needs from the federal government mostly promulgated national standards, technical assistance, and financial contributions only for those communities in which dealing with the impact of poverty is beyond their available resources. Training welfare recipients is just as much of an investment as training any other potential workers. The combination of food stamps, Medicaid, possible public service employment, and wage supplements—EITC or some other form—is clearly a cost, greater in aggregate than that paid out under AFDC only because it puts more income in the hands of the poor. But this added income would be worth the added cost not only because it would reduce deprivation but because it would be based on earned income, the most respected form.

It will become necessary by the close of the 1990s to reassess the size and scope of national expenditures for the middle- and upper-income population. The growth of non-means-tested entitlements over the past two decades has strained the nation's resources, and such spending now by far dwarfs federal outlays in aid of the poor. Shifting the nature of social investment calls for a close scrutiny of the costs and benefits associated with current levels of social security and Medicare benefits and with tax expenditures that disproportionately benefit the well-to-do. It is important that the middle class not perceive itself as having no stake in the welfare system, and yet it is also clear that federal resources should be more carefully husbanded if we are to expand opportunity and alleviate poverty among the least fortunate.

As always, the willingness to augment resources to aid the poor would reflect perceptions about the importance of antipoverty measures among broad national priorities. Antipoverty efforts have fared poorly in the competition for national resources in recent years. But who can say that our priorities will not change? Who would have predicted in the 1950s that poverty and hunger would be powerful issues during the following two decades or that the hippies of the 1960s would become the yuppies of the 1980s? Declining real wages for many have dampened sympathies for those even worse off. But who is to say that tightening labor markets will not assuage competitive concerns or that disillusionment with the distorting income distribution will not rekindle a sense of brotherhood among the entire stymied lower 80 percent. The public could once again turn attention to the pressing needs of the poor. A renewed commitment to the goal of expanding opportunities for all Americans could include the target, not of a war on poverty, but of a pursuit of assisted self-reliance. Only then will the nation meet the challenge voiced by Samuel Johnson more than two centuries ago: "A decent provision for the poor is the true test of civilization."

Notes

1. Hilary Williamson Hoynes, "Work, Welfare, and Family Structure: What Have We Learned?" Working Paper 5644 (Washington, D.C.: National Bureau of Economic Research, July 1996).

2. Ibid.

3. James J. Heckman, "What Should Be Our Human Capital Investment Policy?" in *Of Heart and Mind: Social Policy Essays in Honor of Sar A. Levitan,* ed. Garth L. Mangum and Stephen L. Mangum (Kalamazoo, Mich.: W. E. Upjohn Institute for Employment Research, 1996).

4. Richard B. Freeman, "Why Do So Many Young American Men Commit Crimes and What Might We Do About It?" *Journal of Economic Perspectives* 10 (winter 1996): 41.

5. Andrew Sum, Stephen Mangum, Edward De Jesus, Gary Walker, David Gruber, Marion Pines, and William Sprung, *A Generation of Challenge: Pathways to Success for Urban Youth* Policy Issues Monograph 97-03 (Baltimore: Sar Levitan Center for Social Policy Studies, Johns Hopkins University, June 1997), 75–81.

6. Robert Eisner, "Budget and Taxes," in *Restoring Broadly Shared Prosperity,* ed. Ray Marshall (Washington, D.C., and Austin Tex.: Economic Policy Institute and University of Texas-Austin, 1997), 19.

Index

Library of Congress Cataloging-in-Publication Data

Levitan, Sar A.
   Programs in aid of the poor / Sar A. Levitan, Garth L.
Mangum, Stephen L. Mangum.—7th ed.
      p.   cm.
   Includes bibliographical references and index.
   ISBN 0-8018-5688-4 (alk. paper).—ISBN 0-8018-5713-9
(pbk. : alk. paper)
    1. Public welfare—United States.   2. Economic
assistance, Domestic—United States.   I. Mangum,
Garth L.   II. Mangum, Stephen L.   III. Title.
HV95.L54   1998
362.5´8´0973—dc21   97-15768   CIP